# Jewish Threads

## A Hands-On Guide to **Stitching Spiritual Intention** into Jewish Fabric Crafts

DIANA DREW

WITH

ROBERT GRAYSON

*For People of All Faiths, All Backgrounds*

**JEWISH LIGHTS** Publishing

Woodstock, Vermont

*Jewish Threads:*
*A Hands-On Guide to Stitching Spiritual Intention into Jewish Fabric Crafts*

2011 Quality Paperback Edition, First Printing

**Library of Congress Cataloging-in-Publication Data**
Drew, Diana.
   Jewish threads : a hands-on guide to stitching spiritual intention into Jewish fabric crafts / Diana Drew with Robert Grayson. – Quality pbk. ed.
        p. cm.
   "For people of all faiths, all backgrounds."
   Includes bibliographical references.
   ISBN 978-1-58023-442-9 (pbk.)
 1.  Jewish crafts. 2.  Jewish needlework.  I. Grayson, Robert, 1951– II. Title.
   BM729.H35D74 2011
   746.088'296—dc23
                                                                    2011033114

10  9  8  7  6  5  4  3  2  1

Manufactured in the United States of America

Cover Design: Jenny Buono
Interior Design: Heather Pelham
Graphic Designer/Illustrator: Kevin Greene

*For People of All Faiths, All Backgrounds*
Published by Jewish Lights Publishing
A Division of LongHill Partners, Inc.
Sunset Farm Offices, Route 4, P.O. Box 237
Woodstock, VT 05091
Tel: (802) 457-4000    Fax: (802) 457-4004
www.jewishlights.com

*To Stella Hart Grayson*
*whose love surrounds us*
*and whose example inspires us*

# Contents

# Introduction

## Individual Threads

I came to the fiber arts later in life than most. Growing up, I was drawn to paper more than fabric. A box filled with odd pieces of colored card stock was a joy beyond compare, and colored pens held a singular allure.

Through the years, while I pursued a career as a writer, publicist, and book editor, I kept coming back to sewing from time to time. I found it relaxing, almost a form of meditation, especially if I was creating something for our home, like curtains, or a gift, like a pillowcase for a wedge-shaped pillow for someone who needed a cushion to ease a sore back. Each stitch had a destiny, and I was the one to fulfill it.

At first, I did all this sewing by hand, including curtains for a picture window in the living room (a project that took months!). Then, as an anniversary gift, my in-laws gave me a sewing machine about ten years ago, which prompted me to take a beginners' sewing class at my local craft store. Learning the basics from an eighty-year-old teacher who had been sewing for most of her life, I started making all sorts of fabric crafts, from hats (which I love), to tote bags, cases for makeup brushes, simple jackets, even a headboard cover.

At around the same time, I began editing for Potter Craft, a division of Random House that published books on handcrafts, from sewing and knitting to crochet, handwoven wire jewelry, and more. I loved editing these manuscripts and learned all sorts of interesting tips from the authors. Included among the Potter Craft manuscripts I edited were two of Martha Stewart's books—*Martha Stewart's Encyclopedia of Crafts* and *Martha Stewart's Encyclopedia of Sewing and Fabric Crafts*. Both of these gave me even more ideas on how to work with fabric.

SkyLight Paths—a sister company of Jewish Lights, the publisher of this book—had a hand in my spiritual awakening to the power of Jewish fabric crafts by asking me to edit the manuscript for *The Knitting Way: A Guide to Spiritual Self-Discovery,* by Linda Skolnik and Janice MacDaniels. In this beautifully written manuscript, I discovered that others had found spiritual meaning in working with their hands, just as I had.

Over the years, I came to believe that the Universe was sending me each new manuscript to edit for a reason. If I paid close enough attention, I felt the frisson of meaning intended just for me in each of these projects. So when I started editing manuscripts for Potter Craft and then *The Knitting Way* for SkyLight Paths, I took up knitting once again—something I had learned as a young woman but set aside. The Martha Stewart and other craft manuscripts I edited inspired me to decorate blank greeting cards with Jewish stars or hearts cut out of felt (a fabric that, blessedly, doesn't ravel); to create colorful knitting needle sleeves, adorned with buttons and bows; and to make felt bookmarks, decorated with ribbon, buttons, and embroidered designs.

Dovetailing with the craft manuscripts that had started coming my way was another facet of my life—National Council of Jewish Women. I had never been a "joiner," yet the Universe conspired to make me one of the most active NCJW members, at least on the local level. My involvement began, oddly enough, because of my husband's brother, Lee. As a young man, Lee had been diagnosed with chronic myelogenous leukemia in 1995. The only chance to save his life was a bone marrow transplant, but no one in the family matched his marrow type, and no one in the national marrow donor registry did, either. That meant we needed to reach out to the community to try to find a matching marrow donor. The best chance to find a marrow match would be to find another Jewish person of Eastern European descent, so we organized a series of marrow donor drives, including one at the Jewish Renaissance Fair at the Rabbinical College of America. When we publicized this drive in the mainstream and Jewish press, the co–vice president of NCJW, West Morris Section, Kim Kramer Ganz, called us and asked if we could use some volunteers at the event. We were grateful for all the help we could get, and when seven women showed up that day and stayed the entire time, we felt blessed indeed. Through marrow donor drives like the one at the Rabbinical College, Lee eventually found a marrow donor, Cheryl Wrigley—a stranger to us then; *mishpachah* (family) now—and got a second chance at life.

Later on, my mother-in-law, Stella Hart Grayson, and I were asked to join NCJW, West Morris, and we were happy to become members. Because of the graciousness of these women, their support of a cause dear to my heart, and their commitment to *tikkun olam* (mending the world) through sponsoring marrow donor drives and other meaningful initiatives in the community, I gradually became more and more involved in the organization, rising to the position of co-president. And therein lies the rest of the story.

In the spring of 2001 I had been reading Rachel Naomi Remen's beautiful book *My Grandfather's Blessings,* a collection of essays that included one about Feelie Hearts—soft, stuffed, hand-sewn hearts made by women in Tacoma, Washington, for an organization called Bridges: A Center for Grieving Children. I thought our NCJW section might enjoy making these hearts for Bridges, so I called the organization in the summer of 2001, and the person in charge was thrilled to hear that we wanted to make hearts for the Bridges program to distribute to the grieving children they worked with. We decided to make them out of fleece, because it is soft and doesn't ravel, and to use embroidery floss with a blanket stitch, to give a contrasting color to the finished piece. We planned to make this a fall 2001 community service project.

Then came 9/11.

Living in northern New Jersey, in the shadow of the Twin Towers, all of us were devastated by the terrorist attacks. So we moved up the date of our sewing circle to just after the High Holy Days, and more than twenty-five people came to hand-sew three-inch fleece hearts, destined for the children of the 9/11 victims. These were well-traveled hearts, since they went cross-country to Bridges in Washington State and then came back East. That fall we also sent Feelie Hearts to organizations working directly with families who had lost loved ones in the attacks.

Through the years that followed, NCJW members made these hearts at home and at sewing circles in members' homes, eventually sewing more than twenty-five hundred of them. They went to families all over the United States and in Israel.

Then in 2004, NCJW brought in a speaker for a special event who set us on a new path. Mark Lipinski, a professional quilter, gave a wonderful talk about the art of quilting, which inspired the organization to make a quilted chuppah (a Jewish marriage canopy). This was an immense undertaking, one that took two full years to complete under Mark's tutelage, and was guided by his overall design. It involved design work (Donna Grxoss, one of the *Jewish Threads* contributors, designed beautiful panels with a stained-glass look, all showing scenes of Jewish life), appliqué work by members in a weekly sewing circle or at home, and quilting. The chuppah's pole covers are adorned with grapes, pomegranates, lilies of the valley, and other biblical fruits and flowers; the valances include some of the marriage blessings; and the chuppah itself—the large piece under which the couple say their vows—features the panels of Jewish life plus panels of Jewish stars. (See more about this chuppah in the section titled "Inspirations.")

## Collective Threads

*Jewish Threads* brings together the disparate threads of my own life—Judaism and Jewish observance, sewing and knitting, writing and editing—while stitching together the inspiring stories of fabric artists from throughout the United States and Israel. Collectively, these personal stories and the projects that spring from them form a pastiche of modern-day Jewish life. The part openings, written by my husband, Robert Grayson, place these crafts in historical perspective, with tales from the Jewish tradition that give these fabric crafts added resonance today.

Beyond this storytelling, *Jewish Threads* presents an array of fabric craft projects made with varied needlecraft techniques—quilting, knitting, needlepoint, crochet, embroidery, counted cross-stitch, even felting. Taken together, these stories and their accompanying projects can serve as a catalyst for your imagination, a way for you to translate your own passion for Judaism into beautiful works of handmade fabric art. Both an inspirational book and a craft-making book, *Jewish Threads* draws together the diverse threads of Jewish life and Jewish observance as expressed through Jewish fabric crafts.

Traditionally the purview of women, fabric crafts today appeal to both women and men. While the contributors to *Jewish Threads* are predominantly female, one project comes from Julian M. Brook, a man who loves making tallitot (chapter 26).

In gathering the projects for *Jewish Threads,* I reached beyond the borders of the United States to Israel, the home of two of the contributors—Ruth Lenk and Esther Tivé-Elterman. Their projects reflect the Holy Land's hold on them: Ruth's *Hamsa* Wall Hanging (chapter 2), for instance, includes *hamsa*s, the Hebrew letter *hey,* and other Jewish iconography; Esther's Crazy Quilt *Shulchan* Cover (chapter 7) features a date palm, which grows in abundance in the area outside Jerusalem, where she lives.

For some *Jewish Threads* contributors, the impetus for making a particular piece was to create a contemporary ritual, as Claire Sherman did with her *Ushpizin* Quilt (chapter 15) for Sukkot. Others, like Judith S. Paskind and Vicki Pieser, made their Jewish fabric crafts as gifts for family members. Judy's counted cross-stitch tallit bag for her daughter's Bat Mitzvah (chapter 27) pictures the Garden of Eden, while the *wimpel* Vicki made to celebrate her grandchild's birth (chapter 24) has biblical wishes sewn right in. Several contributors, including Susan Schrott and Eleanor Levie, celebrated life in the Jewish tradition with Tree of Life motifs in their pieces (chapters 1 and 6). Still others felt moved to design a fabric craft with Jewish spiritual intention in response to a loved one's illness or death. Stuart's Healing Quilt, by Holly Levison (chapter 29), and the Shalva Quilts (chapter 30) fall into this category.

Making Jewish fabric crafts like those showcased in *Jewish Threads* gives you a chance to express your creativity, share your love of fabrics and fabric crafts with others, and make an heirloom that those you love can cherish for years to come. A number of the projects presented here, including the Sukkot and Shavuot Torah Mantles (chapters 9 and 10) and the Shalva Quilts, encourage a wonderful sense of camaraderie among groups of needlecrafters. And some, like Lesley Frost's Purim Puppets (chapter 19), enable parents and children to create pieces together, forging a love of Judaism and Jewish tradition in the spaces between stitches.

This book helps you get started by offering easy-to-follow instructions, so if you're captivated by the projects shown here, you can try your hand at replicating these exquisite and meaningful pieces of fabric art and add your own personal touches. While several of these projects are somewhat challenging to make, most of the crafts included here can be done by enthusiastic novices or relative newcomers to fabric crafts as an outlet for their creativity and passion for sustaining Jewish heritage. "Suggested Reading for Beginners" (pages 265–266) offers beginners to fabric crafts some wonderful resources to get started. The "General How-To's for Quilt Making" (pages 245–251) and the "General How-To's for Lettering" (pages 252–254) also give beginners—and even seasoned needlecrafters—a fabulous array of tips on how to make your project go smoothly and how to make it uniquely your own.

I sincerely hope that you enjoy the stories behind the projects in this book and that they inspire you to make your own Jewish fabric crafts, infusing them with love, spiritual intention, and imagination. With the work of our hands, we can each share our life and experiences with others, leaving a richly embroidered legacy that will endure for generations.

—*Diana Drew*

Do you have a special story about a Jewish fabric craft you created? Let me know. You can e-mail me at JewishCrafts18@gmail.com.

*Publisher's Note: Throughout this book, there are project templates that you will need to photocopy in order to complete the projects. Please note this material is covered by copyright (see page ii); the Publisher grants permission to you as the purchaser of this book to copy these templates for your personal use, but not for distribution to others. All rights to other parts of this book are still covered by copyright and are reserved to the Publisher. Any other copying or usage requires written permission.*

# PART ONE

# At Home

Making a Jewish home doesn't require a special occasion; it's an ongoing process that can last a lifetime as we grow and expand our knowledge about and insights into Judaism. Many Jews announce their Jewish home right at the front door—with a *mezuzah*. Though not a fabric craft, the *mezuzah* can set the stage for a home filled with ritual Jewish objects—some handed down through the generations, some newly purchased or created by the homeowner. The Jewish home is the perfect place to pursue your own creativity and find ways to add to the décor of your *bayit* (home) with imaginative fabric crafts that speak to your soul.

Like framed paintings, fabric wall hangings can grace the walls of your home, introducing subjects, colors, designs, and interpretations that create a comfortable setting and make for wonderful conversation pieces. Jewish-themed fabric wall hangings can be fashioned from all sorts of materials, including wool, cotton, rayon, polyester, and silk, in an array of colors and chromatic tones from bright to muted. Choose from myriad design elements, and make yours in a size that fits the space in your home. Techniques for making these beautiful pieces of wall art range from quilting, appliqué, and needlepoint, to knitting and felting. The only limits are your imagination, and that can be nourished by various sources of inspiration, from biblical and talmudic texts to images drawn from Jewish history and tradition.

## Hebrew Words

Many Jewish wall hangings play off Hebrew words, artfully arranged in unusual and even playful designs (see, for example, Arna Shefrin's *Ahavah* Needlepoint, chapter 3). The shapes of Hebrew letters lend themselves to creative designs that prompt viewers to take a step back and consider, in a new light, a word that they may have learned long ago, perhaps as a child.

The word *shalom* springs to mind. In Hebrew, the word *shalom* lends itself to myriad creative expressions, reflecting its many meanings. (See, for example, Hannah Margolis's Woven *Shalom* Wall Hanging, in the "Inspirations" section.) The Hebrew letter *shin,* at the beginning of *shalom,* can be open and wild, exuding a welcoming exuberance that greets people as they arrive in your home. The second letter, the *lamed,* continues the flow, with its graceful, heavenward surge. Large and flamboyant, it draws the eye into the word. The stem of the *lamed* stands high above the rest of the letters like an outstretched arm extending out of a crowd, giving a friendly wave of recognition. The *vav,* a bit timid next to the flamboyant *lamed,* ushers in a sense of calm and order, and the final *mem* puts a square exclamation point on the heartfelt greeting. *Hello, good-bye,* and *peace*—all are embodied in *shalom.*

When combined with other words, *shalom* may imbue a phrase with additional wishes, such as for a peaceful Sabbath (*Shabbat shalom*). So *shalom* on a wall hanging in and of itself suggests a friendly, welcoming place for your family members and guests.

## Doves and Olive Branches

Add a dove to your wall art (as in Susan Schrott's Tree of Life Wall Hanging, chapter 1, and Donna Gross's Quilted *Shalom* Wall Hanging, chapter 4). The story of Noah has forever made the dove and the olive branch symbols of peace. As a result, these tranquil signs perfectly complement the word *shalom* or suggest a quiet, reflective setting of their own. In Genesis 8:8–11, Noah sent out a dove to look for dry land after the Great Flood. When the dove returned with an olive branch, it was a sign that the earth could be inhabited once again.

Doves are seen in wall hangings and other crafts inspired by hopes and dreams for a peaceful world. Scenes of Jerusalem with doves overhead, doves holding up a chuppah at a wedding (or incorporated into the chuppah design, as in both chuppot featured in the "Inspirations" section), or doves flying in midair as the hora is being danced on a grassy pasture below all convey positive, optimistic, and peaceful thoughts.

## The Rainbow

Though it's a scientific phenomenon, the rainbow has religious associations in Judaism as well. Here, again, Noah plays a major role. In Genesis 9:8–17, God showed Noah a rainbow following the Flood. The rainbow symbolized God's promise to never again destroy humanity with floodwaters. So important is the rainbow that the Talmud decrees that a special prayer be recited when beholding a rainbow. In that prayer—"Blessed are You, *Adonai*, our God, Sovereign of the universe, who remembers the covenant, is faithful to that covenant, and keeps God's word"—the rainbow symbolizes God's faithfulness to humanity. That, in itself, would make rainbows a natural for all kinds of Jewish-themed fabric crafts, playing off the *brachah* (blessing), the covenant, and the Flood. Add to those resonances the colorful, fanciful, wondrous nature of rainbows, and they are simply irresistible images for wall hangings, challah covers, and tablecloths—whether in the background or the forefront of the design.

## The *Hamsa* Hand

Renewed interest in Kabbalah—Jewish mysticism—over the past several decades has brought a great deal of attention to the *hamsa* hand as an art form. In Jewish mysticism, the *hamsa* hand is often viewed as God's protective hand, a symbol used to ward off evil and bring good fortune. It is also known as the hand of Miriam. In the Bible, Miriam is the older sister of Moses and one of the few recognized female prophets. The five-fingered hand is sometimes shown with two thumbs and sometimes with one. The *hamsa* is also referred to as the *chamesh* hand. *Chamesh*, meaning "five" (for the five fingers of the *hamsa* hand), is a significant number in Judaism because of the Five Books of Moses and because *hey*, the fifth letter of the Hebrew alphabet, is part of one of God's holy names, *yud-hey-vav-hey*—the Tetragrammaton.

The *hamsa* hand is a symbol recognized in many religions, and archeologists have found evidence that this Middle Eastern icon even predates Judaism. When it comes to Judaism, the *hamsa* hand is more deep-rooted in folklore than in religion, but it's still a very popular ornament. (See Ruth Lenk's *Hamsa* Wall Hanging, chapter 2, and Vicki Pieser's Cross-Stitch *Wimpel,* chapter 24.)

In fabric crafts, the *hamsa* hand is presented in many different ways. Many have a prayer in the center of the hand, written in either English or Hebrew. The prayer can be sewn or painted on and may be long or short. One of the most common prayers found in the center of the *hamsa* hand is the blessing for the home, a prayer seeking harmony and peace in the home and protection for those who live there from sadness, trouble, fear, and conflict. The *Shema* is also found in the center of a *hamsa* hand in some fabric crafts, as are blessings for good health or a return to good health, the traveler's prayer, and prayers for a soldier's safe return. Any type of good wishes can be put in the center of the *hamsa.*

## The Star of David

Another popular decorative addition to any Jewish fabric craft is the Star of David. When David led troops in battle, this six-sided star adorned his shield. *Magen David,* as the star is called in Hebrew, is easily formed by overlapping two equilateral triangles. In 1948, the new State of Israel adopted the Star of David as an official emblem and put it on the nation's flag. One of the most commonly seen Jewish symbols, this star is worked into the motif of many Jewish fabric crafts. (See, for example, Susan Schrott's Tree of Life Wall Hanging, chapter 1, and Zoë Scheffy's Knit Seder Plate, chapter 22.) Sometimes words like *Shabbat* or *Pesach* are spelled out in Hebrew and put in the middle of the star.

## The Menorah

Even before David emblazoned his shield with the now famous six-pointed star, Jewish people used the menorah, or candelabrum, as a symbol of their faith. As one of the oldest ornaments in the Jewish religion—seen in some of the earliest synagogues ever built—the menorah graces many Jewish houses of worship today. Including the menorah in a fabric craft evokes lovely resonances because of the integral role it played and still plays in the décor of so many synagogues.

## The Tree of Life

From a design standpoint, the branches on the menorah closely relate to another spiritual object that takes on some of the same meanings—the Tree of Life, cited in Genesis 2:9. Once again, a symbol more closely tied to Kabbalah than to the Bible, the Tree of Life etched its way into Jewish crafts because it stands for so many things, including wisdom, beauty, protection, bounty, redemption, strength, and the Torah itself. Since there is no definitive way for the Tree of Life to be drawn, it allows for a lot of creative license for those using it in their work. (See, for example, Susan Schrott's Tree of Life Wall Hanging, chapter 1, and Eleanor Levie's Tree of Life Runner, chapter 6.)

## *Chai*

Two letters in the Hebrew alphabet speak volumes when it comes to Jewish-related crafts. The *chet* and the *yud* form one of the simplest yet most powerful words in the Hebrew language—*chai* (literally, "living")—which reflects the importance of life in the Jewish religion and expresses the ultimate in good wishes for a long life. Many thoughts and prayers in Judaism are built around the concept of *chai*, and it is a word that appears freely and often in the culture. *Chai* is a symbol that graces many Jewish homes in one form or another.

Ideas for wall hangings, challah covers, and tablecloths can be expanded and used for blankets, curtains, slipcovers, throws, pillows, and even wearable art like caps, sweaters, and purses (see Barbara D. Levinson's Felted Grapes Purse, chapter 5). Jewish fabric crafts can turn any house into a warm and inviting *bayit*.

—*Robert Grayson*

# 1

# Susan's Tree of Life Wall Hanging

*Project designer:* **Susan Schrott**

S usan Schrott's journey of artistic self-expression took a number of circuitous turns before she picked up quilting and made it her own. Her Tree of Life wall hanging, which uses fusible appliqué and promises to become a family heirloom, exemplifies the life lessons that brought her to this point.

After studying voice and drama at the American Musical and Dramatic Academy and dance at the School of American Ballet and with Martha Graham, Susan ventured into musical theater in her early twenties, appearing nationally with the Jewish Repertory Theatre in New York City. In her late twenties, she went back to college, earning a bachelor of arts degree, and continued on to receive her master's degree in social work and become a licensed clinical social worker. At that point, her creative energies found an outlet in weaving on a four-harness floor loom and other needlework. While she was pregnant with her second daughter, she discovered quilting, and a love affair with this textile art blossomed.

For Susan (www.susanschrottartist.com), quilting the Tree of Life, or *Etz Chayyim*, forges strong connections with nature and our roots in the natural world. It also reflects her desire to think mindfully about others. "I see each Tree of Life as a metaphor for the potential in each of us," she points out. "Trees rarely stand alone, and even when they do, they are often home to birds, squirrels, and other animals seeking food or shelter. We use the Tree of Life for shelter from the sun, for nourishment, and as a place to rest and to explore our physical potential as we climb up and up in life."

The metaphor evoked by the Tree of Life has personal meaning for Susan: "With each Tree of Life I create, ties to the world around me expand and deepen as the tree grows and blooms." Roots sink deep into the earth, offering stability and continuity. The tree trunk—firm and steady—reaches for the sky, while the leaves, which shade all God's creatures on scorching days, draw support from the earth below and the sun and sky above. "Just as we evolve throughout our lives, the shapes and colors of trees change miraculously with the seasons, leaving us breathless and awed. Trees have a natural life cycle, and with it come the wisdom of life and death, and respect for the preciousness of life."

Susan loves creating her own vividly colored, hand-dyed and surface-designed textiles, threads, and mixed media. Besides her Judaica-inspired pieces, like this Tree of Life, she infuses her work with images of women who are courageous, joyful, and inspirational. Her uplifting artwork appears in a number of major collections, including Tel Hashomer-Shiba Hospital / Rehabilitation Center, Rambam Hospital Children's Pavilion, and Karen Yaldenu Youth Center in Rehovot, Israel. She also donates her artwork regularly to the Friends of the Israel Defense Forces for their annual fund-raisers in New York. Dovetailing with her work as a clinical social worker, the award-winning quilting that Susan does with such joy and love enables her to connect with the world in a singularly meaningful way.

# Getting Started

*Finished size:* Approximately 16 inches by 16 inches

Refer to "General How-To's for Quilt Making," pages 245–251.

## WHAT YOU'LL NEED

### *Susan's hints on selecting fabrics for your own Tree of Life:*

Visualize your tree in bloom. Consider the time of year. Are your leaves just budding? Are they in full bloom? Is it autumn, and are the colors changing? On the other hand, don't feel limited by what you think a tree *should* look like. You can use fabrics that have nothing to do with reality—polka dots, squiggles, batiks, even stripes. Or draw inspiration from Shabbat, Purim, Passover, or biblical texts.

Cotton fabrics:

> A fat quarter of light-toned, visually quiet pattern, such as mottled, for background
>
> Contrasting fabric, at least 12 inches square, for tree trunk
>
> 3 different but coordinating fabrics, approximately 12 inches square, for leaves
>
> A fat quarter of a conversation, or novelty, print or other pattern meaningful to you, for borders
>
> A fat quarter, for the backing

Paper-backed fusible web

Batting, 20 inches by 20 inches (optional)

Fabric for backing, 20 inches by 20 inches (optional)

## HOW-TO'S

### *Preparing the Framed Background*

1.  Cut an 18-by-18-inch square from your selected background fabric.

2.  Cut a 9-by-20-inch piece of fusible web and fuse it to the wrong side of your chosen border fabric. Cut 4 strips, each measuring 2¹/₂ inches by 20 inches from the fused fabric. On one long side of each strip, rotary-cut a wavy line, working freehand. Remove the paper backing,

Figure 1.1

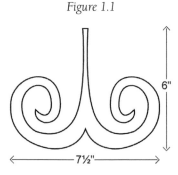

6"

7½"

Figure 1.2

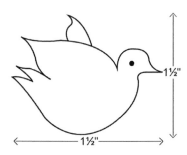

1½"

1½"

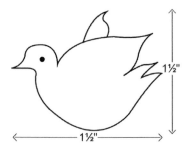

1½"

1½"

1½"

1½"

and arrange the strips on top of the background fabric with the outer edges even. Shift the strips to one side or the other to determine a pleasing look, then trim the ends to align with the background. Fuse the borders in place.

## Tree of Life Design

1.  Enlarge the pattern for the tree trunk at left (Figure 1.1) as marked, and then trace it onto the paper side of the fusible web. Cut out about ¼ inch beyond the traced design lines. Press the fusible web shape to the wrong side of the tree trunk fabric, then cut out directly along the traced lines. Set the tree trunk aside.

2.  Press fusible web to the wrong sides of the leaf fabrics you have selected. Using either scissors or a rotary cutter, freehand-cut a variety of leaves, no more than 3 inches in length. Remove the paper backing from all appliqués.

3.  Center the tree trunk between the sides of the framed background, about 3 inches from the bottom edge. Arrange the leaves, beginning with the center of your tree and working outward, creating a starburst effect. This is when your Tree of Life starts to become utterly unique and personal. Play around with how you choose to arrange your leaves. For example, some may overlap, others may not, or you may decide to create a pattern using your 3 fabrics.

4.  If desired, using patterns at left (Figure 1.2), add doves, a Star of David, or any symbols or shapes that have meaning for you. Trace desired designs onto fusible web, and apply to the wrong side of chosen fabrics.

5.  After the tree trunk and all the leaves and other appliqués are arranged to your satisfaction, fuse everything to the background.

## Finishing

1.  You can now have your Tree of Life matted and framed, to hang in a place of honor.

2.  *Alternatively,* to make it into a quilted piece, layer the quilt top over batting (hold off on the backing), and quilt the design. Consider using decorative stitching and decorative threads. Satin-stitch the outer edges of the tree trunk. Try using some of your machine's decorative stitches, such as featherstitch or honeycomb, on the inner edges of your border fabrics. Consider leaving the edges of the leaves raw, so they fray a bit; free-motion quilt over them to secure them and also to enhance the sense of movement around the treetop. Also free-motion quilt the background fabric to give your piece additional color and dimension.

PHOTO: JONATHAN SCHROTT

3.  Square up the quilted piece, and place it on the backing fabric, cut to the same size, with right sides together and edges even.

4.  Sew around the entire edge of the quilt top using a $\frac{1}{4}$-inch seam allowance, stopping about 5 inches before your starting point. Clip across the seam allowances at the corners to reduce bulk. Reach inside this "pillowcase" and turn the quilt right side out. Fold the edges of the opening $\frac{1}{4}$ inch to the inside and slip-stitch to close. Press the quilt. Hand-stitch a hanging sleeve and a label on the back.

Display your lovely Tree of Life, or present it to someone dear to you with all your good wishes.

# 2  Ruth's *Hamsa* Wall Hanging

- - - - - - - - - - - - - - - - - - - - - - - - - - - - - - - - - - -

*Project designer:* Ruth Lenk

R uth Lenk, a peripatetic photographer, graphic designer, ceramist, and textile artist, takes as her inspiration for this dramatic wall hanging the *hamsa*—a good-luck symbol used to ward off the "evil eye." While viewing an exhibition of *hamsas*, Ruth was captivated by this highly resonant image.

"The hand is a very important means of expression, denoting power, strength, even blessing," she points out. "It can be a symbol of acceptance or exclusion. A write-up accompanying the *hamsa* exhibition noted that, until recently, people felt the need for extra protection in the face of the unknown—usually illnesses for which there were no cures. But I believe we could all benefit from a bit of extra protection."

Currently living in Israel, Ruth notes that the *hamsa's* intricate designs and graphics have always appealed to her, and she has built up a collection of *hamsas* from all over the world. This quilt, arrayed with four different *hamsa* designs, shows some of the myriad styles of *hamsas* seen in far-flung countries.

For this quilted *hamsa* wall hanging, Ruth researched the history, development, and popular themes and iconography used in connection with the *hamsa*. "Each *hamsa* has its own meaning. For example, the salamander symbolizes safety from fire, and the letter *hey* represents the number five—a number with echoes throughout Judaism, including the Five Books of Moses," Ruth observes. "Then I chose colors that I thought complemented each other." Striking details, like bells from India, tassels and mirrors from Israel, and a glass eye from Turkey, give this piece an international appeal, reflecting Ruth's own travels around the world. The *hamsa* wall hanging shown here is nearly as well traveled as Ruth herself: it has appeared in two exhibitions—one in Baku, Azerbaijan, and one in Jerusalem, Israel.

Ruth has always had a passion for visual art. She received a BFA with honors from the Hartford Art School at the University of Hartford. After college, she moved to Israel, where she started working for the *Jerusalem Post* and eventually became the publication's art director. In her free time, Ruth delved into photography, ceramics, and textile work.

Because her husband works for the Israeli Ministry of Foreign Affairs (a government agency equivalent to the U.S. State Department), Ruth relocated with her family to New Delhi, India, a move that allowed her to experiment extensively with quilting and different textiles. As the years passed and the family continued to relocate, Ruth kept discovering new cultures and acquiring new skills.

In 2005, the family was posted in Baku, Azerbaijan, and Ruth created and ran an art program for the primary school at the International School of Azerbaijan. While in Baku, her personal fabric artwork was influenced by the traditional art of carpet weaving. Ruth exhibited her quilted creations, which celebrated local folkways and themes, in the Azerbaijan State Museum for Carpets and Applied Arts.

Now back in Israel, Ruth is teaching art at the Anglican International School in Jerusalem and until recently was working for ILAN (an organization that helps people with disabilities), managing the ceramics studio in ILAN's day center. Living in the Holy Land, she finds Jewish themes, like the *hamsa*, permeating her work. From each place where she has lived, Ruth has absorbed the local patterns, colors, textures, and motifs, weaving them subtly, and sometimes overtly, into her evolving artwork.

# Getting Started

*Finished size:* Approximately 30 inches by 36 inches, not including tassels or hanging loops

Refer to "General How-To's for Quilt Making," pages 245–251.

## WHAT YOU'LL NEED

Cotton fabrics:

> 1¹/₂ yards of black or dark blue, for the background and sashing
>
> ¹/₂ yard yellow, for the large *hamsa*
>
> 3 different blues, 6¹/₂ inches by 8¹/₂ inches, for the small *hamsas'* background
>
> Bright blue, 6 inches by 18 inches, for the large fish
>
> Scraps in assorted colors for details
>
> 1 yard of black, for backing

Batting, 1 yard

Green single-fold bias binding tape

Fabric glue

1 yard each of 2 different, wide jacquard ribbons

Paper-backed fusible web

## *Suggested Embellishments*

1 glass eye bead or charm

5 small bells

5 *shisha* mirrors, 1 inch in diameter

1 jewel pendant

5 large tassels

Assorted ribbons, buttons, beads

Thread in gold and other coordinating colors for quilting

Tulip fabric paint

*Figure 2.1*

*Figure 2.1*

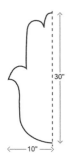

30"

←—10"—→

*Figure 2.2*

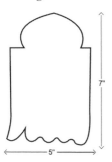

7"

←——5"——→

*Figure 2.3*

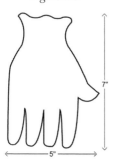

7"

←——5"——→

*Figure 2.4*

7"

←———5"———→

## HOW-TO'S

1.  Enlarge the reduced-size patterns (Figures 2.1 through 2.8) as marked. Draw half the large symmetrical *hamsa* freehand on a 20-by-30-inch sheet of paper, folded lengthwise in half, and cut out to obtain a full pattern. Press paper-backed fusible web onto the back of fabrics you've chosen for the desired appliqué shapes—the smaller *hamsas*, the fish, the salamander, the leaves, and the *hey*—and cut them out.

2.  For the large *hamsa* fingertips, cut out squares from the fusible-backed fabrics in contrast colors: five 2½-inch squares from red, and five 1½-inch squares from blue. Cut a ½-inch hole in the middle of each of the smaller squares, and zigzag-stitch around each hole. Set aside these small squares with holes for now. Arrange the larger squares on the fingertips, as shown (page 12). Center the fish in place. For vines, arrange green bias binding tape in curvy lines, and add leaves as shown. When you're satisfied with the composition, press to fuse everything else in place. Topstitch on both sides of the vines, and zigzag-stitch all other appliqués to secure them. Center a *shisha* mirror on top of each 2½-inch square on the large *hamsa* fingers, and glue it in place. Center a 1½-inch square with a finished hole on top of each of the mirrors, then zigzag-stitch around the edges of each 1½-inch square.

3.  Arrange all the smaller appliqués on top of the smaller *hamsas*.

4.  Secure the appliqués with zigzag stitching around all raw edges, using thread colors to match each appliqué.

5.  Lay the large dark background fabric on a flat surface. Referring to Figure 2.9, arrange the large *hamsa* on one side and the 3 blue 6½-by-8½-inch rectangles on the other. Pin each of the small *hamsas* to its background. Pin horizontal sashing, measuring 6½ by 2½ inches, between the blue rectangles, and vertical sashing, measuring 2½ by 36½ inches,

to the right of the small *hamsas*. Stitch all the pieces together.

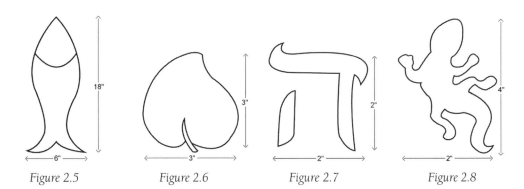

*Figure 2.9*

## Assembly

1. Tape backing to the floor, with right side down. Place batting on top of the backing, and then place the quilt top on top of the batting in a quilt sandwich. Pin the quilt through all 3 layers. Quilt as desired, adding any extra details at this point.

2. Using binding or bias tape over matched raw edges, finish side seams.

3. Make 5 hanging tabs by cutting 5 strips of the background fabric, measuring 2¹/₂ inches by 10 inches each. Fold each strip in half, lengthwise, right side in, and stitch a ¹/₄-inch seam. Turn inside out, and press with the seam in the middle of the back. Match the raw edges, and pin them in place.

4. Fold in the raw edges of the top and bottom quilt edges. Pin the jacquard ribbon over the top and bottom seams, with hanging tabs and tassels in place between the quilt and the ribbon.

5. Topstitch ribbons in place.

Hang your quilted *hamsa* wall hanging on a rod in a place of honor and bask in the good luck it provides you and your loved ones!

*Figure 2.5*   *Figure 2.6*   *Figure 2.7*   *Figure 2.8*

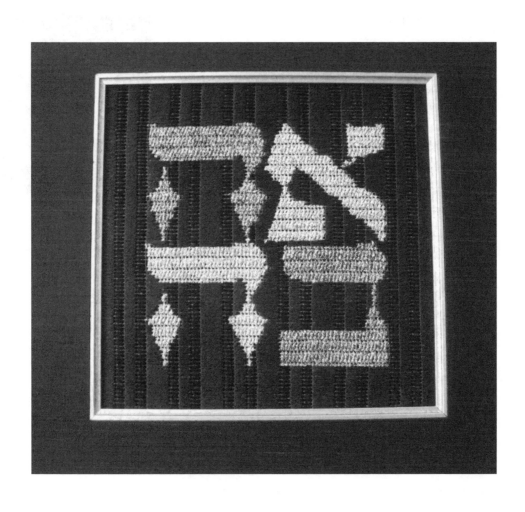

# 3 Arna's *Ahavah* Needlepoint

*Project designer:* Arna Shefrin

A rna Shefrin's *ahavah* (love) wall hanging, done in needlepoint, evokes the iconic *LOVE* sculpture by Robert Indiana. "The theme of this canvas allows me to express my feelings about the importance of love in our lives and about living a Jewish life," says the artist.

Arna grew up in Winnipeg, Canada, known for its strong, vibrant Jewish community. Even though the women in her family didn't have much to do with fabric and fibers, except for making easy clothing repairs, hemming, and simple social knitting, Arna herself has had a lifelong fascination with threads, yarn, and textiles. Both this project and her needle-pointed Jerusalem tallit bag, featured in the "Inspirations" section, lie at the intersection of her Jewish identity and her avocation as a fiber artist.

"I learned how to sew in home economics class and have always loved to create highly detailed things with my hands," recalls the fiber artist, who now calls Menlo Park, California, home. "Early in my twenties, I bought a book, some supplies, and taught myself to crochet. I picked up the fine points while watching a woman on the train work on her project. After that minimal instruction, I went on to teach myself how to read a pattern and to create a somewhat complex crocheted shawl." She discovered needlepoint in much the same way, using the extensive travel time that her career in human clinical research trials required to hone her skills. "I found that needlepoint was a great way to relax while I waited for the next flight."

As with crochet, needlepoint began for Arna with a how-to book and some supplies. Quickly, she mastered the basics on her own and then joined the local needlepointers' guild, where she learned from experts and enjoyed the support and camaraderie of the group. "Some of these members had won national contests by creating pieces that were museum-quality," she notes. "I found that learning advanced techniques, coupled with repetition, was both stimulating and relaxing. For me, it's like painting with threads."

Because the letters for the *ahavah* wall hanging were Hebrew, Arna decided to think of the canvas as somewhat formal. Instead of using red for the letters on a white or colored background, as Robert Indiana had done, she chose silver metallic and hologram threads for the letters and royal blue silk for the background—both traditional Jewish colors. "I wanted to give the canvas an illuminated quality, reminiscent of medieval illuminated manuscripts. Through the vertical columns of the background, I tried to suggest the columns of script in a Torah scroll as well as the image of the generations that came before me," she says. This framed needlepoint canvas is displayed near the entrance to Arna's home—a welcoming and inviting piece of wall art that ushers guests inside.

An injury to her hands from computer overuse forced Arna to retire early from her career in human clinical trials. Fortunately, knitting came to her rescue. "The muscles involved in knitting are different than those involved with using the mouse. Again, lots of books, minimal instruction, inspirational patterns and yarns, and I was off and running," she says, adding that her colorful knit sweaters, vests, and other clothing are like art to wear. "The best part of knitting my own clothes is that strangers approach me and say they can't believe

I made this. I have wonderful conversations prompted by wearing these creations."

Threads, fibers, and textiles have created new connections for Arna throughout her life and have been a source of stimulation for her, as well as great comfort and relaxation. "I volunteer with a local nonprofit that distributes discontinued textile designer samples to individuals, organizations, and schools for creative activities," she points out. "These gorgeous pieces previously went to the landfill. I frequently donate my creations to fund-raisers in support of museums and foundations. In addition, I enjoy finishing items my friends have knit for their grandchildren. This generally involves tea and conversation as I work; it's a meaningful way for me to engage with them and their families. Learning, teaching, and connecting with friends through hands and fibers are the threads—sometimes Jewish, sometimes not—that run through my life."

# Getting Started

*Finished size:* 6¹/₂ inches by 6³/₄ inches
Refer to the "Stitch Guide," pages 255–256.

## WHAT YOU'LL NEED

White needlepoint canvas, 9¹/₂ inches by 9³/₄ inches

Frame or stretcher bars

Splendor 12-ply silk needlepoint yarn, color S859, 1 card

RG Holo FyreWerks hologram ribbon, color FH3, 1 card

RG Holo FyreWerks metallic ribbon, color FM3, 1 card

## HOW-TO'S

*Notes:*

- Attach the canvas to the stretcher bars before you begin. This will keep the canvas square and reduce the amount of blocking that needs to be done by the professional framer once the piece is completed.

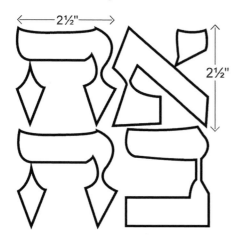

*Figure 3.1*

←——— 2½" ———→

2½"

- Besides referring to a thin, tightly twisted yarn, the word *thread* in needlepoint refers to the intersection of warp and weft (or crosswise) components of the canvas.

## Letters

*Note: Stitch the letters first.*

1. Mark the exact center of the canvas with a light pencil mark. Enlarge the letters pattern at left (Figure 3.1) as marked. With light pencil marks, trace the letters *aleph, hey, vet,* and *hey* onto the canvas. Be sure that the letters are centered on the canvas.

2. *For the* aleph *(upper right) and the* hey *at lower left*: With RG Holo FyreWerks hologram ribbon, color FH3, stitch the letters in slanted Gobelin stitch, 3 threads of canvas tall and 1 thread wide.

3. *For the* hey *at upper left and the* vet *(lower right)*: With RG Holo FyreWerks metallic ribbon, color FM3, stitch the letters in slanted Gobelin stitch, 3 threads of canvas tall and 1 thread wide.

## Background

1. Working from the horizontal center of the canvas, use 6 plies (or enough plies to cover the canvas) of Splendor 12-ply silk to work straight Gobelin stitch over 5 canvas threads, forming a vertical column.

2. Then, following the diagram (Figure 3.2), work straight Gobelin stitch over 2 canvas threads on either side.

3. Stitch straight Gobelin over 3 threads on either side of those columns.

4. Then work straight Gobelin over 2 threads on either side of those columns.

5. Stitch a 5-thread column of straight Gobelin on either side of those columns.

*Figure 3.2*

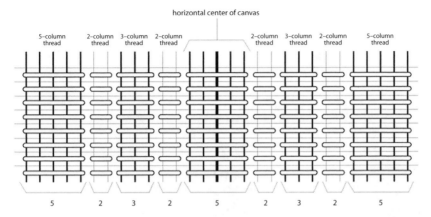

Repeat steps 1–5 until you reach the edges of the canvas, ending with a 5-thread column. Thus, the background is worked with each 3- or 5-thread column of stitches separated from its neighbor by a 2-thread column, starting with 5 threads in the center, working out to the edges, and ending with a 5-thread column, as shown in the diagram.

Have your finished canvas professionally framed by a frame shop familiar with mounting needlepoint canvases using acid-free materials.

Display your *ahavah* wall hanging with love!

# Donna's Quilted *Shalom* Wall Hanging

4

*Project designer:* **Donna Gross**

---

**D**onna Gross's art quilt is a wall hanging inspired by the theme of peace/*shalom*. Peace is very much on Donna's mind because as of this writing, her older son, Philip, is serving in Afghanistan. "He is a captain in the Army Green Berets, and this is his second tour of duty in the Middle East," she notes. "He was in Iraq the first time for eighteen months. Not a day goes by that I do not pray for his safe return."

Donna's younger son, Michael, also served in the Army Green Berets in Afghanistan, earning a bronze star for his valiant actions. He is now pursuing his education in Texas. "I am proud of both my sons for who they are and the fine young men they have grown to be," says the fabric artist, who lives in northern New Jersey.

The peace/*shalom* theme reflects the artist's fervently held wish that peace will come swiftly to all areas of the Middle East—and the entire world. Symbolism abounds in this quilt, from the words themselves, incorporated into the piece, to the earth, with the peace dove protecting her. Speaking about some additional symbols she worked into the quilt, Donna says, "The dove is offering all of us an olive branch. The rainbow is God's promise not to destroy the earth after the Flood. The side borders are embellished with undulating ribbons

25

to represent how all our lives are entwined with one another. The circles on the bottom represent people. They are all different sizes and colors to show the vast diversity on our planet. I placed hearts in the circles because we, as human beings, all have hearts and souls and need to learn to live with one another. I came across the gold stars afterward and decided to add them to represent the seven days of creation." Donna had the greatest fun finding all the embellishments for her *shalom* wall hanging.

Donna began quilting about fifteen years ago because she was curious about the process and wanted to learn how it was done. At the time, she was also painting in oils, which was the main focus of her artistic pursuits. Yet life sometimes takes unexpected turns.

"In 2001, I was diagnosed with multiple sclerosis," she recalls. "I found that painting was not an option anymore because of the MS. I had difficulty holding onto the brush and applying the paint where I wanted it to go. So I turned to quilting—especially art quilts—to take the place of painting and to give voice to my need for artistic expression." Donna started with simple wall hangings and soon discovered a love for the medium and a previously untapped talent for quilting. One of her earlier quilts was selected for the United Synagogue of Conservative Judaism calendar for the year 2006–2007. Her quilted wall hanging graced the October calendar grid.

Since then, she has exhibited her art quilts in juried art shows and won a number of prizes. She has also done commissioned pieces and helped design and craft the chuppah that is the pride and joy of National Council of Jewish Women, West Morris Section. (See the Introduction and the "Inspirations" section for more on the NCJW, West Morris, chuppah.)

Donna was an integral part of the NCJW chuppah project. (See "Donna's Apples & Honey Challah Cover," chapter 13, for a project drawn from the chuppah.) "I designed the squares for the underside—the panel the couple would see when they were under the chuppah—by tying in different Jewish themes, making each design look like a stained-glass panel," she points out. "I put together kits for our members to appliqué. This allowed many of our members to be part of this wonderful project. Once the appliquéd squares were all completed, they were sewn to the Stars of David. The chuppah is now a one-of-a-kind heirloom to be used at many joyous occasions."

While Donna's creativity reaches in many directions, her *shalom* wall hanging embodies her passionate wish for a peaceful world—one in which we all share in the universal spirit of understanding.

# Getting Started

*Finished size:* 26 inches by 24 inches
Refer to "General How-To's for Quilt Making," pages 245–251, and "General How-To's for Lettering," pages 252–254.

> *Notes:*
>
> - You may make this quilted *shalom* wall hanging from any colors you choose, using embellishments that resonate with you and have meaning for your life, your family, or those for whom you are making the quilt.
>
> - Have fun and don't worry about imperfections. This is your artwork, designed to reflect your passions and spiritual intention.
>
> - According to Donna, the wonderful thing about quilting is that there are no rules. You can quilt using any design you like. Donna quilted this piece by following the natural direction of the shapes. So if some other shapes speak to you instead, go for it!

## WHAT YOU'LL NEED

Cotton fabrics:
  Purple for sky, 20 inches by 15 inches
  2 pink rectangles 19 inches by 4 inches, for *Peace/Shalom* backgrounds
  Teal, lavender, and aqua for side borders, 19 inches by 5 inches
  Maroon, 28 inches by 10 inches, for bottom border
Paper-backed fusible web, 1 package of 12 sheets

Figure 4.1

Scraps of various colors for earth, dove, lettering, circles, rainbow, and olive branch

Fabric pencil and acid-free colored pencils

Rickrack, flat trim, and braided trim in metallics and pastels, 1 yard of each

Various heart-shaped buttons, approximately 50

Gold star charms or buttons, approximately 7

Thin gold yarn or cording, 2 yards

Batting, 30 inches by 30 inches

Fabric for backing, 30 inches by 30 inches

Fabric for binding material, ¹/₂ yard

Figure 4.2

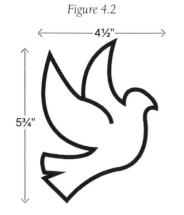

## HOW-TO'S

### *Quilt Top*

1. Enlarge the reduced-size patterns at left (Figures 4.1 and 4.2) to the proper dimensions, as marked. Use colored pencils to trace the design on a large piece of paper and color in the design elements.

2. Referring to the photo for colors (see color insert) or choosing colors and fabrics as desired, lay out the fabric you have chosen onto the large sketch, to see how the overall design and color scheme work together.

3. Cut all the rectangular background pieces to the dimensions indicated, adding ¹/₄ inch to all edges, for seam allowances. Press fusible web to the back of fabrics for appliqués: lettering, doves, rainbow, side border swirls.

4. Use a light box or a sunny window to trace each motif onto the front of appropriately colored fabric, using a fabric pencil. Remove paper backing and then cut out, adding $1/8$ inch to the edges of the rainbow arcs, so you can overlap them, but cutting out all other motifs along the marked lines: the earth, the yellow glow surrounding the earth, the swirls on the side borders, the dove, the olive branch, and the words *Shalom* and *Peace*.

5. *For the sky section:* Arrange the rainbow arcs, with curved sides overlapping and short ends alongside the raw edges of the background. Next, position the yellow glow surrounding the earth, the earth, and the dove. Fuse in place. Add the olive branch and leaves, and fuse them into place. Join the backgrounds for the *Peace/Shalom* lettering to the top and bottom of the sky section. Press the seam allowances toward the center. Fuse the swirls to the side borders. Pin trims in wavy lines on top, then stitch them in place. Stitch the side borders to the bordered sky, and the bottom section across the joined sections. Press seam allowances toward the center.

6. Referring to "General How-To's for Lettering" (pages 252–254), center and fuse the words *Shalom* and *Peace* to the borders as shown. Layer various-sized and various-colored circles over the bottom section and fuse.

## Assembly & Finishing

1. Sandwich and quilt the piece, referring to the photo (page 24). Special touches done here include zigzag-stitching over metallic cord between each rainbow arc, around the dove, and around the earth glow.

2. Bind the quilt (see "General How-To's for Quilt Making," pages 250–251), adding a hanging sleeve. Stitch on stars, buttons, and charms. Add a label.

Hang your heartfelt *shalom* wall hanging with your own prayers for peace.

# 5 Barbara's Felted Grapes Purse

*Project designer:* **Barbara D. Levinson**

For fabric artist Barbara Levinson, the process of felting is imbued with spiritual resonance. "When I'm felting, I feel a definite spiritual connection," she says. "Felting is an ancient form of fiber art, dating back as far as 6300 BCE. After my adult Bat Mitzvah three years ago, I knew that I wanted to include Jewish symbols in my work. The grapes on this purse remind me of family, *Kiddush,* the peacefulness of Shabbat, and our wonderful heritage. I am often complimented on the look and feel of this felt purse, and the uniqueness of the design." Grapes are also one of the seven biblical fruits.

An artist all her life, Barbara attended the Dayton Art Institute in Ohio as a child. But much of her background in fiber arts came from her grandmother, who taught her how to embroider, knit, and sew. After receiving a degree in art education from Ohio State University, Barbara became an elementary school teacher, subtly integrating art projects into all the subjects she taught.

Then, about six years ago, Barbara discovered felting and decided to explore the process further. "I have studied felting with some wonderful artists and attended their workshops," she points out. "Combining colors, design, and fibers is a wonderful journey. I also enjoy the opportunity to create wearable art, such as scarves, purses,

31

and jewelry, and derive great pleasure from seeing people wear my creations." Transplanted from the Midwest, she now lives in the San Francisco Bay area of California.

Felting involves taking a piece of knitting and agitating it in hot water, usually in the washing machine. (Some of us have done this accidentally with a well-loved garment, yielding a doll-size sweater.) This evocative purse is one of the more challenging projects in *Jewish Threads,* requiring a basic knowledge of knitting techniques. Barbara's purse calls for knitting and then felting the base, the branch, the leaves, and the stem, followed by hand-stitching the felted adornments onto the base when all the pieces are dry. The last step involves adding the handles. Along the way, if anything seems puzzling, the artist advises you to check with the folks in your local yarn store. "They're wonderful teachers," she says.

Once you've made this gorgeous purse, be prepared to receive clusters of compliments as you carry your felted grapes bag from home all around town.

# Getting Started

## WHAT YOU'LL NEED

*Note: Do not use superwash wool, as that will not felt.*

3 skeins worsted-weight 100% wool yarn in burgundy (Cascade 220 was used here)

Small amounts (less than half a skein each) of worsted-weight 100% wool in purple, brown, sage green, and olive green

Size 13 circular knitting needles, 20–24 inches

Stitch markers

Tapestry needle

Size 6 double-pointed needles

Sewing needle and polyester double thread in colors matching the yarns for the leaves, branch, stem, and grapes

1 pair leather handles (optional)
(Barbara used Grayson handles,
available at many yarn stores and at
www.jimmybeanswool.com)

## HOW-TO'S

### *Make the Purse*

With circular needles, cast on 30 stitches,
using 2 strands of the burgundy yarn.

Work back and forth on circular needles,
knitting every row for 30 rows (15 garter
ridges). When you reach the last row, do not
turn. Next, pick up 15 stitches along the short
side of the rectangle, then pick up 30 stitches
along the long side of the rectangle, finally
picking up 15 more stitches along the 2nd
short side of the rectangle. You should have
90 stitches total on the needle.

Place marker and knit 60 rounds. Bind off.

### *Make the Branch & Stem*

#### *Branch*

Using the brown yarn and size 6 double-pointed needles, knit the 1st row.
Slide the stitches onto the opposite end of the needle. Now the working
yarn is at the bottom of the row. Knit again, pulling the working yarn up the
back of the piece so you can work on it. Pull tightly. Again, slide the stitches
to the opposite end of the needle. Repeat in this manner. As you pull the
yarn, the back will close up on itself. When the branch is 12 inches long,
bind off and weave in the ends.

#### *Stem*

Using the olive-green yarn and size 6 double-pointed needles, follow directions above for the branch. When the stem is 3 inches long, bind off and
weave in the ends.

## Abbreviations & Techniques

**I-cord handles:** Using size 6 double-pointed needles, cast on 3–6 stitches. Knit the 1st row. Slide the stitches to the opposite end of the needle. Now the working yarn is at the bottom of the row. Knit again, pulling the working yarn up the back of the piece so you can work with it. Again slide the stitches to the opposite end of the needle. Repeat in this manner for as long as you like. As you pull the yarn, the back will close in on itself.

**k2tog:** knit 2 together

**kf&b:** knit front and back

**p2tog:** purl 2 together

**psso:** pass slipped stitch over

**ssk:** slip, slip, knit

### Make the Leaves (make 3)

Using a single strand of sage-green yarn and size 6 double-pointed needles, make a slip knot and then start the following pattern (see "Abbreviations and Techniques" on page 33):

Row 1: Purl, knit, purl.

Row 2: Knit all knit stitches and purl all purl stitches on all even rows.

Row 3: Kf&b, purl 1, kf&b (5 stitches).

Row 5: Kf&b, kf&b, p1, kf&b, kf&b (9 stitches).

Row 7: Kf&b, knit 3, purl 1, knit 3, kf&b (11 stitches).

Rows 8–12: Work stitches as you see them (knit the knit and purl the purl).

Row 13: Ssk, knit 3, purl 1, knit 3, k2tog (9 stitches).

Row 14: Repeat row 2.

Row 15: Ssk, knit 2, purl 1, knit 2, k2tog (7 stitches).

Row 16: P2tog, purl 1, knit 1, purl 1, p2tog (5 stitches).

Row 17: Ssk, purl 1, k2tog (3 stitches).

Row 18: Slip 1 stitch, p2tog, psso (1st stitch).

Pull the yarn through the stitch and weave in the tail.

PHOTO: DR. RON ISRAEL

### Make the Grapes (make 21)

Using a double strand of the burgundy yarn and size 6 double-pointed needles, begin with a slip knot on one needle. Kf&b until you have made 7 stitches in that 1 stitch for a total of 7. Knit the 1st row, then continue in stockinette stitch for 6 more rows—7 rows total—ending with a right-side row.

Bind off stitches as follows: Consider the left-most stitch on the right-hand needle the "1st stitch." Lift the 2nd stitch over the 1st stitch, doing the same with the next stitch, and so on, until you have lifted 6 stitches over that 1st stitch and the "1st stitch" is the only stitch on the needle. The purl side is the right side. Using the double yarn, put it through the last stitch and do a running stitch along the grape edge, beginning and ending in the same place. Pull tightly, double knot, and tuck the ends into the grape.

## Felting

Put all the knit pieces in a zippered pillowcase or a mesh bag. Place the bag or pillowcase in a washing machine, set at the hottest setting, together with a pair of jeans (to add friction). A top-loading machine is best, because it's easy to see when the felting process is complete. Your pieces are fully felted when no knit stitches show. Check your knit pieces often to make sure you don't over-felt.

To dry and block the purse once it is fully felted, put something inside it, such as a plastic container, to hold the shape.

## Assembly

Once all the felted pieces are dry, hand-stitch the grapes, leaves, stem, and branch onto the purse, referring to the photo on page 30. Sew on leather handles according to manufacturer's instructions. *Alternatively*, you could make heavy I-cord handles as long as you'd like, per the directions in the "Abbreviations & Techniques" box (page 33) and sew those on.

Carry your beautiful handmade purse with panache!

# PART TWO

# In the Synagogue

The synagogue, or *shul* in Yiddish, is the centerpiece of any Jewish community and infuses us with both spiritual and creative inspiration. It serves as a sanctuary for reflection and study, and activities conducted there enable us to gain a deeper understanding of and appreciation for Judaism. By drawing on those insights and tapping your own creativity, there are many ways in which fabric crafts can make your synagogue a very special place and services there wonderfully memorable.

The word *shul* comes from a German word meaning "school." That focuses on the synagogue's role not only as a house of worship but as a center of continued study and enlightenment throughout life. *Shul* is one of the earliest references to a Jewish house of worship, which is also referred to as a temple and, in Hebrew, as a *beit k'nesset,* which literally means a "house of assembly."

For many people, early recollections of observing Jewish rituals come from times spent in synagogue. Greeting the Torah during Shabbat services, marching up and down the aisles with Simchat Torah flags, sitting in synagogue with *groggers* ready to drown out the name *Haman* during the reading of the *Megillat Esther* (Scroll of Esther) on Purim, and the lighting of the first Chanukah candle on the big menorah sitting on the bimah—all these play an integral role in the upbringing of most Jewish children. Helping to frame these experiences is the décor of the synagogue, much of which is highlighted by rich fabrics in deep blues and burgundies and in pristine, glittering whites. Precisely embroidered images in silver and gold thread of the Ten Commandments, Stars of David, crowns, lions, and other religious symbols adorn these fine pieces of material and integrate them into the religious experience.

## Torah Mantles

The use of cloth to cover and store the Torah goes back to ancient times and is even mentioned in the Mishnah. According to Latin and Greek literature, in biblical times sacred scrolls were wrapped in cloth in the Middle East. Torah covers, or mantles as they are also known, appear in written references in fourteenth-century Europe as well. During the Middle Ages, artisans created Torah mantles out of heavy and expensive cloth, not fabric seen in everyday life. Books in Germany, dating back to the fifteenth century, record the existence of Torah mantles at that time and use dramatic narrative to describe in detail the intricate design of these Torah dressings. The two openings at the upper end of the mantle, the materials used to make the robe-like coverings, and the decorative motifs sewn on the front of these exquisite pieces fascinated scribes authoring books on European culture in the fifteenth century.

Inspired by tradition and lovingly made with the care reserved for items created for royalty, some Torah mantles fashioned generations ago have survived to this day, and their wear tells the story of their journey to modern times. Torah mantles with significant histories are showcased in museums throughout the world as both art objects and spiritually meaningful pieces of Judaica. It is not unusual for a mantle to remain in use covering the same Torah for decades.

Traditionally, Torah mantles were only changed during the High Holy Days, when the normally colorful mantle was replaced with a white cover to symbolize purity and forgiveness. Now many congregations have a variety of Torah mantles to help dress up the sacred scrolls for various holidays throughout the year. Clever adaptations of holiday-related themes create vivid and spectacular Torah mantles that can make every holiday observance a truly memorable experience as the ark is opened and a Torah clad in a specially designed mantle just for the occasion is taken out of the ark and marched through the sanctuary. (See Judy Snitzer's Sukkot Torah Mantle, chapter 9, and Shavuot Torah Mantle, chapter 10, for modern versions of this ancient form of Judaica fabric art.)

## The Ark Curtain

Unlike Torah mantles, specifics about the *parochet,* or ark curtain, are found in Exodus. Ark curtains can be traced back to some of the earliest arks, and as the structures themselves became more magnificent, so did the curtains that stood in front of them. Again, this is an area where artisans have become more creative through the years, and all types of fabrics, colors, images, and designs now distinguish ark curtains in synagogues throughout the world. From modern creations to more traditional throwbacks, ark curtains are among the most noticeable decorative touches in the sanctuary, since the ark is the backdrop for most prayer settings. Some ark curtains are designed to match the Torah mantles used to cover the scrolls inside the ark. This gives the congregation the opportunity to carry through a holiday theme outside and inside the ark. And like all the fabric crafts in the synagogue, an ark curtain and a Torah mantle can be handmade.

## *Shulchan* Covers

The Torah is usually read on the bimah, a platform that, traditionally, is in the center of the synagogue, to represent the Torah's central role in Jewish life and prayer. But in many contemporary synagogues, the bimah is located in the front of the sanctuary, built in such a way that congregants gather around it—or, at the very least, gather around the stand on the bimah, called a *shulchan,* or "table," that is used to read the Torah. The stand, table, or lectern is often made of wood, and in ancient times, the Torah mantle was often put under the scroll when it was read, as a cushion. The *shulchan* may be straight or, as most are today, slanted to give the reader a better view of the scrolls.

Through the generations, people began making *shulchan* covers that often matched the ark curtain and incorporated the *shulchan* into the overall synagogue décor. The covering for the lectern usually has a fringe all the way around that hangs over the table. Sometimes the fringe of the *shulchan* cover is the focal point of the decorations on the piece, with religious symbols and lettering carefully sewn or painted onto the flap. The center portion of the cover may match the fabric used for the ark curtain. Some artisans making a *shulchan* cover opt for minimal decorations so not to distract the Torah reader. Other *shulchan* covers contain needlework throughout to make the lectern decorative when it's not covered by the Torah. (See Eleanor Levie's Tree of Life Runner, chapter 6, and Esther Tivé-Elterman's Crazy Quilt *Shulchan* Cover, chapter 7, for two contemporary variations of this covering.)

## The *Wimpel*

Another fabric craft that has long adorned the Torah is the *wimpel,* also known as a Torah binder, or *gartl* in Yiddish. (See, for example, Vicki Pieser's Cross-Stitch *Wimpel,* chapter 24.) When the Torah reading is completed, the scroll is held up in front of the congregation by the *magbiah* (the person given the honor of lifting the Torah) to show that the Torah is an open book and belongs to everyone. Then the Torah is rolled up tight, right in the spot where the weekly *parashah* (Torah portion) was just read. The *gollel* (the person who dresses the Torah) is called up to the bimah to tie the Torah with the *wimpel* and to cover the scroll with the mantle, the breastplate, and the crown.

Shortly after the destruction of the Second Temple in 70 CE, the Torah began to be put on two rollers, called *atzei chayyim* (trees of life). That made opening the Torah to the proper *parashah* faster and easier. Ever since then, some form of binder has been used to tie the two Torah rollers together securely.

The *wimpels,* or binders, have a long, symbolic, and fascinating history. One custom linked to *wimpels* can be traced back to European Jewish communities four hundred years ago. At that time, *wimpels* were made out of the cloth that swaddled a newborn son during his *brit milah.* Following the circumcision ceremony, the cloth was washed and then cut into strips of equal length. The strips were each decorated by either embroidery or fabric paints and then pieced together to make a *wimpel* for the Torah. The length of each *wimpel* varied, but it contained the name of the child, the date of birth, and the names of the boy's parents— usually in the same indelible ink used to write the Torah. The *wimpel* also incorporated prayers and good wishes for the child as well as expressions of hope that the boy would grow up to be a man of good deeds.

Depending on the talent of the mothers, some of these *wimpels* were astounding works of art, prefiguring future accomplishments, such as a Bar Mitzvah scene or a marriage scene under a chuppah. Tradition varies, but mothers had about a year or, in some cases, until the first time the child would come to synagogue, to complete the *wimpel* and present it to the congregation. But work would begin on it right after the *brit* to signify the child's immediate bond with the Torah. When the *wimpel* was completed, it was brought to the synagogue and the father of the child would be called up to the bimah as the *gollel*. The mother would bring the *wimpel* to the father, and he would then tie the Torah with it. That particular *wimpel* would remain on the scroll until that Torah was read from again, and then the binder would be stored in the synagogue.

Based on the size of the congregation, a synagogue could have quite a large collection of these *wimpels,* using different ones to tie the Torah from time to time. But the one made specifically for a particular child would be used on the Torah read on the day of his Bar Mitzvah and again on the Torah read on the day of his *aufruf* (traditionally a week before his wedding). The cycle started again when he had a son of his own.

Far from mere decoration, these fabric crafts have figured prominently in the life of the synagogue—and the Jewish community it served—from biblical times to the present. Contemporary crafts, too, like Lois Gaylord's *Sefer* Placekeepers (chapter 8), reinforce the role the synagogue plays in Jewish life as a center for study and prayer. These crafts reflect the artistic sensibility of the congregation, the spiritual underpinnings of the community's Jewish life, and the love of blending tradition with contemporary ritual and practice.

—*Robert Grayson*

# 6  Eleanor's Tree of Life Runner

*Project designer:* Eleanor Levie

-----

Eleanor Levie (www.eleanorlevie.com), the author/editor of *Skinny Quilts & Table Runners,* created this elegant but easy-to-make runner to cover the *shulchan,* or synagogue pulpit, in honor of her son's confirmation on Shavuot. "At the time, our bimah had a rather tired-looking Lucite pulpit, and this piece was meant to dress it up, but also offer a little privacy 'curtain,' should the person standing behind the bimah wish to discreetly scratch an itch," she says with a smile.

During the High Holy Days, when the congregation is too large for Eleanor's synagogue building, services are held in a local church. At those times, this table runner is pressed into valuable service: draped over the church's pulpit, the colorful textile with a Jewish motif hides a carved crucifix.

"Perhaps someday this runner will be hung to show the reverse side," Eleanor points out. "There, the Tree of Life, or *Etz Chayyim,* is just a machine-quilted outline on an elegant ivory fabric, especially appropriate for the Days of Awe. The image comes from the Bible—'It is a Tree of Life to them that hold fast to it, and all of its supporters are happy' [Proverbs 3:18]." *Etz chayyim* is also the term used to describe each of the two wooden dowels, usually ornately carved, that hold and advance the Torah scrolls. Shown here, the graceful, symmetrical motif is drawn from an ancient Sephardic design.

43

Eleanor has recently moved to Center City Philadelphia, joining another synagogue in town where she also teaches art in the religious school. She has produced Rodale's Successful Quilting Library series and *Unforgettable Tote Bags,* a make-it-green book, and she's edited dozens of other needlework and crafts books and magazines. But creating her own original quilting designs remains strictly an avocation, for gifts for friends and relatives and for charity auctions. She travels widely, presenting lectures and workshops for quilt guilds. Wherever she teaches, she encourages, challenges, and inspires. Eleanor contends that this Tree of Life runner is easy to make because the tree trunk and leaves are simply fused in place.

To use the Tree of Life runner as fabric art for a Jewish home, she suggests that you "hang this piece on a door or on a narrow wall; drape it over a railing, dresser, or side table; or spread it along your dining room table or kitchen island, where it is sure to put your family in the mood to celebrate the roots and branches of your own Jewish family tree."

## Getting Started

*Finished size:* 23 inches by 71 inches
Refer to "General How-To's for Quilt Making," pages 245–251.

### WHAT YOU'LL NEED

Fabrics, all prewashed to preshrink and ensure colorfastness:

Purple cotton velveteen fabric: 56 inches wide, $^3/_4$ yard (www.fabric.com); or 42–44 inches wide, 2 yards*

Ivory medium-weight silk or silky fabric, such as dupioni, shantung, or taffeta, 40–44 inches wide, $2^1/_4$ yards*

White flannel, 42–44 inches wide, $1^1/_2$ yards

12 different fancy and cotton fabrics in 18-inch lengths, varying between $1^3/_4$ inches and $4^1/_2$ inches wide, for borders

Yellow-gold medium-weight satiny fabric, for tree, 14 inches by 18 inches

Assorted green scraps—silk, silky, satiny, or lamé, for leaves

*Note: You'll have almost half the length of yardage left over for other projects. Alternatively, you could seam together 24-inch-wide cuts to get the length you need.*

Lightweight fusible web, such as Wonder Under by Pellon, 18 inches wide, ³/₄ yard

Assorted small quantities of metallic and fancy flat trims: jumbo gold rickrack, jacquard ribbon, sheer ribbon, narrow braid, gold metallic mesh

Yellow-gold piping with ¹/₄–inch braid plus lip, 7 yards

Ivory sewing thread, plus rayon thread in yellow-gold and various shades of green for decorative stitching

Zigzag sewing machine with zipper foot and optional darning foot for free-motion stitching

Marking pen

*Figure 6.1*

24"

9"

## HOW-TO'S

### *Appliqué the Tree*

1.  Use the Tree of Life pattern shown at right (Figure 6.1). This is a half-pattern, as indicated by the long dash lines. Omitting the top 3 leaves, enlarge the trunk in two sections so that each takes up a full 8¹/₂-by-11-inch page. Tape the enlarged pieces together so that the half-pattern measures approximately 18 inches in height. Go over the outlines of just the tree trunk with a marking pen, including the ends of the branches that are overlapped by the leaves.

2.  Fold the fusible web lengthwise in half. Open, then lay the web over the pattern, matching the fold line to the long dash lines. Trace the tree trunk. Refold, and cut slightly beyond the marked lines. Open, and fuse to the wrong side of the yellow-gold fabric, following manufacturer's instructions. When cool, cut along the marked lines, and remove the paper backing.

3.  Cut a 24-by-55-inch rectangle from purple velveteen. Place it on a large, flat surface, with the short ends at top and bottom, and the nap (direction of the fibers) running downward. Pin the fusible-backed tree trunk to the velveteen, 1 inch from the bottom and centered between the sides. Place a piece of folded fabric underneath to lightly pad the surface so that the velveteen doesn't get crushed flat, and a pressing cloth on top. Fuse the tree in place.

4. Fuse 2 ½-by-4-inch pieces of fusible web to the wrong sides of green fabrics, to produce at least 32 pieces—more is better. Referring to the actual-size pattern, cut out 32 leaf shapes that vary slightly in length and width. Cut some leaves lengthwise in half, for two-tone leaves. Arrange the leaves along the tree as shown (page 45), using the larger leaves at the bottom and the smaller leaves at the top. When you are satisfied with the placement of the leaves, make sure those at the end of a branch overlap the tips (with the exception of the 3 topmost leaves), and fuse them in place.

## Assembly

*Note: In the following directions, unless otherwise indicated, use sewing thread to match fabrics, or a versatile neutral. Place fabrics together with right sides facing and straight-stitch seams ¼ inch from the edges.*

1. Make borders: Arrange 18-inch strips of various fabrics side by side until they measure at least 32 inches in width. If desired, stitch ribbon or trim across one or more of the strips. Stitch the strips together, right sides facing, and press. Trim the long edges even, then cut across the joined strips for a 12-by-24-inch top border and a 5-by-24-inch bottom border. Stitch trims as desired along the seams or down the center of a wide border strip.

2. Pin a 24-inch strand of piping to the top and bottom of the velveteen, so the lip of the piping is even with the fabric's raw edges. Using a zipper foot, baste the piping in place, close to the cord. Pin the 12-inch border at the top, and pin the 5-inch border on the bottom. Still using the zipper foot, stitch just inside the previous line of stitching, getting as close as possible to the piping. Using a press cloth, press the seam allowances toward the border at each end.

3. Round the corners of the runner: Using a small plate or bowl, trace a curve at each corner and cut along the curve.

4. For a filler that will be less bulky than batting, cut two 26-inch pieces of flannel from selvage to selvage. Butt the short edges, and zigzag-stitch to get a 26-by-80-inch rectangle. Center the Tree of Life "quilt top" on the pieced flannel, and cut the flannel so it's 1 inch larger than

the quilt top all around. Baste the flannel piece to the ivory fabric for the backing, then cut the backing to the same size as the flannel.

5.   Add piping all around the quilt top in the same way as before. Place the quilt top on the backing with right sides facing, and sew around with a zipper foot so that stitches are nestled close to the piping, but leave the top side open. Clip the seam allowances along the curved corners. Pull the quilt right side out through the opening, then pin and slip-stitch the open edges closed.

6.   Working on a large ironing surface, using a spray bottle of water and a press cloth, press the runner so it is as smooth and flat as possible. Insert a few pins or safety pins to keep layers from shifting.

## Quilting & Finishing

1.   Finish the edges and quilt them simultaneously: Use ivory thread in the bobbin, and a yellow-gold rayon thread—or any color(s) you prefer in the top of the machine. Using a darning foot will allow you to free-motion-quilt in any direction, without turning the piece. Sew a fine, medium-width zigzag stitch along all the cut edges of the tree, and zigzag with a narrower setting for the cut edges of the leaves, to keep those edges from fraying. Also zigzag-stitch along the edges of the slender branches to connect the three uppermost leaves to the tree trunk. Then straight-stitch vertically along the tree trunk to simulate the texture of bark, and along the center of the leaves and out to the edges to suggest veins.

2.   Use decorative stitches if your sewing machine has them, making zigzag stitches or simple free-motion patterns, such as loop-de-loop, to quilt along the seams or centers of the border strips.

3.   Between the top border and the top of the tree, stitch wavy lines and curling scrolls, approximately 2 inches apart.

If you're giving your lovely Tree of Life runner to your synagogue, have the rabbi arrange a special ceremony to inaugurate it with blessings. If you made it for your home, display it for a special gathering of friends and family, and savor all the compliments that come your way.

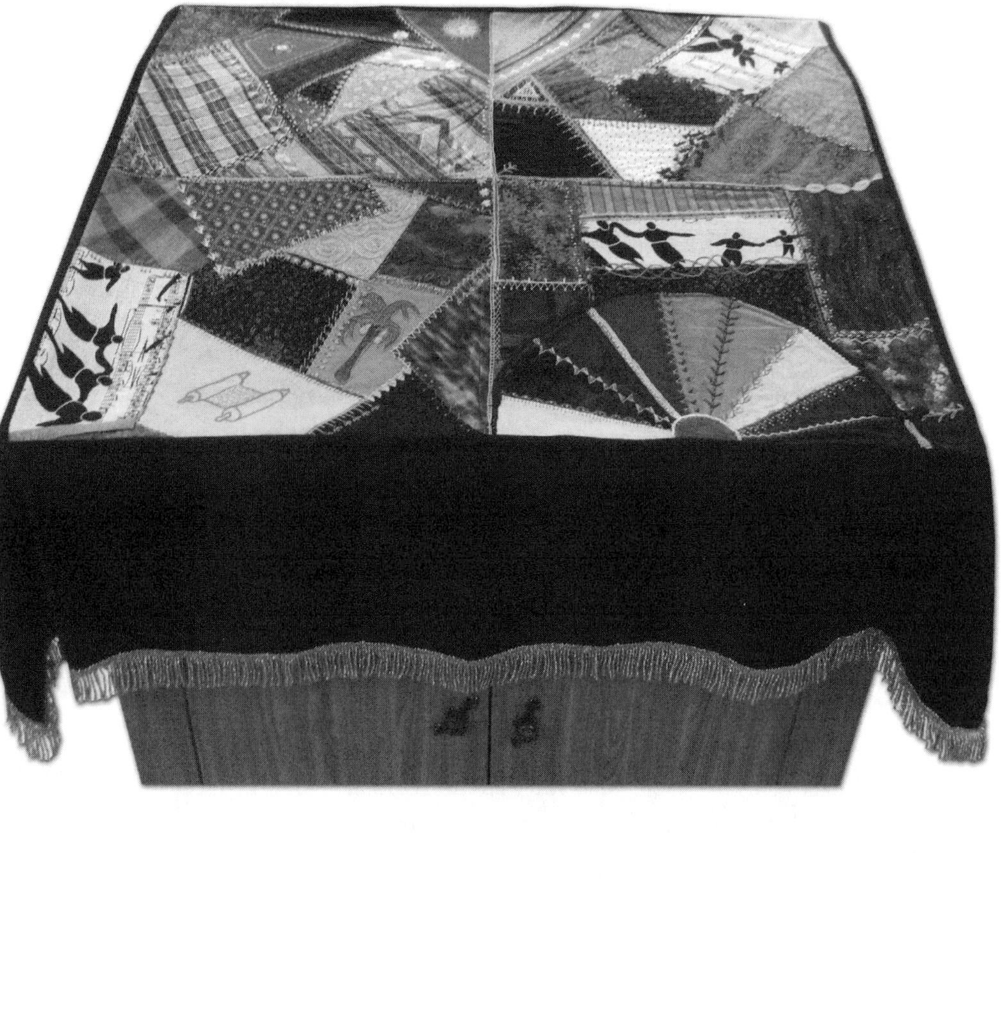

PHOTO: J. R. ELTERMAN

# 7

# Esther's Crazy Quilt *Shulchan* Cover

*Project designer:* Esther Tivé-Elterman

L ove of Jewish life is stitched throughout the fabric art of Esther Tivé-Elterman, a gifted quilter whose home is just outside Jerusalem. A native of Brooklyn, who grew up as an unaffiliated Jew, Esther began to find her way to becoming a fully practicing Jew in her teens, when she forged a friendship with a religious girl. (See more about Esther's background in the introduction to her project Esther's Crazy Quilt Challah Cover, chapter 11.)

A student of art in both high school (where she won an award for printmaking at graduation) and college, Esther pursued a course of study in art education, eventually earning a master's degree in the subject. Through the years, she explored an array of artistic avenues, from drawing and painting to photography and Hebrew calligraphy. Quilting—especially crazy quilting, or patchwork—came later but became one of her favorite forms of fabric art.

After making *aliyah* (immigrating to Israel) in 1996 with her husband and six children, Esther decided to expand her quilting repertoire. She learned how to do Yemenite and other cultural embroidery, which she incorporated in a quilt that was chosen for display at the Menachem Begin Heritage Center Museum in Jerusalem. Done in crazy quilt design, that piece commemorates the destruction of Gush

Katif and the northern Shomron communities. The quilting maven creates personal and custom art pieces, like the quilt that was showcased at the museum, and this exquisite *shulchan* cover.

Esther fashioned this *shulchan* cover for the synagogue where she and her family worship, a Carlebach synagogue that draws people from all over the world and from all different backgrounds and cultures. "Each of them has a new and different insight into what the *shulchan* cover means to them," Esther observes. "The diversity of the people who attend the synagogue is reflected in the variety of fabrics in the piece." Carlebach synagogues, which are based on the philosophy of Rabbi Shlomo Carlebach (1925–1994), promote singing and the experience of joy in prayer.

She presented the *shulchan* cover to the synagogue in 2004, when the congregation moved from a trailer into its new location, in a building used as a bomb shelter. In the trailer, the *shulchan* had been covered with a plain piece of velvet. This colorful and meaningful *shulchan* cover instantly brightened the new space.

Esther's dazzling crazy quilt *shulchan* cover design features fabric prints of dancing people and musical notes. This is "a demonstration of Judaism's emphasis on the joy of life and a reflection of the Carlebach synagogue—a place to pray to God with joy, dancing, and singing," she adds, citing Psalm 100:2, "Serve *Hashem* with gladness, come before God with joyous song." Other fabrics sewn into the *shulchan* cover, in jewel tones of blues and greens and purples and pinks, give the bimah a richness and beauty that enhance the spiritual experience of prayer.

The artist sees a metaphor in crazy quilting for the patterns in life— and in individual lives. Like a crazy quilt, which up close may seem like an array of scattered pieces of unrelated fabric, life, too, may seem scattered, or without coherent meaning, when lived day to day. Yet from afar, the crazy quilt's beautiful patterns emerge, just as life can be seen as a seamless sequence of events, forming a pattern whose meaning as an integrated whole comes to light in hindsight. In pieces like this *shulchan* cover, Esther enjoys expressing this insight—that through serendipity harmony emerges.

# Getting Started

*Finished size:* 58 inches by 58 inches

Refer to "General How-To's for Quilt Making," pages 245–251, and the "Stitch Guide," pages 255–256.

## WHAT YOU'LL NEED

Fabrics:

> 2 yards of muslin, for foundations
>
> Scraps of fancy fabrics in a variety of colors, textures, solids, and prints, for crazy quilting
>
> Blocks or joined sections from other quilt projects (see the pieced fan in the lower right block) or vintage fragments (sometimes available from flea markets or antiques dealers)
>
> 2 yards of cotton velveteen fabric, for borders
>
> 3 1/2 yards of fabric of your choice, for the backing

Assorted ribbons and flat trims in 9- to 12-inch lengths

Number 8 perle cotton in a variety of colors plus gold and silver, for embroidery

7 yards of solid gold fringe trim

### *Additional Tools & Materials*

Embroidery hoop

Embroidery and beading needles

Fabric markers of archival quality

Seed beads of various sizes and colors to match your color scheme

## HOW-TO'S

### *Crazy Quilt Blocks*

1.  For the foundations, cut 4 pieces of muslin, 22 inches by 18 inches.

2.  Work over a muslin rectangle to create one crazy quilt block at a time. Begin at the center and work outward. First, cut an odd-shaped

quadrangle of dark fabric, and pin it to the center of the muslin, right side up.

3.  Cut a different fabric the same size or longer than the right-side edge of the center patch. Lay it on the center fabric, with right sides facing and the right edges even. Stitch along the right edge, ¹/₄ inch from the raw edges. Flip the 2nd fabric to the right side. Finger-press and pin, or press with an iron on a heat setting appropriate to the most delicate of the fabrics you are currently using. Cut a 3rd piece of fabric long enough to cover the bottom edges of the 1st and 2nd pieces. Lay it over these pieces, right sides facing and bottom edges even. Stitch, flip, and press as before. Working clockwise around the center, add patches to the left side and along the top of the center fabric. Occasionally, topstitch a ribbon or other flat trim over a seam, hiding the raw, cut ends of the trim with subsequent seams.

4.  Continue with other rounds, varying sizes, shapes, and colors of patches to form a good balance of textures, as well as some solid or quiet areas where embroidery and fabric drawing can add interest. You can also vary the look and construction by adding patches out to one side or to a corner, covering the raw edges with other pieces or with trims. Use a leftover block or vintage fragment to add richness. Work until the muslin foundation is completely covered. Turn the block over, and trim the edges of the patches even with the muslin.

5.  To embellish each crazy quilt block, refer to the photo (page 48) for suggestions, as well as the Internet or clip art for motifs to print, and a book of embroidery stitches for step-by-step details. Draw motifs meaningful to you with fabric markers; notice Esther's drawings of a Torah, a Jewish star, and a date palm tree, since she lives in the desert and these graceful trees grow there in abundance. Embroider over your drawings with perle cotton, using outline stitches and filling in with satin stitches or

other stitches that fill in the spaces. Add ribbons, seed beads, and combinations of hand-embroidery stitches and French knots, along the seams between 2 pieces of fabric. This can also be done by machine if yours makes decorative stitches.

6. Arrange the 4 crazy quilt blocks together in 2 rows of 2. With right sides facing, stitch the blocks together, press the seam allowances to one side, then stitch the rows together, matching the seams at the center. The *shulchan* cover should measure approximately 40¹/₂ inches by 32¹/₂ inches.

## Assembly

1. Cut 2 pieces of velveteen 9 inches by 32¹/₂ inches and, with right sides facing, stitch to either short side of the joined blocks. Then cut 2 pieces 9 inches by 59 inches and, with right sides facing, stitch to the top and bottom edges.

2. From desired backing fabric, cut or piece together a backing to measure 59 inches square. Place the joined and bordered crazy quilt blocks on the backing, with right sides together and edges even. Sew all around, ¹/₄ inch from the edges, but leaving about 10 inches unsewn. Clip excess fabric. Turn the *shulchan* cover right side out, and sew the opening closed. Press. Sew fringe to the edges of the finished piece. *Alternatively,* fold over the raw edges of the *shulchan* cover, pin them, and sew them all around. Pin and sew the fringe all around. Turn under the raw edges of the backing, and with wrong sides together, pin the backing to the *shulchan* cover and hand-sew the backing to the top.

When you're ready to present your synagogue with this magnificent *shulchan* cover, ask the rabbi to prepare a special *brachah* for it, and then celebrate its debut with a *Kiddush* amid all the oohs and aahs.

# 8 Lois's *Sefer* Placekeepers

*Project designer:* Lois Gaylord

D ating back to our earliest days, Jews have been known as the People of the Book. Education holds a cherished place among Jewish values, and books are treasured by children and adults alike.

Lois Gaylord, a fiber artist who lives in Seattle, decided to show her own reverence for books—especially sacred books—by creating embroidered *sefer* (book) placekeepers for the teachers at Kadima, the Jewish community she belongs to. These beautiful, personalized bookmarks are meant to be brought to synagogue to keep your place in the siddur or another prayer book.

"Every year we have a breakfast and community gathering to pay tribute to the teachers at the Sunday and Hebrew school," she explains. "This event is frequently timed to coincide with Lag B'Omer, when it is traditional to honor teachers. So I decided to make these *sefer* placekeepers for the teachers at Kadima."

This project dovetailed with the decidedly spiritual direction that Lois's work has taken in recent years, as she strives to imbue her fiber artwork with spiritual meaning and create pieces that make the world a better place in the spirit of *tikkun olam* (mending the world). (See more about this spiritual imperative in the artist's work in the introduction to Julia's Bat Mitzvah Challah Cover, chapter 25.)

As she was envisioning how to make these lovely *sefer* placekeepers, Lois gathered the Hebrew names of all the teachers in the school, so she could personalize her pieces. For the image at either end of the Hebrew name, she drew inspiration from an illuminated border design that she found in the Kennicott Bible. "Made in Spain, this Bible, dating from 1476, is considered the finest Hebrew manuscript in the collection of the Bodleian Library at the University of Oxford," she points out.

In designing these beautiful, individualized pieces, the fiber artist pulled fabrics from whatever she had in her "stash." She chose darker colors to contrast with the lighter-colored metallic paints. "The green/copper color combination is one of my favorites," Lois notes. "I chose the embroidery floss colors from what I had on hand that best coordinated with the fabric colors." And, like Lois, you, too, could draw from your stash to turn scraps into gems.

The response to these lovely pieces was heartwarming to Lois. Wrote one teacher: "This bookmark is *so* beautiful. I've never seen anything like it before. And it is personalized—it has my name.... I put it in my siddur, then I moved it to my *Tanach* [Hebrew Bible]. It is beautiful to see the gold Hebrew letters against the page of Hebrew text." And another: "This is a very personal piece of Judaica that will come in handy holding space in both secular and religious texts.... As I read quite a bit, I will use it often ... and be forever reminded of Kadima's gratitude and your personal touch and craftsmanship."

## Getting Started

*Finished size:* 6 inches by 1¹/₂ inches
Refer to "General How-To's for Lettering," pages 252–254, and the "Stitch Guide," pages 255–256.

### WHAT YOU'LL NEED (FOR EACH ONE)

Natural-fiber fabric (cotton, linen, or silk), 4 inches by 7 inches
Medium-weight fusible interfacing, 3¹/₂ inches by 6¹/₂ inches

Metallic fabric paint* (Lois used Lumiere by Jacquard)

6-strand embroidery floss in colors to contrast with fabrics

Tailor's chalk

Dressmaker's tracing paper

*Note: See "Resources," page 257, for a source for metallic fabric paint.*

## HOW-TO'S

### Preparation

1.  Preshrink fabrics and interfacing. Center the interfacing on the wrong side of the fabric, and press to fuse. Then, press the linen edges on all sides $1/2$ inch to the wrong side, and press the entire piece lengthwise in half, with the interfaced side in. Unfold. You will be embroidering within the creased edges on one side of the piece.

2.  Using the patterns on the following pages (Figures 8.1 through 8.3) as a guide, print out, sketch, or draw letters $3/4$ inch tall—with the exception of the few Hebrew letters that have ascenders (such as *lamed*) or descenders (such as *kuf* or final *nun*). Cut and tape, if necessary, to get consistent spacing of letters on the line. Mark the spacing for the letters on the placekeeper with chalk—one horizontal line for the top of the letters and one for the bottom, plus an additional horizontal line $1/4$ inch above or below the 2 main lines, as needed, for ascenders and/or descenders. Cut out the name, and fold the paper crosswise in half, press to crease, and unfold.

3.  Fold the bookmark crosswise in half, press to crease, and unfold. Place the lettering pattern on top, matching the creases and centering the lettering so there is an equal margin above and below. See diagrams and photos. Using a pencil, draw a square (or rectangle), centered $3/4$ inch in from each left and right raw edge. The width of the square (or rectangle) depends on how long the name is.

ILLUSTRATION: KEVIN E. CAIN

*Figure 8.1*

## *Painting*

1. Practice painting on a piece of scrap white fabric. You will probably need to thin the paint with a little bit of water to get it to the consistency of white glue. (Too thick and it will be gloppy; too thin and it will bleed and fail to adhere properly.)

2. Outline the letters, and then fill in the outlined letters and 2 squares of the bookmark with gold paint. Let it dry, then apply a second coat. Let that dry, then heat-set the paint according to manufacturer's directions; lay a press cloth on the bookmark to protect the sole plate of your iron.

## *Embroidery*

1. Copy the scroll design from one of the patterns (Figures 8.1 through 8.3). Place transfer paper underneath it; cut out both sheets, and pin them over the painted square. Working on a firm surface and using a blunt, pointed object, such as a dry ballpoint

*Figure 8.2*

ILLUSTRATION: KEVIN E. CAIN

*Figure 8.3*

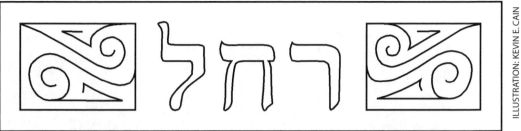

pen or a small knitting needle, trace the scroll design to transfer the image onto the painted square. Lift a corner of the transfer paper to check that the lines appear over the gold square. Repeat to transfer the scroll design onto the second square.

2. Using 2 strands of the 6-strand embroidery floss, embroider the designs in stem stitch. For tight curves, make tiny stitches over stem stitches to couch them in place.

## Finishing

1. Fold the piece lengthwise in half with right sides together. Using a ¹/₂-inch seam allowance, stitch one short edge from the folded edge to the corner. Then turn and stitch about 2 inches toward the center. Do this from the other end, leaving about 2 inches along the middle of the long edge open.

2. Trim corners, and end seam allowances. Turn right side out and press, pressing in the seam allowance at the opening.

3. Slip-stitch the opening closed.

4. Using a fine fabric pen in a color to contrast, sign and date the finished piece on the back.

With special fanfare, present your personalized *sefer* placekeeper to the person whose name graces the front.

PHOTO: ARYEH SCHWARTZ

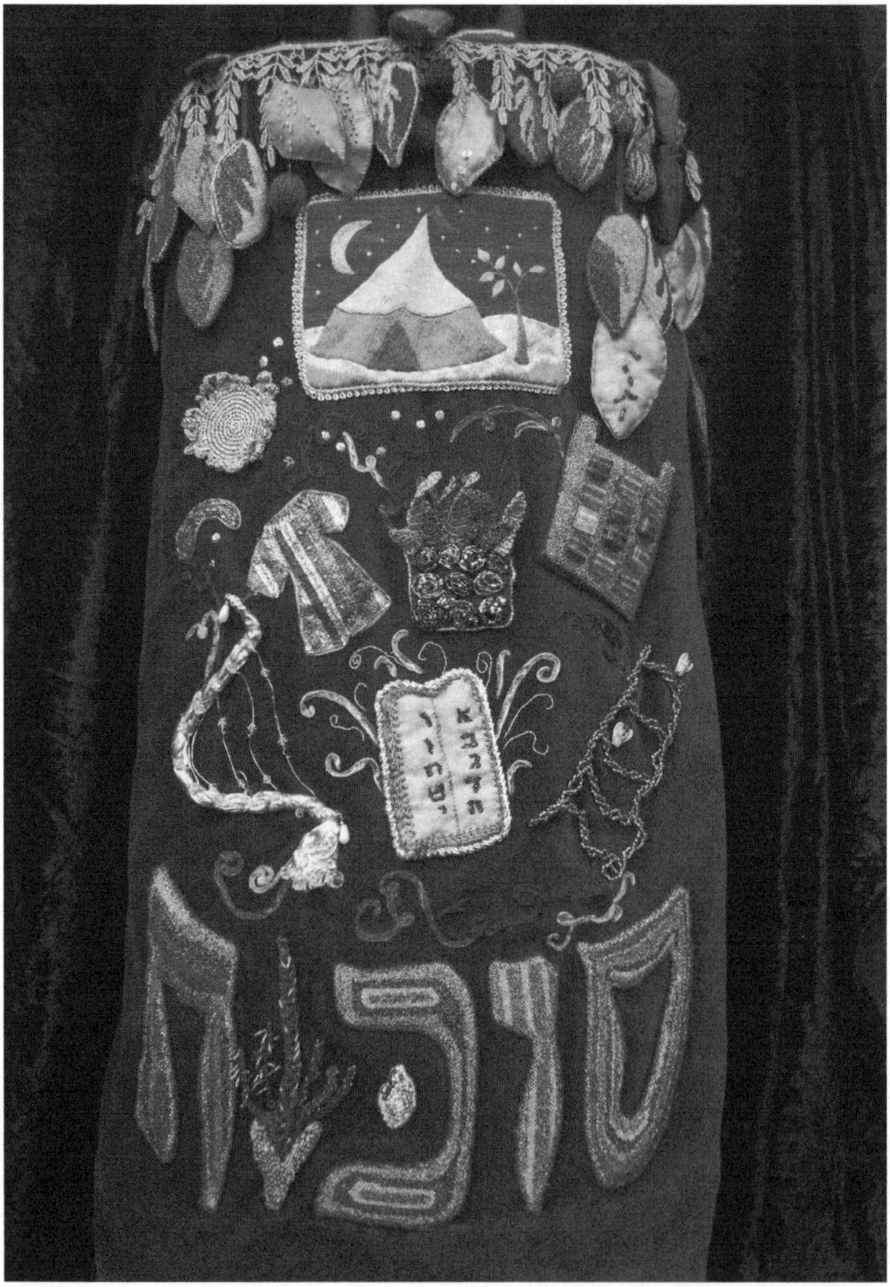

# 9

# Sukkot Torah Mantle

*Project designer:* **Judy Snitzer**

*Committee members:* Catherine Breier, Chana
DeLisle, Alana Riss Fine, Mark Glotter,
Debbie Baumgarten Kusnetz, Judy Shapiro,
and Rita Stough

*Young people who volunteered:* Gabriella Fine,
Zachary Fine, and Shira Kusnetz

Judy Snitzer's synagogue, Darchei Noam in St. Louis Park,
Minnesota, asked her to make mantles for its three *sifrei Torah*
(Torah scrolls). Since there were three Torah scrolls, she decided to
spotlight the "three *regalim,*" the holidays when Jews in ancient times
went up to Jerusalem. This mantle, based on the theme of Sukkot,
was one of three Torah mantles Judy designed with members of the
small congregation—one for Sukkot, one for Pesach (a work in
progress at press time), and one for Shavuot. (See Judy's Shavuot
Torah Mantle, chapter 10.) The Torah mantles are both decorative and
designed to protect the *sifrei Torah,* which are taken out and read during Shabbat and Monday and Thursday morning services.

For the Sukkot Torah mantle, Judy looked for a theme that
would allow many members to contribute independently designed and

executed elements. The theme she chose was the *ushpizin,* or traditional visitors to the sukkah—a different one every night of the week: Abraham, Isaac, Jacob, Moses, Aaron, Joseph, and David. So she designed a motif of Abraham's tent as a focal point of the Torah mantle, because Abraham was renowned in the Bible for welcoming strangers to his tent. Tapping the skills of master embroiderer Rita Stough, Judy asked Rita to create Abraham's tent. The square panel ended up as the central image on the Torah mantle and evokes the sense of a window looking out of the sukkah.

Other key symbols gracing this Torah mantle include Jacob's ladder, which is made out of wire and beads; the breastplate of Aaron, which is needle-pointed and embellished with square beads; and David's harp, which is fashioned from gold fabric wrapped with embroidery floss and adorned with jewels—pieces of a member's earrings. "They were all symbols for each of the *ushpizin* that we translated into a design for the Torah mantle," Judy explains. "We let people come up with their own designs within the overall framework we had established." The letters at the bottom spell *Sukkot* in Hebrew but are curved in the same way as on the Shavuot mantle, to serve as a unifying design element. Judy decided that leaves hanging over the top edge of the Torah mantle would convey the feeling of being in the sukkah, which is usually decorated with fronds of greenery as well as harvest fruits. The fringe of leaves also ties the design together with that of the Shavuot Torah mantle.

As the overall instigator of this wide-ranging community project, Catherine Breier organized activities that allowed the children in the congregation to take part as well. Some young people painted leaves used at the top of the mantle.

Judy was originally approached by the synagogue to make these Torah mantles because her fellow congregants knew that she painted artfully on walls in her own home and those of friends, had made her husband's tallit bag, and had embroidered the *atarah* (neckpiece) on her husband's tallit, using blackwork embroidery. "I copied several ideas from the Israel Museum in Jerusalem," she says.

"I've always sewn small things—doll clothes when I was little, tiny tapestries for a high school project, and a tapestry as a family project. I even taught an elementary school crafts class as a volunteer at an Orthodox day school." And while she has no professional art training herself, she enjoys sharing her love of crafts with others and inspiring them to have fun exploring their own creativity, as she did with the three Torah mantles she fashioned with her enthusiastic corps of fellow congregants.

# Getting Started

*Finished size:* 29 inches long by 36½ inches in circumference
Refer to "General How-To's for Quilt Making," pages 245–251;
"General How-To's for Lettering," pages 252–254; and the "Stitch Guide,"
pages 255–256.

## WHAT YOU'LL NEED

### For the Overall Torah Mantle

Plywood, ³/₁₆–¹/₄ inch thick, or ¹/₈-inch masonite

¹/₂ yard batting

¹/₂ yard muslin

2 yards velvet

2 yards silk or other lining material

1¹/₄ yard leaf-like gold fringe

Curved needle

Sewing thread to match muslin (beige) and velvet

### For the Adornments

Metallic embroidery and needlepoint threads—gold, silver, copper, blue, beige, and green

Green metallic fabric for backing of leaves, approximately ¹/₈ yard

Small amounts of yarn and fabric scraps, in various colors that complement your color scheme, including snippets of gold and silver fabric

Various commercially purchased trims

Tubular needlepoint yarn with a metallic thread running through it, in various colors (Judy used Frosty Rays yarn [see "Resources," page 257])

Size 12 crochet hook

Beading needle

Tapestry needle

Tiny craft iron

6-strand embroidery floss in yellow, gold, brown, red, green, blue, and white (or other colors to match your color scheme)

Small amounts of polyester fiberfill for stuffing individual pieces

Fabric paint in green and other colors complementing your color scheme

## *Additional Materials for Each Adornment*

*Leaves & letters:* 18-gauge needlepoint canvas, ¹/₄ yard; about 30 green seed beads and 50 yellow seed beads

*Knit fruit balls:* Metallic needlepoint yarn in various "fruit" colors

*Abraham's tent:* Gold and silver commercially purchased trims

*Joseph's coat (plus sun, moon, and stars):* Scrap of striped, iridescent fabric (optional: 8 seed beads and scrap of commercially purchased trim); gold-colored yarn (for the sun); scrap of silver felt, approximately 30 gold seed beads (for the moon); 12 sequins, ¹/₂ inch in diameter (for the stars)

*Isaac's altar:* 1-millimeter seed beads (approximately 300) in various colors, including silver, blue, copper, and white, sewn onto small disks of felt measuring 0.5–1 centimeter to suggest rocks; remnants of metallic yarn in gold, blue, red, and silver, crocheted into individual flames

*Aaron's breastplate:* 18-gauge needlepoint canvas, copper metallic thread, 12 large glass beads in various colors

*Jacob's ladder:* Fine-gauge beading wire, 2-millimeter seed beads (approximately 300), 2 African-American porcelain angel beads

*David's harp:* Found objects, such as old earring findings; fine-gauge gold beading wire; gold fabric

*Moses's Ten Commandments:* Scrap of silver fabric, commercially purchased trims, embroidery thread

## HOW-TO'S

### *For the Overall Torah Mantle*

1.  Carefully cut a disk of the plywood so that the disk extends beyond the scroll when the scroll is wound all on one side. (Judy's is an oval measuring 13 inches by 8 inches.) The disk needs to hold the mantle away from the Torah scroll. Carefully cut the holes 3 inches in diameter, or as needed, so they fit over the Torah's *atzei chayyim* (literally, "trees of life," the handles on the scrolls; Judy drew a paper pattern and had a congregant who was handy at woodworking cut it out).

2.  Cover the disk top and bottom with batting, then with a layer of muslin, and finally with velvet. Cut the velvet about ¹/₂ inch larger than the circumference of the disk. Use a curved needle to sew the top and bottom of the batting together, and then sew the muslin together.

3.  Sew the velvet disks together on the plywood disk (right sides facing out) over the muslin, again using the curved needle.

4.  Measure the skirt of the mantle so that there is an overlap at the back of about 6 inches. Make an additional allowance of 1 inch for seams and 2 inches of velvet border on the inside. (To figure the width of the mantle, measure the circumference of the disk + 11 inches. To figure the height of the mantle, measure the length just over the top disks and below the bottom disk + 5 inches. Torah scrolls vary in size, so these measurements will help you make your Torah mantle fit.)

5.  While the Torah mantle is stretched taut, sew the adornments onto the velvet, lightly but firmly, with thread the same color as the velvet. Use as few stitches as you can to secure each one in place.

6.  Cut the lining (Judy used a beautiful silk she bought at a warehouse) smaller than the mantle so that there is a 2-inch border of velvet on the inside. Sew the lining to the decorated velvet mantle, so all the edges are finished, and then sew it to the velvet-covered disk, again using the curved needle. The velvet hem should be 2 inches deep if the seam is ¹/₂ inch.

7. Attach a row of leaf-like gold fringe at the top edge of the disk, using the curved needle to give the top a more finished look. This is the last step after the leaves and fruit are attached.

## Individual Adornments

1. Create the specific adornments as shown or adornments of your choice, following the how-to's below. Cut fabrics or canvas $1/4$ inch beyond the stitching, for seam allowances.

2. With right sides out, trim all soft adornments and backing fabric $1/4$ inch beyond the stitching. Insert the edges $1/4$ inch to the inside. Stuff the adornment lightly with polyester fiberfill, then whipstitch all around the edge.

3. Once completed, sew each adornment onto the Torah mantle with matching thread and a slip stitch, using as few stitches as possible to anchor it in place.

### Leaves:

Draw leaves freehand on 18-gauge needlepoint canvas. Then, using basketweave stitch, needlepoint leaf shapes with metallic threads in green, white, yellow, blue, and other colors of thread that match your color scheme. Place each leaf on a coordinating metallic fabric or the velvet of the cover. With right sides out, insert the edges $1/4$ inch to the inside. Stuff the leaf lightly with polyester fiberfill, then whipstitch all around the edge. Attach trim at one end of each leaf; this will enable it to be hung and will serve as a stem. Make a lot of these leaves, which will form the fringe around the top of the Torah mantle. Have children hand-paint other leaves with fabric paint on fabric scraps, and then have adults sew beads on some of them. Stuff and edge each of these leaves with blanket stitching, then sew trim to serve as a stem. Sew some of the needle-pointed and painted leaves onto the top of the mantle; others will hang gracefully over the edge as part of the fringe. Sew or glue pipe cleaners to the underside of several leaves to help fold them halfway over the mantle top.

*Knit fruit balls (make 10):*
Cast on 16 stitches using size 1 double-pointed needles. First purl one row, then, alternating knit and purl rows, work 11 more rows. Cut the yarn, making sure to leave a 10-inch tail. Draw the yarn through all the stitches, using a tapestry needle, and tighten to close the circle. Close up the side seam using the same piece of yarn, and stuff the fruit ball with polyester fiberfill. Close the ball by drawing the yarn through the cast-on stitches with the tapestry needle. Sew the knit fruit balls so they dangle from the top of the Torah mantle.

*Hebrew letters spelling* Sukkot:
Trace the lettering from the pattern below (Figure 9.1) onto paper, enlarging it to the size of your Torah mantle. Then trace the letters onto an 18-gauge canvas. Needlepoint the letters in basketweave stitch using various colors of metallic thread, following a striping design. Bead the dot in the curve of the *kaf* with yellow seed beads on a piece of felt to resemble an *etrog* (citron)—a symbol of Sukkot. Chain-stitch, using metallic green needlepoint yarns, the willow and myrtle stems in the *lulav* that forms the second *vav*. Sew on green seed beads to suggest willow and myrtle leaves.

*Figure 9.1*

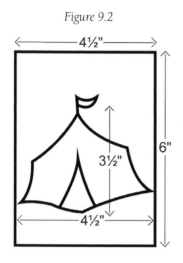

*Figure 9.2*

**The seven Ushpizim**

*(motifs symbolizing the guests invited to the sukkah):*

*Note: The size of these symbols depends on the size of your Torah mantle.*

*Abraham's tent (top center, page 60):*
Enlarge the pattern (Figure 9.2) for Abraham's tent at left (or to the size you desire). With satin stitch, embroider Abraham's tent with the palm tree and the crescent moon, using solid and variegated cotton embroidery floss in yellow, gold, brown, red, green, blue, and white. This forms a window into the sukkah. Frame the tent motif with gold and silver commercially purchased trims.

*Joseph's coat (plus the sun, moon, and stars—upper left, page 60):*
Enlarge and trace the pattern (Figure 9.3) for Joseph's coat at left (or make it the size you prefer). Cut out the striped, iridescent, commercial fabric; fold the narrow edge under, and press using a tiny craft iron. Add beads, embroidery, or trim, if desired. Crochet the sun in the round like a *kippah* (skullcap). Crochet a chain of 4–5 stitches, close the circle, and single crochet with frequent increases as many rounds as necessary to reach $1^1/_4$ inches in diameter. For the sun's "rays," make a short chain of 3–7 stitches, and then crochet back down the chain to the circle. Then go over a stitch or 2 and make another chain, and go back down again. Sew directly onto the velvet cover 12 sequins as "stars," representing the 12 tribes of Israel. For the moon, cut a crescent out of felt, and sew gold or silver beads onto the crescent.

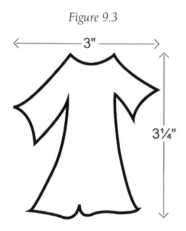

*Figure 9.3*

*Issac's altar (center, page 60):*
Bead the "stones" using beading thread and a beading needle. Sew the beads onto small disks of felt, measuring 0.5–1 centimeters, to suggest rocks or stones. Sew the stones onto a 3-inch-square piece of velvet (the same velvet as the mantle). Back this piece with velvet as well.

Single crochet the "flames," using a size 12 crochet hook and different-colored metallic needlepoint yarns, decreasing into a point. Sew the flames to the back of the altar so that flame tips hang loose.

*Aaron's breastplate (upper right, page 60):*
Cut a 3-by-4-inch piece of 18-gauge needlepoint canvas, with tabs for "shoulders." Needlepoint this canvas in basketweave stitch using copper metallic needlepoint yarn. With a beading needle, sew the 12 beads onto the needle-pointed breastplate to look like stones adorning the shield.

*Jacob's ladder (lower right, page 60):*
String beads on fine-gauge beading wire, then twist it to form a flexible ladder (see photo on this page). Sew 2 tiny African-American porcelain angel beads directly onto the velvet mantle as if they were scaling the ladder.

*David's harp (lower left, page 60):*
Twist a scrap of gold fabric and wrap a piece of gold beading wire around it so you can shape it into the harp body. Decorate the harp with found objects, such as old earring findings and jewels. String three pieces of gold beading wire with intermittently spaced jewels from the top of the harp body to the bottom, securing them in place by wrapping the wire around the harp body. Embellish with gold and copper beads.

*Moses's Ten Commandments (center toward the bottom, page 60):*
With a scrap of silver fabric, cut out the tablets of the Ten Commandments and embroider the letters *aleph* through *yud* with blue and gold embroidery thread. Quilt the embroidered fabric. Trim with silver, gold, and white commercially purchased trims. Embellish with silver Frosty Rays trim.

Have everyone who contributed to your Torah mantle accept the heartfelt blessings of the congregation when the Torah with its gorgeous mantle is brought out for the first time.

# About the Additional Contributors

**Catherine Breier**, a business owner with degrees in social work and architecture and the instigator of the whole Torah mantle project, decided that the Darchei Noam *sifrei Torah* were badly in need of new mantles to replace their worn and patched ones. First thought: What a great collaborative project for members of the synagogue (tried that first idea and scrapped it). Second thought: Get Judy Snitzer to design the Torah mantles and assign members parts to work on. Third thought: Wow! Judy managed to bring together people with diverse skills to produce beautiful mantles that truly embodied the spirit of Darchei Noam.

**Chana DeLisle**, an emergency department physician, found little time during medical school and residency for recreational quilting, a skill she learned early on that has come in handy for suturing lacerations. Happily, suturing has kept up her skills, and she has time again for more recreational types of needlework.

**Alana Riss Fine**, who holds a PhD in clinical health psychology from Yeshiva University, began to admire Judaic needlepoint when she went to a *swanee* in the Sephardic (Syrian) community in Brooklyn. In a *swanee,* the groom and his family send the bride trays of gifts, flowers, silver, and perfumes, while the bride's family prepares a similar table for the groom, with books, electronics, and religious items. On the groom's table was a beautiful needle-pointed tallit bag the bride had made for her fiancé. At that moment Alana decided that when she got married, she would make one for her husband (and she did!).

**Mark Glotter**, a manufacturer's representative, travels all over the world. His mother used to own a needlepoint store, and he learned how to needlepoint from her.

**Debbie Baumgarten Kusnetz**, a speech-language pathologist, works in a hospital with people who have had strokes or other neurological impairments. She started crocheting when she was about twelve, determined to learn how to make *kippot* (skullcaps)—first for her brothers and later for the other men in her life.

**Judy Shapiro** is a social worker who has been obsessed with needle-point for thirty-five years. She "specializes" in Judaica pieces like tallit bags, *mizrachs* (ornamental wall hangings), and Torah-mantle letters and leaves, and she loves doing it!

**Rita Stough** learned how to embroider little doilies from her mother when she was about five or six years old (in the 1950s). After that, she didn't do much needlework until the late 1960s, when she embroidered flowers all over her jeans and shirts. Her husband, Bruce, bought her a book called *The Art of Crewel Embroidery,* by Mildred J. Davis, and she's been embroidering ever since.

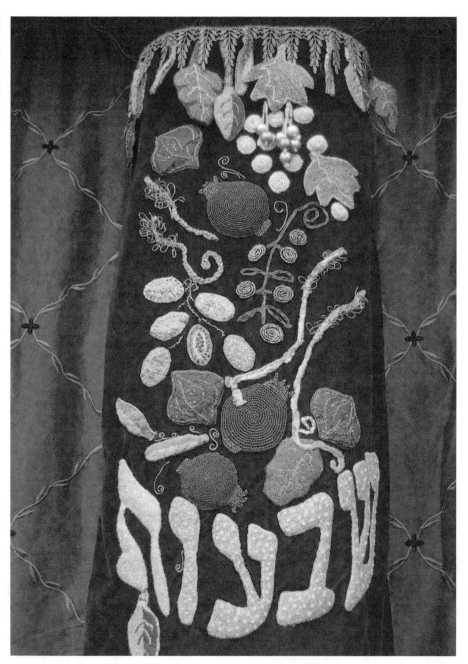

# Shavuot Torah Mantle

10

**Project designer:** Judy Snitzer

---

*Committee members:* Hanna Bloomfield, Catherine Breier, Alana Riss Fine, Debbie Baumgarten Kusnetz, Debbie Mintz, Judy Shapiro, and Rita Stough

---

*Young people who volunteered:* Dahlia Krebs, Yonit Krebs, Shira Kusnetz, Shoshana Kusnetz, Raya Israelson, and Rafaella Slager

L ike the Sukkot Torah mantle showcased in chapter 9, this Shavuot Torah mantle—one of three handcrafted by members of Darchei Noam synagogue in St. Louis Park, Minnesota—also sprang from the imagination of Judy Snitzer. A microbiologist by profession, who enjoys painting on walls and doing embroidery, Judy put her talents to work on this very special Torah mantle as well.

Darchei Noam, which rents space in a Montessori school, had been given several *sifrei Torah* (Torah scrolls) from defunct synagogues—including one from Holland that had been rescued from the Holocaust. "Creating the mantle for a Torah that survived the Holocaust and would now be in use once again felt very life-affirming," Judy notes. "We chose a theme that many members could participate in. The creation of this mantle was one tiny piece in the ongoing continuum of rebuilding

Jewish life, over and over again, throughout the centuries. If I were looking to find God in this process, I would look in the space between the elements of the design and between the years when this *sefer Torah* [Torah scroll] was in use."

Catherine Breier, a member of Darchei Noam, asked Judy if she would coordinate making a custom Torah mantle for the Dutch *sefer Torah*, since it was unusually tall and a standard Torah mantle would not cover it. Interested members of the congregation volunteered to help her bring the project to fruition. Some needle-pointed, some crocheted, and some embroidered. After Judy came up with the overall design concept, each person's skills were matched to a piece of the design. For example, the pomegranates were crocheted by Debbie Baumgarten Kusnitz, a member who had crocheted *kippot* (skullcaps) and figured out how to add the crown. (Notice how much each of these resembles a *kippah* [skullcap].)

"We ended up with crocheted pomegranates and grapes, needle-pointed leaves and letters, painted grapes, beaded olives, and knotted and beaded wheat and barley, as well as a few embroidered figs and dates," Judy points out. "Eventually, I collected all the individual pieces. Each piece was stuffed to give it a three-dimensional look and then backed using a blanket or whipstitch, with fabric that was attractive but unlikely to ravel, to ensure that the pieces would not fall apart during use and would be easy to reattach if they did come off.

"Once all the pieces were completed, I set about tacking them onto the Torah mantle with a minimal number of stitches. The velvet was stretched using my husband's version of an Amish quilting stretcher, so that I could hold the needle above and below the velvet cover. The pieces were then arranged and pinned in place. Care was taken to leave the sides of the mantle free of decoration so that the design elements would not be handled as much while the Torah is carried around. The Torah cover was finally put together using directions Marian Kugelmass, a member of the Pomegranate Guild of Judaic Needlework, kindly gave me over a very long phone call. Jewish geography helped me learn of her existence."

In creating the Shavuot Torah mantle, Judy enjoyed working with different fabrics and interacting with her fellow committee members. Watching as the pieces of the Torah mantle came together made all the hard work worthwhile. "I'm grateful to have been asked to do it," she says. "For me, making the Torah mantle was all about the pleasure of combining the talents of diverse members."

Judy relished the challenge of taking a traditional Torah mantle and giving it a more contemporary look. "Instead of fringe, we had leaves hanging down," in line with the sense of Shavuot as a celebration of nature and the spring harvest. The Torah mantle incorporates the seven species the Torah associates with Israel, reflecting the harvest theme of Shavuot.

Speaking about the spiritual intention behind the Shavuot Torah mantle, Judy notes that she doesn't consider herself a spiritual person. "I'm more community-based—more horizontal than vertical. For me, it's more about the pleasure of working with other people to accomplish something the whole community can appreciate," she explains. Still, the work of her hands—and that of her fellow congregants—clearly reflects the intention of bringing beauty, biblical resonance, and a touch of whimsy to the synagogue from which she draws spiritual sustenance.

# Getting Started

*Finished size:* 33 inches long by 36¹⁄₂ inches in circumference
Refer to "General How-To's for Quilt Making," pages 245–251;
"General How-To's for Lettering," pages 252–254; and the "Stitch Guide,"
pages 255–256.

## WHAT YOU'LL NEED

### *For the Overall Torah Mantle*

Plywood, ³⁄₁₆–¹⁄₄ inch thick, or ¹⁄₈-inch masonite

¹⁄₂ yard batting

¹⁄₂ yard muslin

2 yards velvet

2 yards silk or other lining material

1 yard leaf-like gold fringe

Curved needle

Sewing thread to match muslin (beige) and velvet

## For the Adornments

Metallic thread—gold, silver, copper, and green

Green metallic fabric for backing of leaves, approximately $1/8$ yard

Transparent nylon tubing with metallic needlepoint thread running through it, in various colors, for leaves on olives as well as connecting design elements (Judy used Frosty Rays thread [see "Resources," page 257])

Embroidery needle

Tiny craft iron

Size 12 crochet hook

Small amounts of polyester fiberfill, for stuffing

## Additional Materials for Each Adornment

*Leaves & letters:* 18-gauge needlepoint canvas, $1/4$ yard

*Wooden grapes:* Approximately 12 wooden ball beads, $5/8$ inch in diameter; purple metallic craft paint

*Crocheted grapes:* Purple metallic yarn, fine, 1 small spool

*Figs:* Olive-green satin scraps, copper 6-strand embroidery floss, approximately 30 copper seed beads

*Pomegranates:* Metallic red and gold needlepoint yarn, 3 spools (the Darchei Noam needlepointers used number 12 Krienik tapestry needlepoint yarn)

*Wheat and barley:* Approximately 100 gold and copper seed beads, scraps of yellow or gold cotton knitting yarn, scraps of metallic needlepoint yarn

*Dates:* Scraps of yellow satin, 6-strand white and gold embroidery floss, approximately 150 gold seed beads

*Olives:* Approximately 200 green 1-millimeter seed beads; beading wire; 9-by-12-inch piece of olive-green felt

## HOW-TO'S

### For the Overall Torah Mantle

See general instructions for making the overall Torah mantle in chapter 9, "Sukkot Torah Mantle," pages 65–66.

### Back of the Torah Cover

On the back of the Darchei Noam Shavuot Torah mantle is the emblem of the Dutch community where this Torah scroll originated. The phoenix is the symbol of the Portuguese-Spanish communities that immigrated to Amsterdam. Judy and her coworkers photocopied the symbol onto fabric, and Rita Stough painstakingly embroidered it. Then they sewed this embroidered symbol onto the back of the Torah mantle. Says Judy, "Although it is the most beautiful piece on the Torah cover, it is on the back because we added it a year after the mantle was completed."

### Individual Adornments

See general instructions for making individual adornments in chapter 9, "Sukkot Torah Mantle," page 66.

#### Leaves:

Draw each leaf freehand on 18-gauge needlepoint canvas. Then needlepoint the leaves with metallic threads, using basketweave stitch. Place each leaf on a coordinating metallic fabric. Make lots of these leaves to serve as part of the fringe around the top of the Torah mantle, and appliqué a few more onto the cover itself.

#### Wooden grapes:

Paint wooden ball beads with purple metallic paint. (*Note: Children do a great job painting these wooden balls.*) When they're dry, hang them from the top seam with metallic cords.

### Crocheted grapes:

Crochet grapes in the round using metallic purple yarn to $1/2$–$3/4$ inch in diameter, just as you'd make a tiny *kippah*. Crochet a chain of 4–5 stitches, close the circle, and single crochet with frequent increases as many rounds as necessary to reach the desired diameter and make each grape somewhat convex. Then pull the yarn through the last stitch to make a knot. Weave in the ends. Sew crocheted grapes onto the Torah mantle, behind the painted wooden grapes.

### Figs:

Cut fig shapes freehand out of olive-green satin, roughly 3 inches by 2 inches. Fold edges under to form a narrow hem, using a tiny craft iron. Embroider with copper thread around the edges and into the fig itself, using chain stitch. Sew on a scattering of copper beads.

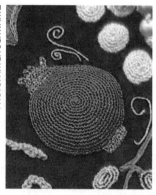

### Pomegranates:

Crochet as you did the grapes. Using metallic red yarn for the body of the pomegranate, make a chain of 6 stitches, close the chain, and single crochet with frequent increases to make each pomegranate $1^{1}/2$–3 inches in diameter and somewhat convex. For the crown of the pomegranate, add 4–5 chain stitches up and then back down in gold and red yarn. For the bottom of the pomegranate, add 3–4 chain stitches up and then back down. When sewing the stuffed pomegranate to the Torah mantle, leave the tips of the crown hanging freely, unsecured.

### Wheat and barley:

Single crochet to your desired length a chain for the stalk out of scraps of cotton knitting yarn twisted with metallic needlepoint yarn, and then sew on beads with metallic threads. Add loops of metallic threads at the top of each stalk, pulling through with a crochet hook.

### Dates:

Cut ovals $1^{1}/4$ inches by $2^{1}/2$ inches from yellow satin. Iron under a narrow hem. Embroider each date with gold and silver threads, and sew beads on for added dimension.

### Olives:

String green beads onto wire (a good project for children) and twist them into circles. Then, using a couching stitch and green sewing thread, sew the strung beads onto ovals of green felt measuring approximately 1 inch by ⅝ inch. *(Note: Varying the size of the olives makes this design element more interesting.)* Sew olive leaves directly onto the Torah mantle, using transparent needlepoint thread (Judy used Frosty Rays).

### Hebrew letters spelling Shavuot:

Enlarge the curved letters in the pattern below (Figure 10.1) to the desired size, and trace them onto 18-gauge needlepoint canvas. Judy's measured 5½ inches by 2¾–3½ inches, but adjust the measurements to the dimensions of your Torah mantle. Using basketweave stitch, needlepoint each letter in gold, with silver specks. Cut out each letter, leaving a ¼-inch border of canvas around it, then machine-stitch around the edge of the canvas to reinforce the canvas. Back each letter using the same technique as for the leaves.

Share your beautiful work with the entire congregation amid blessings and celebration, and have everyone who contributed to your Torah mantle stand up and take a bow.

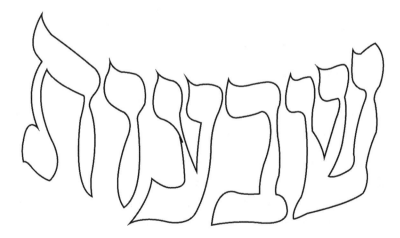

*Figure 10.1*

# About the Additional Contributors

**Hanna Bloomfield**, a physician researcher, likes to crochet and do calligraphy in her spare time.

**Catherine Breier**, a business owner with degrees in social work and architecture, was the instigator of the whole Torah mantle project.

**Alana Riss Fine** holds a PhD in clinical health psychology from Yeshiva University. She began to admire Judaic needlepoint when she went to a *swanee* in the Sephardic (Syrian) community in Brooklyn, where the bride and groom exchange gifts. On the groom's table was a beautiful needle-pointed tallit bag the bride had made for her fiancé. At that moment Alana decided that when she got married, she would make one for her husband (and she did!).

**Debbie Baumgarten Kusnetz**, a speech-language pathologist, works in a hospital with people who have had strokes or other neurological impairments. She started crocheting when she was about twelve, determined to learn how to make *kippot*—first for her brothers and later for the other men in her life.

**Debbie Mintz**, who holds a master's degree in occupational therapy from New York University, grew up doing needlepoint, embroidery, and crocheting. Thanks to Judy Snitzer, she is now able to put her skills to use. She is happy to be part of the group making Torah mantles and loves seeing them on Shabbat.

**Judy Shapiro** is a social worker who has been obsessed with needlepoint for thirty-five years. She "specializes" in Judaica pieces like tallit bags, *mizrachs* (ornamental wall hangings), and Torah-mantle letters and leaves, and she loves doing it!

**Rita Stough** learned how to embroider little doilies from her mother when she was a child in the 1950s. After that, she didn't do much needlework until the late 1960s, when she embroidered flowers all over her jeans and shirts. Her husband, Bruce, bought her a book called *The Art of Crewel Embroidery*, by Mildred J. Davis, and she's been embroidering ever since.

# PART THREE

# Celebrating Holidays

Holidays offer ready-made inspiration for needlecrafts. The theme is already there—it's just a matter of taking the story behind the holiday and developing it into an extraordinary piece that will make your home, office, or synagogue wonderfully festive for the occasion.

Jewish holidays stem from ancient epic tales of bravery, miracles, persistence, sacrifice, the drive for freedom, strength of faith, and triumph over evil. Outlawing the observance of Jewish holidays was one of the strategies used by those who oppressed the Jewish people to try to destroy the religion. Yet, steadfast in their beliefs, many Jews continued to celebrate these holidays even if they had to do so surreptitiously and at great personal risk. Eating matzah on Pesach, lighting candles on Chanukah, reciting the prayers on Rosh Hashanah, and fasting on Yom Kippur all came under attack by one tyrant or another but survived to be passed down through the generations.

## Chanukah

Oppression of the Jews is the genesis of several Jewish holidays, including the wintertime celebration of Chanukah. The Festival of Lights has its origins in the ruthless Syrian-Greek regime of King Antiochus IV, which started in 175 BCE. The king demanded that all

Jews embrace Zeus, and to accomplish this he ordered the burning of the Torah and Jewish prayer books; banned the observance of Jewish holidays, including Passover and Sukkot; and had all who failed to convert killed. King Antiochus IV ruled the Seleucid Empire. The empire, based in Syria, was formed from the eastern conquests of Alexander the Great, after the military leader's death in 323 BCE. Judea, the southern part of Israel, had been ruled by the Seleucid Empire since 200 BCE.

Through the efforts of the Maccabees and a small band of freedom fighters, the Jews fought back against the edict of the king, defeating the more experienced and superior army of King Antiochus IV and reestablishing the Jewish religion and culture in 165 BCE. Among the whimsical crafts celebrating this historical triumph are Eleanor Levie's *Chanukiah* Vest (chapter 16) and Ruth Lenk's ChanuCats Quilt (chapter 17).

## Pesach

The oldest continually celebrated Jewish holiday is the springtime festival of Pesach, or Passover. The celebration of the Israelites' escape from Egyptian tyranny, some thirty-five hundred years ago, is known for its seders, Haggadot, special foods, *afikomen*, bitter herbs, Elijah's cup, and, of course, the retelling of the riveting Exodus story. The special symbols of Pesach give fabric crafters plenty of opportunity to spin their handiwork for this holiday. You can always embroider a spiritually meaningful symbol onto the linens that are put into use during the annual weeklong event that begins on the fifteenth day of Nisan. (See Shellie Black's Ten-Plagues Matzah Cover, chapter 20; Claire Sherman's *Afikomen* Envelopes, chapter 21; and Zoë Scheffy's Knit Seder Plate, chapter 22.)

## The High Holy Days

Rosh Hashanah and Yom Kippur—the High Holy Days, which fall in early autumn—are deep-rooted in self-reflection. (See Heather G. Stoltz's High Holy Day Inspiration, chapter 14.) The High Holy Days

**Susan's Tree of Life Wall Hanging**

Susan Schrott (Chapter 1)

**Ruth's *Hamsa* Wall Hanging**

Ruth Lenk (Chapter 2)

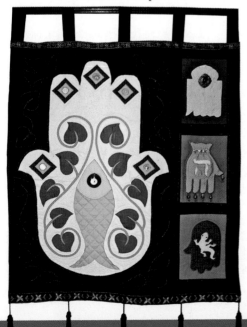

**Barbara's Felted Grapes Purse**

Barbara D. Levinson (Chapter 5)

**Arna's *Ahavah* Needlepoint**

Arna Shefrin (Chapter 3)

**Donna's Quilted *Shalom* Wall Hanging**

Donna Gross (Chapter 4)

**Eleanor's Tree of Life Runner**

Eleanor Levie (Chapter 6)

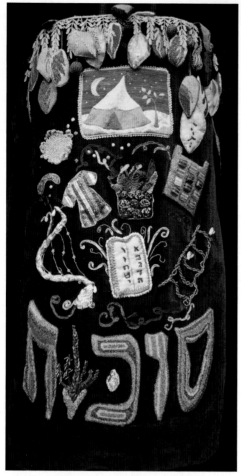

**Lois's *Sefer* Placekeepers**

Lois Gaylord (Chapter 8)

**Sukkot Torah Mantle**

Judy Snitzer (Chapter 9)

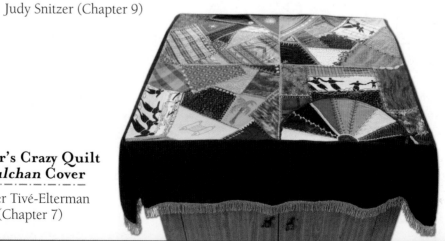

**Esther's Crazy Quilt
*Shulchan* Cover**

Esther Tivé-Elterman
(Chapter 7)

### Esther's Crazy Quilt
### Challah Cover

Esther Tivé-Elterman (Chapter 11)

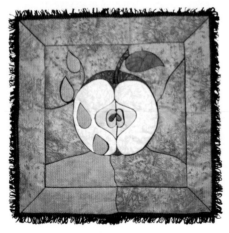

### Donna's Apples & Honey
### Challah Cover

Donna Gross (Chapter 13)

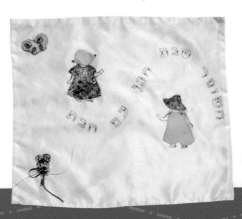

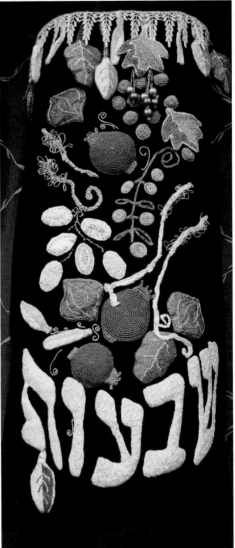

### Shavuot Torah Mantle

Judy Snitzer (Chapter 10)

### Menorah's Challah Cover

Menorah Lafayette-Lebovics
Rotenberg (Chapter 12)

**Heather's High Holy Day Inspiration**

Heather G. Stoltz (Chapter 14)

USHPIZIN
אושפיזין

**Claire's *Ushpizin* Quilt**

Claire Sherman (Chapter 15)

**Lesley's Purim Puppets**

Lesley Frost (Chapter 19)

**Ruth's ChanuCats Quilt**

Ruth Lenk
(Chapter 17)

### Zoë's Knit Seder Plate

Zoë Scheffy (Chapter 22)

### Julia's Bat Mitzvah Challah Cover

Lois Gaylord (Chapter 25)

### Claire's *Afikomen* Envelopes

Claire Sherman
(Chapter 21)

### Shellie's Ten-Plagues Matzah Cover

Shellie Black (Chapter 20)

### Eleanor's *Chanukiah* Vest

Eleanor Levie
(Chapter 16)

PHOTO: ED ANISMAN

### Julian's Traditional Tallit

Julian M. Brook (Chapter 26)

### Hannah's Baby Quilt

Claire Sherman (Chapter 23)

PHOTO: RICK APITZ

### Vicki's Cross-Stitch *Wimpel*

Vicki Pieser
(Chapter 24)

For this child I prayed and The Lord granted my petition. I will give thanks to the Lord with my whole heart~

BLESSED IS HE WHO ENTERS

### Debra's Tallit & Tallit Bag

Susan H. Rappaport (Chapter 28)

### Dancing Hamantaschen

Ellen Muraskin and Marcy Thailer
(Chapter 18)

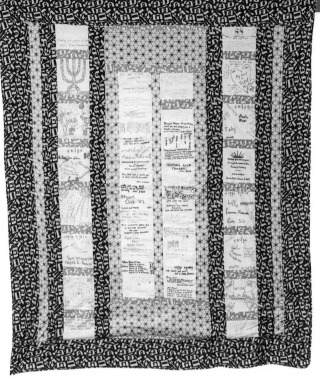

## Stuart's Healing Quilt

Holly Levison (Chapter 29)

## Judy's Garden of Eden Tallit Bag

Judith S. Paskind
(Chapter 27)

## Shalva Quilt

The Quilting Group with No Name (Chapter 30)

PHOTO: EDWIN BERNBAUM

# Beyond *Jewish Threads*
## Inspiration from Talented Professionals

### Another Chuppah
Ursel Behr Eichengreen-Fuchs
(Inspirations)

### NCJW, West Morris Chuppah
National Council of Jewish Women, West Morris
(Inspirations)

### Hannah's Woven *Shalom* Wall Hanging
Hannah Sue Margolis
(Inspirations)

### Arna's Tallit Bag
Arna Shefrin
(Inspirations)

### Women's Torah Project Bimah Cloth
Lois Gaylord (Inspirations)

focus on self-examination and moral improvement, as we evaluate our lives and look toward correcting past mistakes. While Rosh Hashanah is joyful, it is also a time to make heartfelt resolutions about how we live our lives and how we treat one another. It is about becoming a better person.

Rosh Hashanah begins a ten-day period of repentance (in Hebrew, *Aseret Yemei Teshuvah*), which ends on Yom Kippur. During this period, we face the mistakes we have made over the past year, ask for forgiveness from others and from God, and begin working on ways to avoid making the same mistakes again. One of the most recognizable symbols of this period is the shofar, which finds its way as a theme into many fabric crafts fashioned for the High Holy Days. Also traditional at this time of year are apples and honey, signifying the wish for a sweet new year. (See Donna Gross's Apples & Honey Challah Cover, chapter 13.)

## Tu B'Shevat

Long before environmentalists started calling attention to saving the earth, Jewish people were caring for our planet all year round and especially on the fifteenth of the month of Shevat, by observing Tu B'Shevat, the New Year of the Trees, which occurs in midwinter. On Tu B'Shevat, many Jewish people plant trees in their own backyard or on the grounds of their synagogue or make donations so trees can be planted in Israel. The holiday dovetails nicely with a Tree of Life motif, which can be incorporated in all sorts of fabric crafts. (See Susan Schrott's Tree of Life Wall Hanging, chapter 1, and Eleanor Levie's Tree of Life Runner, chapter 6).

Jewish families have traditionally planted a cypress tree on Tu B'Shevat when the holiday takes place after the birth of a girl and a cedar tree after the birth of a boy. When the child marries, branches from the tree would be cut down and used to make a chuppah for the wedding ceremony.

Some people host a dinner similar to a Pesach seder to celebrate the New Year of the Trees. Weather permitting, the Tu B'Shevat seder may be held outdoors, and a picnic quilt—perhaps handmade especially for Tu B'Shevat—may be used to cover the ground to create a table-like setting. If the weather doesn't cooperate, the quilt can be used as a tablecloth indoors. Flowers, plants, and greens of all sorts grace the Tu B'Shevat seder table, along with fruits, vegetables, and nuts, to give the seder an outdoorsy feel. Hosts include as many different and unusual fruits and vegetables in the Tu B'Shevat seder meal as possible. Figs have a special place at this seder because they represent peace. Nuts are significant because they can be soft, medium, or hard—traits that people share as well. Water, and its important role in maintaining the earth, is also feted during Tu B'Shevat. The fifteenth day of Shevat is a time for us to recommit ourselves to saving the earth and all it produces.

## Sukkot

Another holiday with an outdoor flavor is Sukkot, an eight-day autumn harvest festival that starts on the fifteenth day of Tishri. Today, the holiday centers around the sukkah, a hut made of natural, unprocessed material such as wood and decorated with fruits and vegetables that might have been harvested in ancient times by Jewish farmers in the Promised Land. A symbol of protection and peace, the sukkah dates back twenty-five hundred years. Sukkahs were built by Jewish farmers who needed to be close to their crops during the fall harvest. By living in their sukkahs out in the field, farmers could quickly gather crops damaged during a sudden storm, thereby limiting any loss. Quickly constructed and easy to take apart, sukkahs were also used as shelters by the Jewish people, who wandered in the desert after the Exodus from Egypt (noted in Leviticus 23:42–43). So the sukkah recalls both the Exodus and the autumn harvest in the Land of Israel. The holiday of Sukkot was a way to thank God for a good harvest. Grapes were a popular crop in the Holy Land at the time and are often used in fabric crafts made with a Sukkot theme in mind. (See Judy Snitzer's Sukkot Torah Mantle, chapter 9, and Claire Sherman's *Ushpizin* Quilt, chapter 15.)

## Simchat Torah

Simchat Torah is observed eight days after Sukkot. Each year the Torah is read from beginning to end, and Simchat Torah celebrates reaching that end and beginning once again. The last few verses of Deuteronomy, the end of the Five Books of Moses, are read to mark the conclusion of the reading of the Torah. The process is started again for another year with the reading of the first few verses of Genesis, the first book of the Torah.

All the Torah scrolls are usually taken out of the ark for this holiday and the congregation dances around the scrolls. As the Torahs are carried through the synagogue, children parade behind them and are showered with candy to add to the festivities. A joyful celebration of the Torah, Simchat Torah honors the Torah and all the lessons we learn from it.

## Shavuot

Like Simchat Torah, Shavuot honors the gift of the Torah. Shavuot is the springtime festival of the giving of the Torah. It occurs seven full weeks after the second day of Pesach, so the two holidays are linked. Shavuot is also called the Festival of Weeks, because it took the Jewish people seven weeks (or forty-nine days) to travel from Egypt to Mount Sinai. On the fiftieth day, God gave the Torah to the people of Israel at Mount Sinai. Shavuot is celebrated to remind Jewish people throughout the world that the deliverance from Egypt and a life of bondage was not completed until the Torah was received. According to tradition and a ritual called counting the *omer* (*omer* being a measurement, traditionally of grain), a special prayer is said every day after the beginning of Pesach, noting the count in days and weeks to Shavuot. Excitement builds as the holiday approaches, and on the fiftieth day it is customary to stay up all night studying, signifying our readiness to receive the Torah at any time. (See Judy Snitzer's Shavuot Torah Mantle, chapter 10, for ways to incorporate a Shavuot theme in a Jewish fabric craft.)

# Purim

Purim commemorates the story of Queen Esther, who saved the Jewish people from the evil Haman in Persia around the fifth century BCE. A springtime holiday, it is celebrated on the fourteenth day of Adar. The Persian king, Ahasuerus, issued a decree that all the Jewish people in Persia be killed. But it was actually his close adviser Haman who wanted the Jewish people annihilated. When the beautiful Queen Esther, who was Jewish, got word of the decree, she convinced the king to rescind the order. The king went a step further and ordered Haman killed.

One of the highlights of the holiday is the reading of the *Megillat Esther,* or Book of Esther. Noisemakers are used to drown out the name of Haman every time it is mentioned during the *Megillah* reading. In many synagogues, the reading is done before a congregation dressed in costumes, representing characters from the Purim story. Usually handmade, these Purim costumes offer fabric craftspeople endless opportunities to exercise creative license. Among imaginative approaches to the Purim story are Ellen Muraskin and Marcy Thailer's Dancing Hamantaschen, chapter 18, and Lesley Frost's Purim Puppets, chapter 19.

# Shabbat

In traditional Jewish homes, preparations for Shabbat are rigorous. Fine linens are put on the table and special foods prepared, with the aromas from these tantalizing dishes filling the house as if to alert all those who enter that Shabbat is not far off. Challah, the traditional egg-twist bread, is covered by a special cloth to decorate the Shabbat table. (See Esther Tivé-Elterman's Crazy Quilt Challah Cover, chapter 11, and Menorah Lafayette-Lebovics Rotenberg's Challah Cover, chapter 12.) Finally, as the sun sets on Friday evening and Shabbat arrives, it comes as a day of leisure, a day to reflect, to study Torah, to renew our commitment to Judaism.

For those who do not observe Shabbat, this weekly holiday may seem like a day full of restrictions. But those who understand it realize that the Sabbath is actually a gift from God—a day to take a break from our daily labors, to set aside our ongoing concerns and focus on the more meaningful things in life, such as family and lessons drawn from the Torah. Shabbat is much more than just a day to pray or a day to eat special meals. On Shabbat Jews do these things in a more leisurely fashion, taking time to savor aspects of life that are often hurried through and taken for granted during the rest of the week. Shabbat is a joyful occasion that gives us time each week to refresh our spirituality and reset our sights on living a life rooted in the teachings of Torah.

—*Robert Grayson*

# 11 Esther's Crazy Quilt Challah Cover

*Project designer:* **Esther Tivé-Elterman**

Esther Tivé-Elterman found her way to Jewish observance by a circuitous route, somewhat akin to the crazy quilting, or patchwork, that has become her passion. In certain ways, her evolving love for Judaism dovetailed with her evolving love of art.

Growing up in Brooklyn as an unaffiliated Jew, she went to art museums with her family and watched her father, a pharmacist by profession, sketching people on the New York City subway trains—her biggest inspiration to pursue art as a vocation. Meanwhile, as a teenager, Esther became friends with a religious girl, and that friendship had a tremendous impact on her. Gradually, she became a fully practicing Jew.

After studying art education at Hunter College and Buffalo College and pursuing a graduate degree in the subject at Pratt Institute, Esther took a life-altering four-month backpacking trip through Europe and Israel. In addition to seeing firsthand the amazing artwork she had been studying for years, she was drawn inexorably to the Land of Israel.

Art became Esther's livelihood and lifeblood, as she taught in after-school art programs, at sleepaway camps, and in a public school. "I continued drawing, painting, photography, and Hebrew calligraphy," she recalls of that time after college and before her marriage. "I drew my own *ketubah* [marriage contract] when I got married to my husband, Arthur." A neighborhood friend piqued her interest in quilting, and Esther then took a quilting course, finding yet another outlet for her artistic impulses.

Through the years, the artist nurtured her love of Eretz Yisrael (Land of Israel), and in 1996, Esther and her family—her husband and six children—made *aliyah,* settling in Mitzpeh Yericho, twenty minutes east of Jerusalem in the Judean hills overlooking Jericho and the Dead Sea. There she began to quilt once again, making special gifts for B'nei Mitzvah, weddings, and other celebrations.

An accomplished quilter, who has exhibited her work at the Menachem Begin Heritage Center Museum in Jerusalem, Esther sees a profound connection between crazy quilting and Judaism—one that infuses her art with meaning and spiritual intention. "Up close, crazy quilts seem like scattered pieces of fabric, an array of different colors and patterns," she points out. "But, looking at a crazy quilt from a distance, you see the picture and it comes together. Likewise, in Judaism, sometimes when you look up close, you see scattered situations or practices, seemingly without meaning. Yet, in retrospect, you can see that they follow an orderly, orchestrated sequence of events.

"I have always enjoyed the crazy quilt style because of its serendipity. With this challah cover, I have animated this very concept of bringing together scattered pieces with the harmonizing principle of serendipity."

Seeking to create art that would encompass and enhance life, Esther uses her challah cover every Shabbat and encourages others to bring their own *kavannah,* or spiritual intention, to stitching a piece like this.

## Getting Started

*Finished size:* 22 inches by 22 inches
Refer to "General How-To's for Quilt Making," pages 245–251,
"General How-To's for Lettering," pages 252–254; and the "Stitch Guide,"
pages 255–256.

## WHAT YOU'LL NEED

Fabrics:

  1 solid-colored fabric, silk or cotton, 10½ inches by 10½ inches square, for center

  Small scraps of at least 8 different cotton fabrics to coordinate with the center

  Muslin or thin cotton, 10½ inches by 10½ inches, for stabilizer

  Desired fabric for backing, 24 inches by 24 inches

  Muslin or thin cotton, 24 inches by 24 inches, for stabilizer

Seed beads in colors to highlight

Number 8 perle cotton thread or 6-strand embroidery floss (using only 3 strands at a time) in assorted colors, including black

Tracing paper, to transfer lettering

1⅓ yards of flat jacquard ribbon, ¾ inch wide

2½ yards of fringe trim, 1½ inches wide

Embroidery hoop

Beading and embroidery needles

Fabric paint in various colors (optional)

## HOW-TO'S

1.  For the center, cut a 10½-inch square of the fabric chosen for the center. Enlarge the Hebrew lettering (see Figure 11.1), which reads *L'Kvod Shabbat V'Yom Tov*—"For the Honor of the Sabbath and Holiday." Trace the lettering onto the center of the fabric, following the photo. Baste the center square to the muslin, cut the same size, to stabilize your work.

2.  Chain-stitch the outline of the letters in number 8 black perle cotton. Within the traced outlines of the Hebrew letters, use various colors of perle cotton to featherstitch each word over the space. *Alternatively,* using fabric paint, paint the letters within the penciled outline. Let the paint dry overnight, and heat-set the paint per

*Figure 11.1*

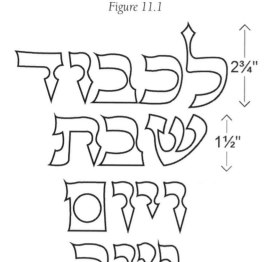

2¾"

1½"

manufacturer's instructions. Then chain-stitch the outline in black perle cotton.

3. For the crazy quilting, cut a 24-inch-square of muslin for a foundation. From the various fabric scraps, cut straight-sided shapes with edges ranging from 2 inches to 8 inches. Start by placing a piece right side up at the top center of the muslin square. Place a different piece wrong side down on top, with the right edges even. Stitch along the right edges, leaving a ¹/₄-inch seam allowance. Unfold the 2nd fabric, and press the seam. Add a 3rd piece of fabric in the same way, working around the fabric clockwise, and continuing until the muslin foundation is covered around the edges.

4. Embroider all seams between crazy quilt patches, using various stitches as shown in the "Stitch Guide" on page 255. Add beading to further embellish the embroidery along crazy quilt seams.

5. Pin or baste the embroidered square to the center, so that the foundation is completely covered. Pin ribbon all around the center square. Topstitch by machine to secure, covering all raw edges. By machine or by hand, zigzag-stitch all around the inside edges of the ribbon.

6. Referring to the detail photo at right, pencil a wheat stalk in each corner of the center square, and embroider over the marked lines with yellow perle cotton (or your desired color) in chain stitch. *Alternatively,* use fabric paint to paint in the wheat stalks.

PHOTO: J. R. ELTERMAN

7. Place the crazy quilt square on your choice of fabric for the backing, right sides facing. Stitch around the edges, leaving a 6-inch opening. Trim backing edges, clip corners, and turn challah cover to the right side. Press. Pin fringe trim all around and stitch by machine. *Alternatively,* fold over the raw edges of the quilt top, pin them, and sew them all around. Pin and sew the fringe all around. Turn under the raw edges of the backing, and with wrong sides together, pin the backing to the quilt top and hand-sew the backing to the top.

Celebrate Shabbat and other Jewish holidays in grand style with your imaginative crazy quilt challah cover!

# 12 Menorah's Challah Cover

*Project designer:* **Menorah Lafayette-Lebovics Rotenberg**

**M**enorah Lafayette-Lebovics Rotenberg feels blessed that her parents gave her such a distinctive name—one with a strong Jewish resonance. A psychotherapist, writer, and fabric artist who enjoys making pieces for her family, Menorah seeks to create images in her work that reflect her life and her sense of Jewish tradition.

Menorah made her first challah cover at Ramaz School in New York City, when she was in the third grade, and she has been making them ever since. Eventually, she graduated from challah covers to quilts, which she made for each member of her family. Says the artist, "I made my first quilt for my eldest son, Josiah, who was born in 1970. His personalized quilt was finished almost in time for the birth of our second son, Ethan, in 1972." Menorah made a quilt for Ethan, and then one for her daughter, Elizabeth, her third child.

As a writer and psychotherapist, highly attuned to the power of words, Menorah often incorporates meaningful phrases from sacred scriptural and liturgical Judaic texts into her work. "The objects I stitch, both by hand and by machine, are to beautify and lend additional significance to our family's Jewish ritual and life-cycle events. The Rabbis had a term for this—*hiddur mitzvah*—the enhancement and illumination of a commandment," she says.

Menorah's fabric artwork combines embroidery, appliqué, and, as embellishments, sequins, beads, and mirrors. While primarily self-taught, she has taken many classes over the years in quilting, manuscript illumination, painting on silk, and some specific embroidery stitches. She also gives workshops on the construction of personalized tallitot.

In creating this challah cover, Menorah interweaves three key factors: her love of Jewish texts and melody, her experience as a quilter, and the birth of her daughter in 1975. Growing up, her family always sang *zemirot* (special words and lyrics, many written in the Middle Ages by Jewish sages) at the Shabbat dinner table and after Shabbat lunch. These are a kind of Jewish *tafelmusik* ("table music," a term from the sixteenth century usually referring to background music at feasts and banquets, much of it composed by Telemann and others of that period).

As her children were growing up, Menorah kept hearing the words and melody of one of the *zemirot* they had been singing for years. The song, "Blessed Is the One Above," has as its refrain "*Hashomer Shabbat haben im ha-bat*—Those who keep the Sabbath with their sons and daughters...." These lyrics resonated with Menorah, and so, when her daughter was born (now that she had both sons *and* a daughter), she decided to create yet another challah cover, this one based on this beloved text.

She drew on a longtime quilting tradition, replicating the Counterpane Twins, a pair of twins (a boy and a girl) often appliquéd onto squares sewn into quilts. One is called Recollect; the other Remembrance.

Menorah used fabric markers for the letters. She deliberately chose a font of Hebrew lettering that has spaces between the upper half of the letter and the lower half. Into those spaces, she sewed small purple beads. The flowers at the lower left represent the flowers that decorate her Shabbat table each week, and the butterfly at the upper left was added as a touch of whimsy and joy—elements that suffuse Shabbat for Menorah and her family.

## Getting Started

*Finished size:* 22 inches by 18 inches

Refer to "General How-To's for Quilt Making," pages 245–251, and the "Stitch Guide," pages 255–256.

## WHAT YOU'LL NEED

White fabric, 23 inches by 19 inches, for the decorated top (Menorah used silky white rayon because it "shone"; cotton or linen also works well)

Fabric scraps for the hats, the girl's dress, and the boy's overalls, plus the butterfly and the floral bouquet

Thin-tipped fabric markers in colors that suit your taste and match your fabric scraps

Dressmaker's transfer paper (optional)

Purple seed beads (or seed beads of any color that match your overall color scheme), approximately 35

2 thin ribbons, 11 inches each

2 small sew-through buttons

6-strand embroidery floss

Thin, iridescent silk embroidery thread

Embroidery and beading needles

Lightweight cotton, 24 inches by 20 inches, for the backing

## HOW-TO'S

*Note: Lay out your entire design on the fabric cover before you begin to paint or sew.*

### Decorated Top

1. Enlarge the patterns (Figures 12.1 through 12.9) on the following pages as indicated for the curved Hebrew phrase, the boy and girl figures (including their hats), and the butterfly and floral bouquet.

2. Pin the enlarged patterns to the fabric you've chosen for each piece, and cut out the fabric for the bodies and hats of the boy and the girl, plus the butterfly and the floral bouquet. (You may also use dressmaker's transfer paper for this purpose.) For the boy and the girl, plus their hats, use needle-turn appliqué (or any appliqué technique you like) to eliminate the raw edges. Pin the appliquéd boy and girl fabric pieces in place on the white fabric. Appliqué the boy

Figure 12.1

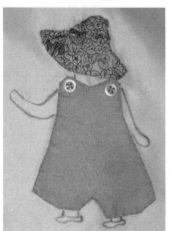

and girl figures onto the white fabric using a running stitch with matching-color thread.

3. Using a thin-tipped fabric marker, draw the arms, hands, feet, and shoes of the boy and girl, following the close-up photos at left. Using a thin-tipped fabric marker in another color (based on your color scheme), trace the curved Hebrew lettering onto the white fabric, following the photo on page 94. Using embroidery floss in a color that matches the painted arms and legs, sew the buttons at the top of the boy's overalls.

4. Embellish the butterfly with beads, if desired, or with fabric scraps. To add fabric-scrap details, as Menorah did, pin small pieces of the same fabric used for the girl's dress onto the butterfly, placing embroidery floss around the border of each one and sewing it in place with a couching stitch using iridescent silk thread, following the close-up photo on page 99.

5. Pin the butterfly and the floral bouquet in place, following the photo on page 94. Place embroidery floss around the border of each one, and sew it in place with a couching stitch, using iridescent silk thread. Tie the 2 ribbons into a bow, and tack the bow to the bouquet

Figure 12.2                    Figure 12.3

Figure 12.4    Figure 12.5

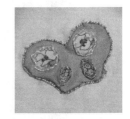

above the "stem" with a few stitches. Sew through the knot of the bow and the appliqué.

6. Sew 4 beads on the left side of the girl's hat and 3 on the right. Sew beads in the middle of each Hebrew letter, as in the photo on page 94. Carefully press the decorated piece, ironing around the beads.

## Assembly

1. Position the decorated top piece on the backing material, cut 1 inch larger all around, with right sides facing and edges even.

2. Machine-stitch along 3 sides of the top, as you would a pillowcase. Then trim the backing fabric even with the decorated top, and clip across the seam allowances at the corners. Turn the challah cover to the right side, insert the raw edges of the opening ¼ inch to the inside, pin, and slip-stitch the opening closed.

3. Carefully press your finished challah cover.

Then make your Shabbat table wonderfully memorable with this handmade heirloom decoration.

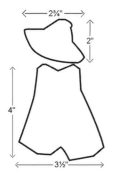 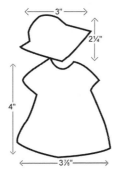 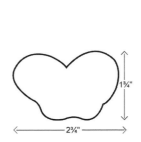 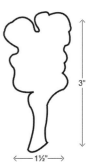

Figure 12.6     Figure 12.7     Figure 12.8     Figure 12.9

# 13

# Donna's Apples & Honey Challah Cover

*Project designer:* **Donna Gross**

------------------------------------

**D**onna Gross is one of the few contributors to *Jewish Threads* I know personally. She's an active member of National Council of Jewish Women (NCJW), West Morris Section, the organization for which I serve as co-president. Donna herself is co-president of the Sisterhood at Morristown Jewish Center–Beit Yisrael in Morristown, New Jersey. She is also a talented quilter, who makes beautiful quilted tote bags.

The fabric artist generously lends her time and talents to numerous organizations throughout northwest New Jersey, where she lives, and one of the most magnificent projects she's worked on is the quilted chuppah made by NCJW, West Morris, which is the inspiration for this book. (See more about this in the introduction and the "Inspirations" section.) Bringing a wonderful sense of spiritual understanding to the chuppah project, Donna designed twelve gorgeous square panels for the underside of the chuppah, each representing one aspect of Jewish life. Then she made up kits for members to sew as appliqués. The kits included all the fabric needed for the panel, pattern pieces to be used to cut out the fabric, a diagram of where each piece of fabric was to go, and the special silk thread needed to sew the panel. Donna chose a stained-glass motif for these panels, which gives them a distinct sense of dimensionality at eight feet off the floor. Once all the panels were done, they were sewn together and then quilted—a monumental project overall, which took more than two years to complete.

One of these panels pictures apples and honey, representing the promise of a sweet New Year for Rosh Hashanah. I asked Donna to re-create that piece for *Jewish Threads* as a quilted challah cover for the Days of Awe, which take place in early autumn. This piece would make a lovely hostess gift for the holidays—one that would be cherished for generations to come.

# Getting Started

*Finished size:* 17 inches by 17 inches
Refer to the "General How-To's for Quilt Making," pages 245–251.

## WHAT YOU'LL NEED

Cotton fabrics in solids or mottled hand-dyed batiks with overall visual texture:

   $1/2$ yard black cotton

   1 fat quarter of turquoise, for background

   Small amounts of white, gold, red, beige, and green

Thin batting, 17 inches square

White fabric marking pen

Light box (optional)

Black fringe (or any type of edging treatment of your choice—ribbon, pompoms, or whatever strikes your fancy)

## HOW-TO'S

*Note: Because this design simulates stained glass, be sure to keep the black fabric visible between the different-colored fabric shapes to provide a leading effect. Donna used the needle-turn appliqué technique to appliqué the color onto black fabric, but any appliqué technique will work.*

### Appliqué

1.   Cut the black fabric in half, and put half aside for the backing.

2. Enlarge the pattern at right (Figure 13.1), so you can mark the borders and the pool of honey on a 17-inch square. Trace the full design onto the black material, using a white marking pen so it will show up. Use a light box, if possible, or work over a sunny window. Keep ⅛ inch between all the different-colored shapes to let the leading show through.

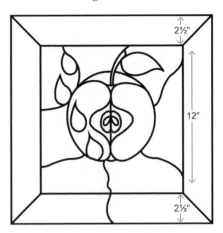

*Figure 13.1*

3. Trace the different appliqué shapes onto the appropriately colored fabrics, referring to the photo (see color insert)—the apple peel on red, the leaf on green, the honey on gold, and so on. Using the appliqué technique of your choice, appliqué the shapes onto the corresponding areas of the background, making sure to leave space in between shapes for the black fabric to show through. There is no need to finish the outside border edges. When otherwise completed, press, and then square off the piece to 17 inches by 17 inches.

## Assembly

1. With right sides facing and edges even, place the appliquéd piece on a same-size piece of black fabric, for the backing. Center a same-size square of batting on top, and pin all around. Sew around, ¼ inch from the edges, leaving a 5-inch opening. Trim the batting close to the seam, and clip across the seam allowances at the corners. Pull the piece right side out through the opening, and pull the corners out with a pin. Slip-stitch the opening closed, and press the piece.

2. Hand-quilt along the black lines between fabric appliqués.

3. Attach the fringe or trim of your choice around the outer edges with topstitches.

Cover your round challah with this beautiful handmade cover as your guests gather round to receive heartfelt wishes for a sweet New Year.

# 14 Heather's High Holy Day Inspiration

*Project designer:* Heather G. Stoltz

S everal years ago, professional fiber artist Heather Stoltz (www.sewingstories.com), who lives in New York City, joined the Journal Quilt Project and committed herself to creating a small art quilt each month. The Journal Quilt Project was organized by Karey Patterson Bresenhan for the International Quilt Festivals in Houston and Chicago as a free-form exercise in creativity, designed to encourage quilt artists to stretch their talents by trying new methods; by experimenting with color, image, composition, materials, and/or technique; and by keeping an informal journal to record the influences on their experimental work and their own reactions to this work. For Heather, it was fitting that the first piece she was making for the Journal Quilt Project would be for the month of Elul, preparing her for both the High Holy Days and her birthday, which fell on Rosh Hashanah that year.

Reflecting on this serendipitous confluence of factors, Heather notes, "The year that was ending had been a year of transitions—a year of finding myself. On the cusp of a new year on the Jewish calendar and a new year in my life, I was ready to break out of the confusing fog and fly toward a new life. Sewn into this piece is a recording device that plays the sound of the shofar when the button under the butterfly is pushed—a call to make these changes with courage and intention."

Heather first discovered her love of fiber art while pursuing a master's degree in Jewish women's studies at the Jewish Theological Seminary in New York. Since then, she has been translating texts of the Jewish tradition into textile art, bringing her own interpretation to the ancient words. The multifaceted fiber artist also holds a BS degree in mechanical engineering and a BA in Jewish studies from Lafayette College in Easton, Pennsylvania. Although she no longer works as an engineer, she draws on these skills in the design of her quilts.

Heather's work has been exhibited nationally in many venues, including the Park Avenue Synagogue in New York City and the Jewish Orthodox Feminist Alliance's Tenth Anniversary International Conference. Her pieces have also appeared in several publications, including *Creative Quilting: The Journal Quilt Project,* edited by Karey Patterson Bresenhan, *Zeek,* and *Practical Matters.*

Co-president of the New York Chapter of the Women's Caucus for Art, Heather was an arts fellow at the Drisha Institute and served one year as a Poretsky artist-in-residence at the National Havurah Committee Summer Institute in Rindge, New Hampshire. She teaches fiber art workshops at synagogues and conferences throughout the Northeast. She also creates commissioned pieces sparked by the needs and desires of her clients, as well as Judaica items, including tallitot, chuppot, and Torah covers.

While this quilt is more abstract in design than most of the others in *Jewish Threads,* it conveys the soaring spirit that often accompanies a new year, a new perspective, and new challenges to take on as we move into the season of awe. The sounds of the shofar, embedded in this quilted piece, also evoke the quiet moments when we feel the shofar blasts resonating in our soul.

# Getting Started

*Finished size:* 8¹/₂ inches by 11 inches or 12 inches by 12 inches (but you can make yours any size that works for you)

Refer to "General How-To's for Quilt Making," pages 245–251.

## WHAT YOU'LL NEED

Background fabric, roughly 12 inches by 12 inches

Steam-a-Seam 2 fusible webbing (or another double-sided fusible web)

Layers of fabrics in colors that inspire you

Various embellishments: tulle, netting, yarn, beads, ribbon (to add texture, dimension, and meaning to your quilt)

Parchment paper

Sewing needle and thread

Fabric glue

Batting, slightly larger than 12 inches by 12 inches (optional, for quilting)

Muslin or other backing material, slightly larger than 12 inches by 12 inches (optional, for quilting)

Solid fabric as a border, 2 pieces 12 inches by 1¹/₂ inches, 2 pieces 14¹/₂ inches by 1¹/₂ inches (optional, for border)

## HOW-TO'S

*Note: These instructions are more "free-form" than most of the others in* Jewish Threads. *While they do show how Heather made her piece, they encourage you to view this piece as a springboard for your own imagination and make an art quilt all your own—one that reflects your sense of what the High Holy Days mean to you.*

## Inspiration

To make an art quilt that is meaningful to you, the designer advises you to begin by thinking about the themes of the High Holy Days. For example, she points out that during the month of Elul, leading up to Rosh

Hashanah, "We reflect on the past year and think about the things we want to change in the coming year. Is there anything you regret from the past year? Have you strayed from your desired path? Do you want to reconcile with a friend or loved one? This is the time of *teshuvah* [repentance; literally, 'return'].

"If you aren't inspired by these questions, think about prayer—prayer in general, a specific prayer that has special meaning for you, or a particular moment of transformative prayer. What words, thoughts, or images come to mind?"

As you brainstorm in this way, write down whatever occurs to you. Once you have compiled your list, choose one or two words or phrases to focus on, such as *new beginnings* or *emerging*.

## Design

What colors, images, lines, symbols, or textures best reflect the words you have chosen? For example, cool colors (blue, purple, green) can be used to depict calm, relaxing moments, while warm colors (red, orange, yellow) evoke more energetic feelings. Similarly, straight and angled lines and edges generally suggest structure, anger, or rigidity, while soft curves indicate tranquility or fluidity.

As you start to sketch your piece, don't worry about how it will be made. Keep in mind that there are no rules in fiber art, and anything you imagine can somehow be created. Try not to overthink the design. Go with your first instincts, and concentrate on overall colors and shapes. The design process will continue as you create the piece; this sketch is just a starting point.

## Making Your Quilt Top

### Background and Appliqué
The best way to create your piece depends on your unique design. These instructions will describe the process of creating a piece with raw-edge appliqué, but feel free to use other techniques if you have sewing or quilting experience and feel that another method would work better for your design.

1. Choose a 12-by-12-inch or 8½-by-11-inch piece of cotton fabric for the background of your piece. (Other fabrics can also be used, but 100% cotton is the easiest to work with for the background.) You can leave much of this background showing, cover the entire thing with other fabrics, or do something in between.

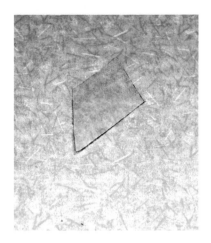

2. For raw-edge appliqué, Heather uses Steam-a-Seam 2, a double-sided fusible webbing that allows you to add layers of fabric to a piece without doing any sewing. Simply remove the backing from one side of the webbing, stick it to the desired fabric, and cut out your shape (see photos at right). Next, peel off the remaining paper backing (making sure to leave the webbing in place), place the shape on your background, and iron it in place when you're ready. The shape will temporarily stick to the background before ironing so you can move it around until you're happy with it. It will become permanent once ironed.

3. Using layers of fabrics and Steam-a-Seam 2, create your piece based on your sketch and guided by your source of inspiration. As you work, think about what other elements will help express your prayer, such as tulle, netting, yarn, beads, or ribbon. These embellishments add dimension, texture, and meaning to the finished art quilt. For Heather's piece, white tulle was folded in layers over the orange background fabric. To create the illusion that the fog was thinning, each added layer stopped farther away from the center, allowing more of the background to show through in the less covered

areas. While you should think about what elements will be added and where they might fit best, do not add them until all the layers underneath have been ironed in place. (Says Heather, "I have learned the hard way that many of these embellishments are not friends of the iron.")

4. When you have your fabric layered the way you want it, place parchment paper over your piece and iron everything in place. The parchment paper serves as a pressing cloth that will not stick to any stray pieces of Steam-a-Seam 2 that are showing. If you have incorporated a variety of fabrics, use the iron setting appropriate for the most delicate one in your piece.

   *(Note: If the iron touches the Steam-a-Seam 2 directly, everything gets gummy—the iron, your piece, and the ironing board. Keep in mind that if you cannot find Steam-a Seam 2, you can use any other double-sided fusible webbing or fabric glue.)*

*Embellishments*

1. Now you're ready to embellish!

   *(Note: If you are planning to machine-quilt your finished piece, you may want to layer and quilt before adding embellishments. Adding heavier embellishments after layering will also help distribute the weight more evenly and keep your piece together.)*

2. Beads, ribbons, tulle, feathers, and anything else that you can imagine can be added to your piece with a needle and thread or fabric glue. Whatever speaks to you can find its way into your quilt.

   *(Note: This is the stage at which Heather inserted the recording device in her quilt that plays the sound of the shofar when the button under the butterfly is pushed. When layering the piece, Heather cut a hole in the batting the size of the thin recording device and nestled it between the layers. She then hand-stitched through all the layers to keep it from sliding out of position.)*

## Fiber Art versus Art Quilt

Congratulations! You have completed a piece of fiber art. Fiber art is just what it sounds like—art made from mainly fiber-based materials. Technically, if you used other items in the embellishment phase, you created a mixed-media piece, but let's not worry about the details.

1. If you wish to make an art quilt from your piece, see "General How-To's for Quilt Making," pages 245–251.

2. Decide whether or not you want to add a border to your piece. (Heather didn't.) Will a frame of solid fabric help call attention to your piece, or will a small binding be sufficient? More complicated borders can also be considered.


Mazel tov! Your quilt is complete. Take a step back and enjoy it!

# 15 Claire's *Ushpizin* Quilt

*Project designer:* Claire Sherman

The autumn harvest festival of Sukkot is a holiday that revolves around inviting people together to forge and strengthen interpersonal connections in a beautiful setting, under the stars—a holiday redolent of seasonal fruits and vegetables. Sukkot enables us to reconnect with nature as we reconnect with family members and friends within the walls of the sukkah, designed as a temporary shelter, open to the elements. Decorated with fruits of the season, the sukkah also tantalizes the senses with enticing scents and vivid colors.

As Claire Sherman was designing her colorful *ushpizin* quilted wall hanging, her *kavannah,* or spiritual intention, was to enhance the meaning of the gathering in her sukkah and the connection between the friends and family members eating dinner there. She also wanted to use the wall hanging as a touchstone for a contemporary ritual to invite into the sukkah the guests who couldn't be there, either because of their distance or because they had passed on.

"I've been welcoming guests into my sukkah for years, but this year I welcomed a new kind of spiritual, or virtual, guest. I called these guests *ushpizin,*" Claire notes. "*Ushpizin* simply means 'guests' in Aramaic. If you look in a traditional prayer book, there is a prayer, called *Ushpizin,* which welcomes seven biblical 'faithful shepherds' to the sukkah each night, following a mystical tradition from the *Zohar*. Since Sukkot lasts for seven nights, the custom is to invite a different biblical guest each night. However, every night the other six tag along, too. The traditional guests are Abraham, Isaac, Jacob, Joseph, Moses, Aaron, and David. I have also seen contemporary groupings of seven women guests, including seven drawn from among the following list: Sarah, Rebecca, Rachel, Leah, Miriam, Esther, Ruth, Dinah, Deborah, Hannah, and more."

Speaking about what prompted her to make this lovely quilted wall hanging, Claire points out, "I'd wanted to create some kind of *ushpizin* ritual before, but for some reason, I hadn't been able to do it without a ritual object. Once I hung this *ushpizin* quilt on the wall of my sukkah, I felt empowered to begin. As soon as we started talking about who was missing from the table, we began to write down the names of our mystical guests.

"Another intention I brought to this quilt was to keep alive the connection between my children and their grandparents, who are no longer alive."

Surprisingly to both Claire and her family and friends, this simple *ushpizin* ritual was immensely powerful. "Tears were shared when we talked about our loved ones who weren't at the table," the designer recalls. "The families whose children were away at school were especially grateful to be able to symbolically invite their distant offspring into the sukkah to be with them at this time."

Because Claire lives in Berkeley, California, most evenings during Sukkot are warm enough for her to entertain in her sukkah. Besides making quilts like her *ushpizin* piece, the artist conducts workshops throughout California in paper cutting and Jewish ritual objects for adults and children. A member of the Quilting Group with No Name, whose Shalva Quilts are featured in chapter 30, Claire enjoys chanting Torah and leading services at her local synagogue, Congregation Netivot Shalom. She and her husband, who have two daughters, were among the synagogue's founding members. Claire is now tutoring her younger daughter for her Bat Mitzvah at Netivot Shalom.

This *ushpizin* quilt reflects Claire's welcoming nature and her love of sharing her home with guests. Creating your own ritual objects, as Claire did with this wall hanging, and then inventing your own contemporary rituals—these are among the joys of making your own Jewish fabric crafts.

# Getting Started

*Finished size:* 40 inches by 24 inches

Refer to "General How-To's for Quilt Making," pages 245–251, and "General How-To's for Lettering," pages 252–254.

## WHAT YOU'LL NEED

Cotton fabrics:

   Sky print, 10 inches by 12$^1/_2$ inches

   Green print, 4$^1/_2$ inches by 12$^1/_2$ inches

   $^1/_3$ yard of blue for the lettering background and bottom bar front

   $^1/_8$ yard of purple, for the inner border

   $^1/_3$ yard of lavender, for the outer border and the background for the names

   Scraps of various magenta prints, for the letters

   Scraps of wood-grain, fruit-motif prints, and leaf-themed fabric, for the sukkah, the sukkah decorations, and the foliage

   Fabric for the backing, 28 inches by 44 inches (or pieced to that length)

1$^1/_4$ yards of quilt batting

$^1/_2$ yard of paper-backed fusible web

$^2/_3$ yard of Velcro hook and loop tape

Fabric pencils

Parchment paper, as used in baking

## HOW-TO'S

*Note: Claire's first decision was which words to put on her* ushpizin *quilt. To make it simple, she chose to write* ushpizin *in English and Hebrew letters. (*Ushpizin *is Aramaic, but Aramaic is written with Hebrew letters.) Other options might be "We welcome these mystical guests to our sukkah," or "Sit, sit, exalted guests," from the* Ushpizin *prayer in the prayer book.* Ushpizin *is the masculine plural form, which grammatically encompasses both genders. If you want to specifically include women, the feminine plural is* ushpizata, *not* ushpizot, *as Hebrew speakers might guess. "I wouldn't have known this except that a woman rabbi told me a story about making that mistake on her paper* ushpizin," *Claire adds.*

### *Appliqués*

1.  Begin with the sukkah scene. For a background, join the sky fabric piece to the grass fabric piece along the 12¹/₂-inch edges. Press paper-backed fusible web onto the back of each fabric to be used as an appliqué. Although you could enlarge the sukkah graphic presented at left (Figure 15.1), Claire recommends that you design your own. Another option is to ask a child to draw one for you. A simple sukkah drawn by a child as young as seven and cut from fabric would be charming. (Claire's sukkah design was drawn by her twelve-year-old daughter, Shira.) Using a light box or a sunny window, place each shape under the fabric you'd like to use, referring to the photo (page 112) for suggested prints. Trace the shape with fabric pencils in colors to contrast. Cut out each

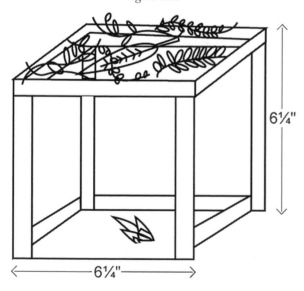

*Figure 15.1*

6¼"

6¼"

fabric piece, then peel off the paper backing from the fusible web. Arrange the shapes for the sukkah on a sheet of parchment paper, and fuse the appliqués together. Peel them off when cool, and position them on the background. (Although you could fuse everything directly onto your backing fabric, this gives you the flexibility to change your mind and the ability to fix mistakes.) When you are happy with the sukkah design, fuse it in place. Add foliage and flowers, again with pieces cut from fusible web–backed fabrics.

2. For lettering, follow directions in "General How-To's for Lettering" (pages 252–254) to create patterns 4 inches tall at the most for the word *ushpizin* or the words of your choice. (See the patterns in Figure 15.2 for the English and Hebrew words used in Claire's design.) Choose different magenta fabrics for the letters to get a "scrappy" look, in keeping with the way our foremothers sometimes made quilts. Press fusible web to the wrong side of each magenta fabric, and then cut a 3-by-8-inch rectangle. Each piece will accommodate two letters, approximately $2^{1}/_{2}$ inches by 3 inches for each letter, except for letters such as the final *nun*, which measures 4 inches long. Use a light box or a sunny window and fabric pencils to trace the English and Hebrew letters onto the right side of the fusible web–backed fabrics. Cut out each letter with small, sharp scissors, and remove the paper backing. After the quilt segments are joined, arrange the letters on the large blue fabric bar; see step 3 under "Assemble the Quilt Top."

*Figure 15.2*

אושפיזין

# USHPIZIN

3.  Using clear monofilament in the top of the machine and sewing thread in the bobbin, zigzag-stitch around most of the fused pieces.

## Assemble the Quilt Top

1.  Frame the scene with an inner border: Cut 2-inch-wide strips of purple fabric, and join them to the side edges of the scene. Then join strips to the top and bottom edges. Trim and press seam allowances toward the center.

2.  Add an outer border: Cut 2 strips of lavender fabric 5 inches by 17 inches—or the length of the scene. Sew a strip to either side of the bordered sukkah scene. Trim off the excess, and then add 4-by-24-inch top and bottom borders.

3.  For a lettering background, cut one rectangle from blue fabric, $10^3/_4$ inches by 24 inches; another blue rectangle, 6 inches by 24 inches, for the bottom section; and one magenta strip, $1^1/_2$ inches by 24 inches. Join the large blue rectangle to the top edge of the double-bordered quilt top. Arrange the letters on the blue background fabric at the top, fuse, and zigzag-stitch around the letters, for stability. Finally, join the magenta strip, then the remaining blue strip to the bottom of the quilt top.

## Finishing

1.  Make a quilt sandwich, and quilt as desired. Trim and bind the quilt, including a hanging sleeve at the top. Refer to "General How-To's for Quilt Making," pages 250–251.

2.  Write the names of the guests you are inviting on a separate piece of lavender fabric, 6 inches by 24 inches. Iron a piece of parchment paper to the back of the fabric to stabilize it so it's easier to write on. Use a permanent marker or a fabric marker, and iron to heat-set the lettering. Stitch corresponding dots or strips of Velcro to the signed fabric and the bottom of the wall hanging, so you can easily attach this extra piece. When friends want to add more names, simply detach the fabric from the quilt so the names can be written while

sitting at the table. If you prefer, you can use a new piece of fabric to make a new "guest" list every year and never run out of space to write their names. Another quilted wall hanging or a lap quilt to warm you in the sukkah could be made from these "guest" lists.

## Afterword

Since Claire's *ushpizin* quilt wasn't finished until after Sukkot, during the holiday she pinned the pieces of it that she had completed to the wall of her sukkah. She also pinned up a blank sheet of paper, on which she and her guests wrote the names of the missing "guests" that year. Next Sukkot her completed quilted *ushpizin* wall hanging will make its debut. "Originally, I intended to write the names of the guests directly on the quilt, on the lavender fabric that borders the sukkah. However, once it was finished, I couldn't bear the idea of people writing with a permanent pen on my artwork. So I changed the design yet again, inserting the piece at the bottom affixed with Velcro for the names," she points out, showing how simple it is to adapt a design like this one to your own spiritual urgings.

# 16 Eleanor's *Chanukiah* Vest

*Project designer:* Eleanor Levie

Eleanor Levie (www.eleanorlevie.com) brings out this *chanukiah* (menorah) vest during the Festival of Lights every year and wears it at every opportunity. "At holiday parties, it's a bold but good-hearted way to identify as someone with my own set of lively traditions," says the designer. And having recently moved to Center City Philadelphia, she especially loves showing off her creativity at Congregation Rodeph Shalom, where she's a new member and art teacher for the religious school. At Shabbat services when menorahs and Shabbat candles are lit, says Elly, "The littlest children sitting behind me can kindle the *chanukiah*—no risk of burnt fingers!"

As her "day job," Elly is a book producer—one of her recent publications, *Unforgettable Tote Bags,* is a make-it-green collection of "twenty designs too cool to leave in the car." She relishes inspiring others to create pieces that showcase individual imagination and personal passions. "Whether tote bags or embellished clothing, wearable art can serve as a billboard for your creative talents wherever you go," she points out.

Elly is a firm believer in keeping it simple and getting it done. With appliqués cut from felt, there's no need to finish edges that might otherwise unravel. And this crocheted vest, which bears her motif designs, once sat on a table at a thrift shop. Working with any knit or crocheted

121

surface as a background means you'll probably need a stabilizer to prevent the edges from stretching. But Elly suggests that any simple garment will do. And if you're using a garment constructed from sturdy woven fabric, such as a jeans jacket or a classic blazer, you can simply fuse the felt shapes in place for no-sew, quick-and-easy fun, and use permanent markers to draw letters on the dreidels. For longtime use, however, it's a good idea to secure the edges of the appliqués with zigzag stitching. That means you'll be able to rededicate yourself to enjoying Chanukah in style for many years to come.

## Getting Started

*Finished size:* Chanukiah motif, 11 inches by 13 inches; dreidel motif, 5 inches by 6 inches

*Figure 16.1*

### WHAT YOU'LL NEED

Simple vest or jacket

9-by-12-inch acrylic felt "squares": gold heather, white, yellow-gold, purple, tan, sage green, kelly green

Paper-backed fusible web, 1 yard

Permanent marker

For knitted or crocheted surfaces: tearaway interfacing in black or white, to match vest

### HOW-TO'S

1. Enlarge the half-pattern above (Figure 16.1) for the *chanukiah* until its height (without candles) fills the width of an 8½-by-11-inch sheet of paper. Other patterns will be enlarged to full size at this same proportion. Trace the *chanukiah* onto paper folded in half, with long dash lines along the fold line. Cut out the patterns and unfold the *chanukiah* pattern to obtain a full, actual-size pattern.

Also trace the middle sections of the dreidel, and substitute the Hebrew letters *hey* and *shin* for the *nun* and *gimel.*

2. Following manufacturer's instructions for fusible web and instructions for fusible appliqué on pages 248–249, press the web to 1 side of the felt. Pin patterns to pieces of fusible-backed felt, referring to the photo (see color insert) or your imagination for colors. Cut pieces out along the edges of the patterns, then remove pins, patterns, and the release paper that covered one side of the fusible web. In this way, cut out one *chanukiah*, 9 candles and flames, and 2 sets of dreidels (5 separate dreidel pieces). Arrange the pieces on a work surface, turning the 2nd set of dreidel pieces so they look like a mirror image of the first. Use the pattern and a permanent marker to write in the Hebrew letters.

3. Position the pieces on a vest or jacket, referring to the photo or making use of the empty areas on your garment. For the dreidels, leave 1/8 inch between the top, bottom, and side pieces, so that the background fabric peeks through. Let each dreidel handle overlap the top. On the *chanukiah,* layer the Jewish star on top; leave space above and below the candles. Using a press cloth to protect the iron and your ironing surface, press all pieces of fusible-backed felt in place.

4. If you are working over a thin fabric or a stretchy one, like this crocheted vest, pin tearaway stabilizer behind the appliqués. Do all machine appliqué as instructed below. After stitching is completed, tear away or carefully cut away the stabilizer beyond the stitches.

5. Using thread to match the appliqués, sew along all cut edges, with a narrow, open zigzag stitch.

6. Using black thread and a fine, narrow zigzag stitch (satin stitch), go over the marked Hebrew letters on the dreidels.

Share the triumphant spirit of Chanukah everywhere you go as you wear this lovely vest sporting the symbols of the Festival of Lights.

# Ruth's ChanuCats Quilt

*Project designer:* **Ruth Lenk**

R uth Lenk, who has traveled throughout the world with her family, finds that creating fabric crafts grounds her wherever she goes. A native of the United States, Ruth now lives in Israel, where her husband works for the Israeli Ministry of Foreign Affairs (a government agency equivalent to the U.S. State Department).

The fiber artist, who has always loved the visual arts, earned a BFA with honors from the Hartford Art School at the University of Hartford. After college, Ruth moved to Israel, where she started working for the *Jerusalem Post* and eventually became the publication's art director. In her free time, Ruth delved into photography, ceramics, and textile work. Together with her family, she has lived in such far-flung places as Azerbaijan and India, drawing artistic inspiration from the disparate cultures she has called home.

While Ruth is not a "cat person" per se, this whimsical ChanuCats quilt sprang from her imagination in response to a call for entries in a competition sponsored by the Simplicity Creative Group, the makers of Simplicity patterns. Called the "Seasonal Holiday Celebration Contest," the competition required entries to be based on Simplicity patterns.

Ruth's inclination was to design a quilt that echoes the uplifting character of the Jewish seasonal (winter) holiday of Chanukah, which celebrates the triumph of Judah the Maccabee and his small band of freedom fighters in the second century BCE against the oppressive Syrian-Greeks. However, all of Simplicity's holiday patterns had Christmas motifs—in costumes, decorations, and ornaments. None focused on Chanukah.

Undaunted, Ruth decided to improvise, basing her design on one of Simplicity's baby blanket patterns and adjusting it for a different "Holiday Celebration"—the Jewish Festival of Lights, Chanukah. Hence, ChanuCats, a fanciful take on the *chanukiah* (menorah) that's especially appealing to cat fanciers (including the author of this book). "I found the cats on a baby blanket pattern, and I figured I could rearrange the cats to make them into a *chanukiah*," Ruth recalls. "Then I added the flames to reinforce the idea that they were the candles."

Ruth's ChanuCats quilt (which won second place in the Simplicity contest!) exemplifies how, by taking one design and reinventing it to make something else, you can give voice to your own passions. (See Ruth's *Hamsa* Wall Hanging, chapter 2, for another piece Ruth created by tapping into her own spiritual source.) And while many Jewish fabric crafts—like Torah mantles, *shulchan* covers, and matzah covers—have specific ritual purposes, others, like this ChanuCats quilt, reflect Judaism's lighthearted spirit and bring a smile to the faces of children and adults alike as they celebrate the triumph of the Maccabees over their oppressors more than two millennia ago.

## Getting Started

*Finished size:* 56 inches by 30 inches
Refer to "General How-To's for Quilt Making," pages 245–251.

### WHAT YOU'LL NEED

Cotton fabric (9 prints overall):

Blue print, 53 inches by 19 inches, for background

Dark blue print, 53 inches by 13 inches, for border

Blue solid, 53 inches by 9 inches, for *chanukiah* base

Brown print, 16 inches by 16 inches, for *shammas* (large center candle) and corner patches

4 different brown prints, 10 inches by 12 inches, for 8 other feline candles

Mottled yellow, 12 inches by 18 inches, for flames

18 small sew-through buttons, for eyes

2 yards small white rickrack, for whiskers

Backing fabric (muslin or whatever you choose for the back side of the quilt), 60 inches by 34 inches

Batting, 60 inches by 36 inches

1½ yards paper-backed fusible web, 36 inches by 24 inches

6 yards yellow double-fold bias binding tape, or you may use ½ yard of any of the fabrics in the quilt for binding

## HOW-TO'S

1. For the background, stitch the 53-inch sides of the solid and print blue rectangles together. Trace the actual-size cat pattern on page 128 (Figure 17.1) for the smaller cats. Enlarge a second cat to 13½ inches tall. Cut out the 2 cats. Trace around the cats on the paper backing of fusible web—once for the large cat, 8 times for the smaller cats. Fuse the marked paper-backing web to the wrong side of the fabrics chosen for the cats. Cut out the cat shapes, leaving a ¼-inch sewing allowance. Remove the paper backing, and position the cats on the background, beginning with the large cat at dead center and slightly off the bottom edge, then spacing 4 cats to either side along the seam line. Fuse in place.

2. Place a piece of muslin or tearaway stabilizer behind the cats. Zigzag-stitch over the raw edges of the cats.

3. To make the flames, cut free-form shapes from the fusible web, ironing them onto the wrong side of the yellow fabric, and cutting them out, leaving a ¼-inch sewing allowance. Then, as with the cats,

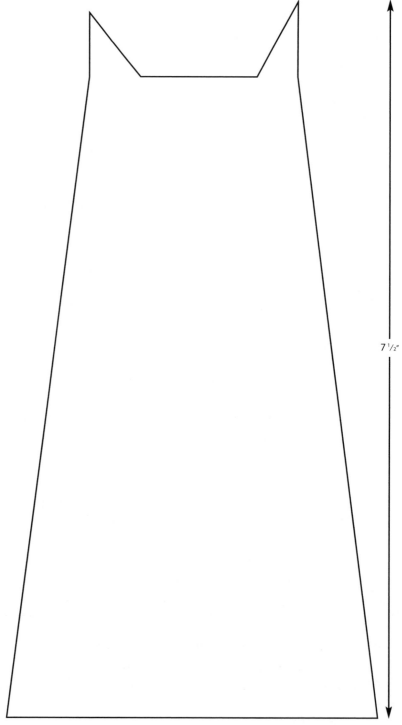

7 ¹/₂"

*Figure 17.1*

remove the paper backing, iron them in place, and then zigzag-stitch them in place.

4.  For the border, cut 2 strips, 4½ inches by 52½ inches, and sew them to the top and bottom of the quilt top. Next, cut 2 strips, 4½ inches by 22½ inches, and four 4½-inch squares. Sew the squares to the ends of the 2 shorter strips, and then sew them to the sides of the quilt top.

## Assembly

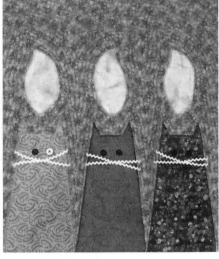

1.  Cut the backing fabric 2 inches larger all around than the quilt top. Trim the batting the same size as the backing. Sandwich the layers and quilt, referring to the photo on page 124 for suggested quilting lines.

2.  Trim the batting and backing even with the quilt top, and square up.

3.  Add binding, enclosing a hanging sleeve at the top edge.

4.  Mark the placement for the eyes on each cat, then sew buttons in place.

5.  For whiskers, cut rickrack into approximately 4-inch lengths; crisscross 2 pieces on each cat's face, and stitch down in the center to secure it in place. You can also tack down the ends so they don't flop around, if you like.

Bring out your ChanuCats quilt on the first night—and every night—of Chanukah to applause all around!

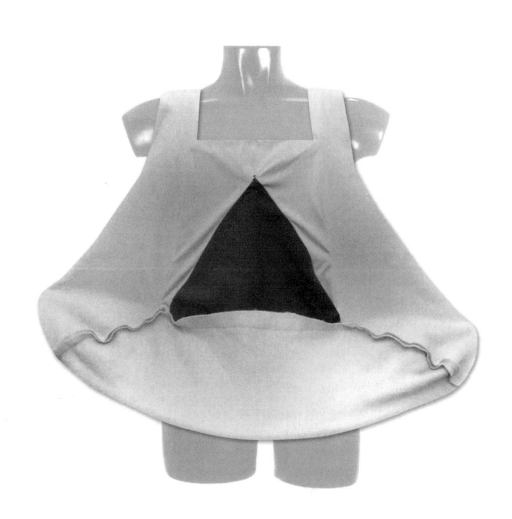

# 18 Dancing Hamantaschen

*Project designers:* **Ellen Muraskin and Marcy Thailer**

T he Purim story, as recounted in the Book of Esther (*Megillat Esther*), echoes with majestic themes—the triumph of good over evil, the courage of one woman to stand up for her people, the love of family exemplified by Mordechai's love of Esther. Yet the celebration of Purim still calls for a sense of silliness rarely seen in Jewish observance.

In line with that fun-filled Purim spirit, the members of Adath Shalom synagogue in Parsippany, New Jersey, who work on the Purim *shpiel* (Yiddish for "play") every year, came up with these "Dancing Hamantaschen," or "Hamantaschenette" costumes, with an eye toward elevating the general merriment of Purim. The actual costume designers, Ellen Muraskin and Marcy Thailer, wanted to give their Purim *shpiels* some added pizzazz, and the response from the Purim revelers—both the *shpiel* attendees and the players themselves—has been wildly enthusiastic.

Says Ellen, "Perhaps it speaks to the closet Reconstructionist in me (and plenty of other nominally Conservative Jews), but the Judaism I want to practice incorporates as much group creativity as humanly possible. Marcy had designed a hamantasch costume for her kids, and that sparked our imagination."

Marcy adds, "In making my kids' Purim costumes one year, I was trying to go for a more Jewish approach to Purim, rather than having them dress up as Spider-Man or Ariel, the Little Mermaid. Once I'd figured out how to make those costumes for my children, it was on to bigger sizes for the *shpiel*."

Working together, Ellen recalls, "We synthesized Purim traditions and early television to come up with the Hamantaschenettes, in the style of the dancing cigarette-pack chorus lines of '50s TV." Ellen sewed the costumes, following Marcy's directions, and the Dancing Hamantaschen were a smashing success. In their debut performance in 2006, the "Hamantaschenettes" act was a commercial break from the *shpiel* itself, a hilarious series of sketches—mostly TV show parodies—hung on the *Megillah* plot. Now an obligatory homegrown tradition, these Dancing Hamantaschen costumes have been unpacked and worked into a different *shpiel* every year since.

In the process, the Dancing Hamantaschen costumes have been worn by fearless male congregant/performers as well as women, and they've taken on roles outside their initial commercial dance numbers. "The year we did 'Morty [Mordechai] Wonka and the Hamantasch Factory,' the Dancing Hamantaschen assumed the character of Oompa-Loompas and took advantage of the syllabic meter match to sing their own Oompa-Loompa/Hamantaschen song," Ellen recalls. As a grand finale, five of them got in a line and turned around in unison, spelling out *Purim*.

A widely published writer/copywriter on high-tech topics in accessible, low-tech language, Ellen has written and edited for trade media, the popular press, marketing departments, and PR firms. Once a year she dons her playwright hat, as part of the core *shpiel*-writing team at Adath Shalom. Marcy, an actuary by profession, is always happy singing, dancing, doing needlecrafts, and making good use of her many glue guns, all of which come in handy when preparing for a Purim *shpiel*.

These simple costumes—made of felt, stretch knit, and part of a hula hoop—propel the Purim spirit to a whole new level. The camaraderie involved in making them—and performing in them—has made Adath Shalom's Purim *shpiels* one of the most highly anticipated events on the synagogue calendar.

# Getting Started

*Finished size:* 18 inches wide at shoulders, 35 inches from front shoulders to bottom hem, and 35 inches from shoulders to hem in back
Refer to "General How-To's for Lettering," pages 252–254.

## WHAT YOU'LL NEED (FOR EACH HAMANTASCH)

Refer to the patterns on page 134.

For dough pieces A, B, C, and F: 2 tan felt panels at least 45 inches square

For filling piece D: 15-inch square of cotton velveteen in orange for apricot filling or purple for prune filling

For inset E: Tan stretchy knit, at least 15 inches by 16 inches

Hula hoop

Hacksaw or matte knife (to cut the hula hoop)

Parchment paper

1 1/2 yards of black felt, for appliquéd letters (optional)

## HOW-TO'S

1. Referring to the patterns on page 134 (Figure 18.1), enlarge and draw patterns on large sheets of parchment paper. Pin pattern pieces to fabrics as indicated in the "What You'll Need" list, and cut out the pieces. With right sides together and leaving 5/8-inch seam allowances, sew triangular "filling" piece D to inset piece E, along the top right side of the triangle. Clip the seam at the top of the triangle. Sew the top left side of the triangle to piece E. Turn the top of piece E under 1/4 inch, and stitch across for a clean finish.

2. With right sides together, and placing piece E 8 inches down from the top of piece A (to form an opening for the wearer's head and a shoulder strap), sew Hamantasch front side A along the long straight edge to piece E, leaving the last inch of the seam unsewn to fold E under and finish with hand- or topstitching. With right sides together, and placing piece E 8 inches down from the top of piece B,

*Figure 18.1*

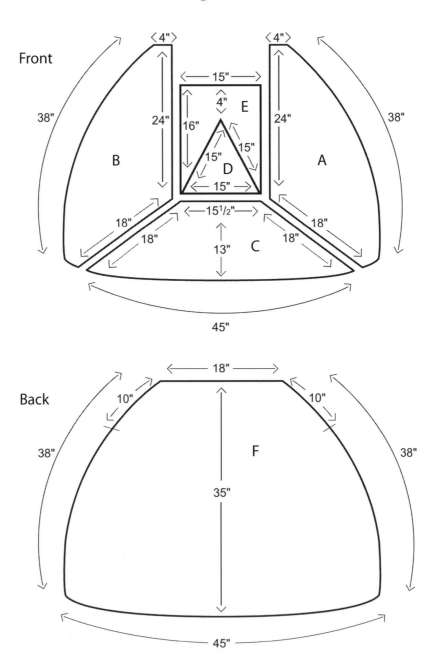

sew Hamantasch front side B along the long straight edge to piece E, leaving the last inch of the seam unsewn to fold E under and finish with hand- or topstitching.

3. With wrong sides together and a ¾-inch seam (so this looks like pinched dough), sew the front bottom C to the bottom sides of B-D-A.

4. With right sides together, sew Hamantasch back piece F to the assembled front, on the shoulders. Leaving 10 inches unsewn at the top for armholes, sew the sides and around the wide corners on the bottom till you're an inch or two into part C, leaving the rest of the bottom open. This leaves encased corners into which you insert the hula-hoop piece. Turn armhole edges under to the wrong side, and stitch.

5. Using a hacksaw or a matte knife, cut out ⅓ of the hula hoop and discard. Slip the open hoop into the bottom of the Hamantasch front, with either end stretching into the Hamantasch corners. Fold under the front bottom edge to form a casing, and enclose the hoop. Sew this closed by hand.

6. *Optional:* Cut out black felt letters, 24 inches high: *P, U, R, I,* and *M.* Hand-sew one letter to the back of each of five Hamantaschen costumes, so dancers can spell out Purim (see photo below).

Serve with milk. Or schnapps.

# 19 Lesley's Purim Puppets

*Project designer:* Lesley Frost

For Lesley Frost, a native of the United Kingdom and a Jew by choice, raising Jewish children posed a challenge. Trained as a teacher, Lesley believed that children learn by doing, and she found herself on the other side of the teacher's desk as she immersed herself in Judaism, Jewish traditions, Jewish food, and Jewish holidays, learning everything she could about her adopted religion and its distinctive culture. "The teacher in me then began to pass on all I had learned to my children, and this became the way I bonded to my chosen religion and to my children," she recalls.

When her children were young, Lesley created a set of five Purim hand puppets as a mitzvah project for her synagogue's Hebrew school. The puppets represented each of the key players in the Purim story—Queen Esther, Mordechai, Haman, Queen Vashti, and King Ahasuerus. "My idea was to create fabric hand puppets that a mother and child could make together and then play with to reenact biblical events and stories," she notes.

Through the years, Lesley has given away numerous sets of these puppets, sold them through a crafts business she ran with a neighbor, and used them at school puppet shows and as holiday table decorations at home. In making these puppets and presenting puppet shows

137

with them in New Jersey, where she has settled, Lesley formed connections with people in many Jewish organizations and with other talented craftspeople. "Each new contact has enriched my understanding and deepened my connections and commitment to Judaism, and its traditions and holidays," the gifted artisan points out.

A former president of the National Council of Jewish Women (NCJW), West Morris Section, Lesley has earned the prestigious Hannah G. Solomon Award, the highest honor in NCJW, for her inspiring volunteer work, her compassion, and her commitment to the Jewish imperative of *tikkun olam,* mending the world. Her community service work has included serving as a crisis response counselor for victims of domestic violence; chairing the Rachel Coalition, the MetroWest community's response to domestic violence; organizing the first Passover Survivors' Seder for victims of domestic abuse; coordinating shipments of snacks and personal items to soldiers serving in Iraq and Afghanistan; overseeing the NCJW, West Morris Section's sixth-grade diversity contest, called "What Prejudice Means to Me"; volunteering at marrow donor drives to help those desperately searching for matching marrow donors; and hosting sewing circles for Feelie Hearts for grieving children. (Feelie Hearts are small, soft, stuffed, fleece hearts that are shipped throughout the United States and Israel free of charge.) She has also earned the Phenomenal Woman award from Morristown (New Jersey) Neighborhood House, which celebrates the accomplishments of women from the surrounding community whose outstanding achievements often go unrecognized.

Wholeheartedly embracing Judaism and its mandate to mend the world, Lesley brings a wonderful sense of hands-on Yiddishkeit to her whimsical Purim puppets.

# Getting Started

*Finished size:* Approximately 12 inches tall

## WHAT YOU'LL NEED

$1/4$ yard of fabric for robe or gown

$1/8$ yard of flesh-colored fabric for head and hands

Plastic doll eyes, $1/4$ inch in diameter, 2 per puppet

Scraps of pink or red felt, for the mouth (optional)

Yarn in desired color, for hair

Curly chenille yarn, for beards (optional)

$1/4$ yard of felt, for a vest

Small amount of polyester fiberfill, for the head

Braid, ribbon, rickrack, strips of sequins, beads, lace, and other assorted embellishments

Tacky glue

Compass

## HOW-TO'S

### *Drafting and Using Patterns*

*Body—actually a robe:*
Following Figure 19.1 (enlarging as marked) and using a pencil and ruler, draft the robe or gown onto a sheet of paper, and cut it out. Fold the fabric crosswise and lengthwise in half, and pin the dash line along the fold of your fabric. Cut it out, to get 2 pieces—a front and a back.

*Head:*
Use a compass to draw a $4^{1}/_{2}$-inch-diameter circle on paper. Draw a line across the bottom of the circle. From the center of the circle, draw a line to the bottom of the circle, where it meets the horizontal line. Measure $1^{1}/_{2}$ inches on

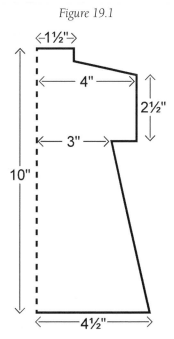

*Figure 19.1*

*Figure 19.2*

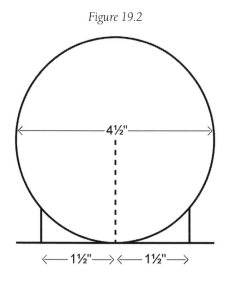

4½"

1½" — 1½"

either side of the intersection of these 2 lines (see Figure 19.2). Connect the end points to the line at the bottom of the circle. This forms the neck. Cut around the head and neck, as shown with solid lines. Place this pattern on flesh-colored fabric and cut out 2 pieces, for the front and back of the head.

*Hands:*

Refer to Figure 19.3 and draw a 2½-inch by 1¾-inch rectangle on paper. Mark the midpoints of the top and bottom and connect them, as shown by the vertical dash line. Mark the sides 1 inch from the top and connect them, as shown by the horizontal dash line. Round the top corners as shown. Cut out the resulting shape, pin it on flesh-colored fabric, and cut out 4 pieces.

## Assembly

1. Pin the neck edges of one head and one body/robe together, with right sides facing. Stitch across, ¼ inch from the edge. Press seam allowances toward the robe. Repeat with the 2nd head and body/robe piece.

2. Pin each hand, with the straight edge centered on the sleeve ends, and with right sides facing. Stitch across, ¼ inch from the edges. Press seam allowances toward the robe.

*Figure 19.3*

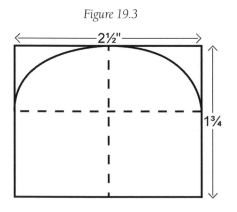

2½"

1¾

3. Pin the 2 joined pieces for front and back together, with right sides facing and edges even.

4. Fold four 6-inch strands of yarn in half, and insert them between the 2 head-pieces, with the fold along the top edge and the strands tucked well inside.

5. Sew the 2 bodies together, starting at the bottom of the body and continuing around the hand and head. Make sure you catch the folds of the yarn strands into the stitching at the top of the head, but none of the ends of the strands. Continue around the 2nd hand and back to the bottom. Turn up the bottom edge of the robe $\frac{1}{4}$ inch twice and sew, for a hem. Clip the fabric up to the stitching at the inside corners—at the bottom of the neck and at the armpits. Turn the body right side out and press (see Figure 19.4).

*Figure 19.4*

### Puppet Face: A Mommy & Me Project

1. Stuff the head with a small fistful of polyester fiberfill—enough to give it shape and definition, but not so much that you cannot push your finger up into the back of the head when using the puppet.

2. To complete the hair, use the same type of yarn already attached to the head. For a male puppet: Cut twenty-four 8-inch lengths of yarn. For a female puppet: Cut twenty-four 24-inch lengths of yarn. Divide the lengths into 4 bundles. Referring to Figure 19.5, place 1 bundle of yarn lengths between strands A and B, and tie the strands in a tight knot around the bundle. Repeat this with the other 3 bundles by placing and tying 1 bundle between strands C and D, 1 between strands E and F, and the last one between strands G and H.

3. Brush the yarn back off the face, and trim the ends neatly.

4. Position doll eyes on the face (see Figure 19.6 for guidance). Use a strong glue or stitch in place, as appropriate.

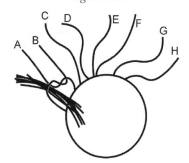

*Figure 19.5*

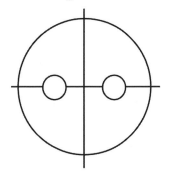

*Figure 19.6*

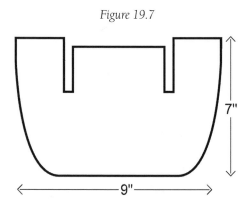

*Figure 19.7*

7"

9"

5. For the mouth, use a small piece of pink or red felt. Draw a mouth shape on it, then cut it out and glue it onto the face. *Alternatively, for a male puppet, glue a 4- to 5-inch piece of curly chenille, in black, brown, or gray, under the eyes; for a female puppet, tack a piece of lace onto the face as a veil.*

## *Puppet Vest*

1. Enlarge Figure 19.7 on paper and cut it out. Pin it on the felt and cut it out. Lay the vest flat, right side up, and decorate it with braid, ribbon, rickrack, or strips of sequins attached with glue or sewn in place.

2. When all the embellishments are dry, turn the vest over so that the nondecorated side is facing you. Fold the 2 sides toward the middle. Turn the vest over and stitch or glue along the top of the front shoulders, where they show above the back. Slip the vest onto the puppet.

## SPECIFIC CHARACTER SUGGESTIONS

*For Queen Esther:*
Use a silky or satiny fabric for her gown in a light color. (Be sure to turn under and sew any raw edges.) Add a ring of star garland for a tiara, tacking it in place with 1 or 2 stitches. Cut a small square of lace, and use a few stitches to tack it over her face as a veil. Glue metallic leaf bangles to the edges of her vest.

*For King Ahasuerus:*
Use a copper or gold satiny fabric for his robe, and purple felt for his vest (again, turning under and sewing any raw edges). Decorate the vest with jewels fit for a king. To make his crown, sew or glue together lengthwise a small strip of purple satin. Wrap it around his head, then overlap the edges to form a crown, tucking the raw edge under and tacking it in place. Glue or sew on a regal gold embellishment. Tack the crown in place.

*For Mordechai:*
Jazz up his vest with an array of sequins or beads in parallel rows.

*For Queen Vashti:*
Add a ring of star garland for a tiara, tacking it in place with a stitch or 2, and tack a small square of lace over her face as a veil. Sew or glue some glittering beads to her vest.

*For Haman:*
Use a black satiny fabric for his robe, decorated with black shiny buttons or sequins. Make him a hat by taking a strip of black satin, sewing or gluing it together lengthwise, and then overlapping the edges in the center, tucking the raw edge under and tacking in place. Add a bead in the center of the hat. Tack the hat in place.

Have a grand time playing with your Purim puppets!

# 20

# Shellie's Ten-Plagues Matzah Cover

---

*Project designer:* **Shellie Black**

P reparations for Pesach (Passover) in a traditional Jewish house-hold can be highly stressful—clearing the house of *chametz* (any food with leavening), switching to separate sets of dishes, cleaning the house from top to bottom. Sometimes, taking a break to create a family treasure imbued with spiritual intention, as Shellie Black did back in the 1990s, can infuse the holiday with special meaning and even a touch of whimsy.

Shellie and her family had moved to Ra'anana, Israel, in the summer of 1996, and they lived there for six years. "Since my Hebrew was terrible and I was busy raising two daughters and adjusting to life in Israel, I decided that it was a good time for me to learn how to quilt," she recalls. "It was something I had always wanted to do, but I had little time for it while I was living in the States, raising two little girls, and working as a social worker."

Seeking out someone to teach her the intricacies of quilting, Shellie met a wonderful woman, named Susan Trachtenberg, in her English-speaking book club. Susan generously offered to show Shellie how to quilt, and they became fast friends. "We spent lots of mornings while the girls were in school sewing together. We had a wonderful time! I made a few baby quilts, and a couple of lap quilts," the enthusiastic quilter notes.

As Shellie was learning to quilt, her daughters became fascinated by the process and wanted to learn, too. Then her daughters' friends showed a keen interest as well, so Shellie started a kids' quilting group. "We had great fun creating projects in the afternoons," she says. "I thoroughly enjoyed that time with my daughters and the other children who came to my classes (including a couple of boys!). It was a fun little business that I developed over the years that we lived in Israel."

One thing led to another, and Shellie herself joined an English speakers' quilting group that met once a month in Herziliah. People of all quilting levels participated, and they all enjoyed showing each other what they were making and learning from the amazingly skilled quilters among them. They all shared fabrics, books, and stories about their quilts, too.

In her quilting group, Shellie met Terry Mozowski, a highly accomplished quilter, who offered to work with her. "I talked to her about my desire to make a matzah cover, and she guided me and shared some wonderful fabrics and thoughts on how to accomplish this," Shellie recalls. "This cover is not quilted—it's merely pieced. And there are three sections sewn into the cover for the three matzot used for the seder."

Shellie had a grand time searching for fabrics to represent each of the ten plagues. Her greatest challenge was finding a print to represent the plague of lice: "Since Israel doesn't have amazing quilt shops, like those in the United States, and online shopping hadn't evolved as it has now, we found a ladybug fabric in Terry's stash and decided that that would work just fine." Yet another challenge was inherent in the design itself: there are ten plagues, but the Attic Windows design she chose calls for three rows of three blocks in a square—only nine places. So for the last two plagues—darkness and the slaying of the firstborn—she grouped the two together in one block. "I decided to use the gray and silver heavenly theme to convey the power of *Hashem* [God], rather than a baby fabric." Shellie embroidered the names of the plagues in Hebrew under each panel and used a border print with celestial images to suggest the overarching majesty of *Hashem*.

"Although I did get ready for Pesach 1998 on time, I also managed to get this matzah cover done for our seder table. That was a lot more fun than the tedious chores of Pesach preparation!" says Shellie, who now lives in Seattle. "We use this matzah cover every year, and it brings back memories of my time in Israel—the wonderful days of my sewing machine humming away and my little girls sharing that time with me. I am so grateful for that part of my life."

# Getting Started

*Finished size:* 16¹/₂ inches by 16¹/₂ inches; each finished Attic Windows block measures 4³/₄ inches square, including "windowpanes"
Refer to "General How-To's for Quilt Making," pages 245–251, and "General How-To's for Lettering," pages 252–254.

## WHAT YOU'LL NEED

Cotton fabrics:

   Novelty or conversation-print fabrics to represent each of the 10 plagues, 5-inch squares of each

   1 fat quarter each in dark and light colors, to complement novelty fabrics, for "windowsills"

   1 fat quarter print, for border

   17-inch square of one of the above fabrics, for the back of the cover

Muslin, 1 yard, for lining and matzah pockets

Single-fold bias binding tape, 2 yards

Blue 6-strand embroidery floss

Embroidery hoop

## HOW-TO'S

### Blocks

1. Arrange your print fabrics representing the 10 plagues in a tic-tac-toe format. For the full squares, use a rotary cutter to cut the fabrics 4¹/₄ inches square, centering the motifs.

2. For each square that will be divided into 2 triangles, known as a half-square triangle (there are 2 here), cut out a 4³/₄-inch square in each of the 2 fabrics you've chosen for that half-square triangle. Then, using a rotary cutter and a good ruler, mark the diagonal and cut out 2 triangle shapes, setting one aside. Make sure the fabric motifs will be upright when the 2 triangles are joined, with the diagonal division going from lower left to upper right. Also try to align the 2 short edges of each triangle with the horizontal and vertical grain of the fabric. Place the 2 triangles together with right sides facing and stitch along the long edge of the triangle, with a ¹/₄-inch seam allowance. Clip excess fabric, and press the seam allowance toward the darker fabric.

### Attic Windows Sashing

1. From each of the solid light and dark fabrics, cut 9 rectangles, each measuring 5¹/₄ inches by 1¹/₂ inches. Pin a dark strip to the left edge of a square or half-triangle square, with right sides facing and raw edges even along the left and top edges. The strip will hang down beyond the square. Turn the piece so the square is on top. Stitch from the top, ¹/₄ inch from the edges, and stop ¹/₄ inch from the end. Press the seam allowances toward the sashing.

2. Pin a light strip to the bottom edge of a square or half-triangle square, with right sides facing and raw edges even along the right and bottom edges. The strip will extend beyond the left side of the square. Turn the piece so the square is on top. Stitch from the right side, ¹/₄ inch from the edges, and stop ¹/₄ inch from the end. Press the seam allowances toward the sashing.

3. To miter the sashing strips at the bottom left corner of each square, fold and press the block diagonally in half from lower left to upper right, with right side in and the 2 sashing strips extending, following the illustration on page 149 (Figure 20.1). Place the sashing strips so that one overlaps the other. Fold the bottom sashing strip under at a 45-degree angle and press. Line up a ruler along the diagonal fold

and on the top sashing strip, and draw a line onto the top sashing strip. Hand- or machine-stitch from the corner of the square outward along the marked mitering line. Press seam allowances toward the dark fabric, and trim excess fabric.

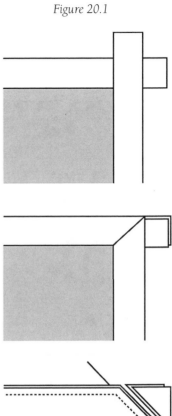

*Figure 20.1*

### Finishing the Top

1. Arrange blocks in 3 rows of 3. Stitch blocks together in rows, and press seam allowances toward the dark sashing. Then stitch the rows together, matching seams. Again, press seam allowances toward the dark sashing.

2. Add borders on top and along the right: First, cut 2 fabric strips 2 inches by 17½ inches. Stitch to the edges with excess border fabric extending at the upper right corner. Miter and trim the excess, following step 3 under "Attic Windows Sashing" on page 148.

3. Placing your quilt top in an embroidery hoop, embroider the names of the plagues, following "General How-To's for Lettering," pages 253–254. (Shellie wrote the words in washable marking pencil and embroidered over them.) Use 3 strands of 6-strand embroidery floss to chain-stitch the Hebrew words for each of the plagues on the Attic Windows sashing, centered below each square (see Figure 20.2 on page 150).

4. Press and square the patchwork. Make a lining as follows: With right sides facing, pin the patchwork top onto a same-size piece of muslin. Stitch all around the edges, leaving about 4 inches unsewn. Clip corners, turn it right side out, and press. Hand-sew the opening closed.

*Figure 20.2*

דם
צפרדע
כנים
ערוב
דבר
שחין
ברד
ארבה
חשך
מכת/בכורות

## Assembly

1. Measure the top layer and add ¹/₄ inch all around. Cut 1 square of backing fabric and 1 square of muslin to this size. Cut 2 rectangles of muslin 1 inch longer on one side; set these aside.

2. For the back of the cover, pin the backing fabric to the same-size muslin square, with right sides facing and edges even. Stitch all around, leaving about 4 inches unsewn. Clip corners; turn right side out, and hand-sew the opening closed. Press. See photo above.

3. Create pockets: On each of the 2 remaining muslin rectangles, turn one short edge ³/₄ inch to the wrong side twice; press, and topstitch. (Shellie used a fancy stitch to add pizzazz to the pockets.) Place together, right sides facing and hems aligned, and stitch all around the raw edges. See photo on page 151.

## Finishing

Pin together along 3 sides (not the bottom opening) the assembled, lined front patchwork panel (right side out), the "pillowcase" with the opening at the bottom, and the lined back cover (right side out). Pin the binding along the 3 sides, covering all the edges. Topstitch through the binding and all pieces of the matzah cover.

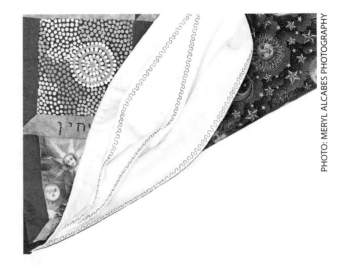

Decorate your seder table with your beautiful handmade matzah cover, and sit back (recline, that is, as instructed in the Haggadah) as you receive kudos from all your guests!

# 21 Claire's *Afikomen* Envelopes

*Project designer:* Claire Sherman

Most Jewish households evolve a set of traditions that give Passover (Pesach) special meaning and create memories that last a lifetime. Far-flung family members gather around the seder table each spring to read the story of Moses and the Exodus from Egypt, often drawing comparisons to more contemporary struggles for liberation from bondage and oppression.

Among the traditions that surround the observance of Pesach is the search for the *afikomen,* the middle matzah broken during the seder and "hidden" for children to find. According to Jewish tradition, the "hiding" of the *afikomen* was a strategy for keeping children engaged in the seder all the way to the end. The word *afikomen* comes from the Greek, meaning "that which comes after" or "dessert," and it is generally the last thing eaten at the seder.

While most families simply wrap one piece of the middle matzah in a napkin and hide it for the children to retrieve, Claire Sherman designed an ingenious *afikomen* envelope—actually, several of them—to make the "hunt for the *afikomen*" especially memorable.

"My spiritual intention in designing the *afikomen* envelopes evolved from my feeling that the hunt for the *afikomen* shouldn't have losers—only winners," she explains. "My daughters are four-and-a-half years apart in age. To give the younger one a chance at finding the *afikomen,* we started hiding as many *afikomen* as there were children at the seder. With each one wrapped in a napkin, that's a lot of matzah crumbs all over the house!

"At first, I came up with the idea of making *afikomen* envelopes from paper. But the fabric version is more ecologically sound, since it lasts longer and doesn't require any trees to be cut down. In addition, according to the Jewish precept of *hiddur mitzvah,* the object that you use to perform a mitzvah [commandment] should be as beautiful as possible. So rather than *afikomen* envelopes from flimsy stapled paper, *hiddur mitzvah* suggests that the *afikomen* be placed in a lovely envelope to elevate the mitzvah of hunting for the *afikomen.*"

Claire, who lives in Berkeley, California, thrives on making all sorts of Jewish ritual objects, teaching workshops on both fabric crafts and paper cutting for adults and children throughout California. She is also a member of the Quilting Group with No Name, whose Shalva Quilts are featured in chapter 30. Two other pieces she designed herself also appear in this book— Claire's *Ushpizin* Quilt (chapter 15) and Hannah's Baby Quilt (chapter 23).

These *afikomen* envelopes exemplify how easily you can devise a simple solution to a problem (matzah crumbs from multiple pieces of *afikomen*) with some imagination and a flair for fabric. Using fabrics suggestive of the holiday, such as frogs or prints with Hebrew letters, as on the lining of the chocolate-covered strawberries envelope, these whimsical envelopes enhance the mitzvah of the *afikomen* and add unexpected pizzazz and panache to your seder. (You may be wondering what chocolate-covered strawberries have to do with Pesach. Simple: they are Claire's favorite Pesach dessert!)

## Getting Started

*Finished size:* 8¹/₂ inches by 5¹/₂ inches

### WHAT YOU'LL NEED
### (FOR EACH *AFIKOMEN* ENVELOPE)

2 pieces of fabric, each 13 inches by 8¹/₂ inches (consider prints, in complementary colors, evocative of the holiday)

1 piece of interfacing with fusible web on both sides, 13 inches by 8¹/₂ inches *(Note: If you can't find interfacing, you may use fusible web)*

Black elastic cord, 3 inches

Large shank-type button

## HOW-TO'S

PHOTO: ED ANISMAN

1. To make your envelope firm—so the matzah within is more likely to stay intact—position the fabrics, right side out and edges even, on each side of the fusible interfacing. Press to fuse.

2. Fold this sandwich (fabric + interfacing + fabric) crosswise, almost in half, leaving 2 inches extending at the top. This 2-inch area will become the flap of the envelope. Iron the crease at the bottom of the envelope to flatten it further. Your envelope will measure 8¹⁄₂ inches by 5¹⁄₂ inches once you fold the flap down, but don't fold it down quite yet. If you prefer a rounded edge, trim the corners off the flap with scissors, as in the chocolate-covered strawberries envelope.

3. Zigzag- or satin-stitch with a sewing machine across the top inside edge of the envelope. (This is the edge that will be overlapped by the flap). Then stitch in the same way along the folded sides of the envelope, penetrating both layers. Continue stitching around the edge of the flap to give it a more finished edge. *Alternatively,* you may sew the sides closed by hand, using a thimble to help you whipstitch or overcast stitch through the double-layer sides.

4. Fold the flap down, and press it with a hot iron.

5. Tie a knot in each end of a 3-inch piece of black elastic cord. Tie another knot about 2 inches from the first knot. Trim off the elastic cord ends beyond the knots. Fold the cord in half, bringing the knots alongside each other. Sew the 2 knots to the center of the flap on the inside, using close satin stitches.

6. Hand-stitch a button to the envelope to correspond with the elastic loop.

Now that you've made an *afikomen* envelope, think of the other kinds of envelopes you could make, following the same directions. How about an envelope made of Chanukah fabric to put a present in? Or a very small envelope, in which a child could place a treasured baby tooth. According to Claire, the possibilities are limited only by your imagination!

# 22

# Zoë's Knit
# Seder Plate

---

*Project designer:* Zoë Scheffy

Zoë Scheffy's life and heritage—plus her approach to Judaism—embody the very essence of diversity. Zoë is both Jewish and African-American. "I was raised by my mother in Los Angeles, and my upbringing was heavily influenced by the traditions, celebrations, and culture of my German-Jewish relatives," the fabric artist recalls. "I have fond memories of Chanukah and Passover celebrations, and as the only child (and thus the youngest participant) present for many years, I had the opportunity to read the Four Questions and search for the *afikomen* (and always get the prize) for much of my childhood."

Zoë's maternal grandmother, Ruth, was a seamstress, who taught the youngster how to sew at a very young age, sparking a love of traditional handcrafts, fiber arts, and handmade items that has led her on a wonderful journey. Says Zoë, "My grandmother used to sit me on her lap, and we would sew stuffed animals and clothes at her sewing machine. In her studio hung a photo of the Wailing Wall, and she had Israeli textiles, clothes, and Judaica throughout the house. I miss her; she passed away when I was twenty-eight. My grandfather, Gerard, turned ninety-seven this past spring, and it is wonderful to have him in my life still. We talk online every Thursday."

After fleeing Germany in 1933, most of Zoë's grandmother's family immigrated to Israel, while members of her grandfather's family came to the United States and other countries. Through her grandmother Ruth's influence, Zoë picked up embroidery and other textile arts and later took up knitting while studying abroad in Norway. Zoë traveled back to Scandinavia in 1999 to complete a doctorate in folklore on Sami handicraft and artistry in Sweden. Today, she knits for pleasure and also designs knitwear, home goods, and Judaica through her website, Seaside Knitting Patterns (www.seasideknittingpatterns.com).

In recent years, Zoë's children, Nelleke, eight years old, and Magnus, five, have become interested in participating in the Passover seder, so she wanted to create for them—and for her home—a personal seder table. "My husband, Clark, is not Jewish, and he and I are raising our children in the traditions of both of our families," notes Zoë, who now lives in Cambridge, Massachusetts. "We are not a very religious family, but I am proud of my Jewish heritage and embrace it in the cultural education of my children."

As she was looking for a seder plate that fit her own, personal aesthetic, Zoë considered whether she wanted something traditional or modern; metal, glass, or ceramic; with Hebrew words or English. "There are so many beautiful options, but none truly spoke to me," she points out. "While I inherited various items for celebrating Chanukah from my grandmother and mother, I did not have any Passover heirlooms. Therefore I decided to create my own."

Drawing on the various strands of her life as a knitter, her mix of heritages, and her diverse household, she decided to fashion something new, something unique for her own Passover seder, rather than adopting a creation of others. With that in mind, she designed this imaginative knit seder plate. Fashioned after a traditional plate in the round, this knit version offers a framework for the seder foods, while allowing the host to exercise personal preference and creativity in dish selection. The knit seder plate can be integrated into the rest of the table settings, while maintaining a separate space for the seder foods. She adds, "I used Hebrew words on the plate because I like the connection and community they create.

"When I designed the knit seder plate, I had in mind several inspirations: the traditional round seder plate; the knit hexagon, which is easily created with regular decreases (like knitting a hat); and the six points of the Star of David. By adding box pleats toward the center of the hexagon, I was able to guide the fabric toward a star shape at the center of the piece. I then added an embroidered Star of David to finish the seder plate and bring the shaping and color patterns together," she explains. (See some coordinating accessories, including table runners, on Zoë's website.)

While Zoë had a solid Jewish upbringing, throughout her life she has had to navigate her way as a mixed-race woman—a Jewish woman and an African-American woman. "Being true to myself, my identity, and my family has offered me a space to be creative, new, different, and develop a voice of my own," she notes. "My knit seder plate furthers this discussion."

# Getting Started

*Finished size:* 18 inches in diameter

## WHAT YOU'LL NEED

### Yarn

2 balls (approximately 328 yards) of sport-weight cotton yarn for Main Color (MC)

1 ball (approximately 164 yards) of sport-weight cotton yarn for Contrast Color (CC)

(Sample shown with KnitPicks Simply Cotton sport-weight yarn; MC colorway Camel Heather; CC colorway Reindeer Heather)

1 ball (approximately 100 yards) of sport-weight self-striping yarn for the outside border, Star of David, and center star embroidery (sample shown with Noro Chirimen; colorway number 3—Kiwi, Yellow, Tan)

### Needles & Notions

Size 4 circular knitting needles

Size 4 double-pointed knitting needles

## Abbreviations

**k2tog:** knit 2 stitches together

**M1:** make one (an invisible increase). Pick up the strand of yarn, or horizontal "ladder" that extends between stitches, and place this on the left-hand needle. Knit this lifted strand through the front. An additional stitch is now made.

Tapestry needle

Stitch markers

Cable needle

1 yard of cotton or linen fabric for lining (optional)

## GAUGE

24 stitches and 32 rows = 4 inches in stockinette stitch

## HOW-TO'S

### Colorwork Tip

Be sure to stop working and adjust the tension on the back side (purl side) every 20 stitches or so. This will ensure that the colorwork does not pull together too much and that the words are legible when the seder plate is complete. For a look at Zoë's matching seder table runners, visit Zoë's website at www.seasideknittingpatterns.com.

### Outside Border

Cast on 342 stitches onto size 4 circular knitting needles in the self-striping sport-weight yarn for the outside border, and place stitch markers after stitches 57, 114, 171, 228, 285, and 342.

Begin working in the round, making sure not to twist the stitches.

Round 1: Knit.
Round 2: Purl.
Round 3: Knit.

### Hebrew Stranded Colorwork

1.  Change to sport-weight cotton MC yarn, and begin working according to the Hebrew colorwork charts (Figures 22.1 and 22.2).

2.  Attend to decreases on rounds 3, 5, 7, 9, and 11 by using k2tog on either side of each stitch marker. (See "Abbreviations" above.)

*Figure 22.1*

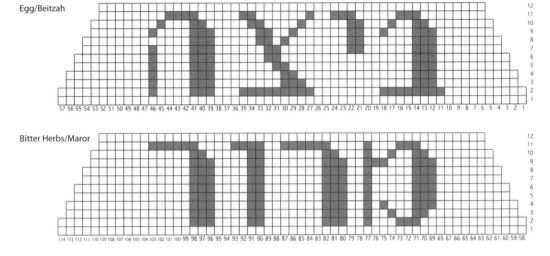

Egg/Beitzah

Bitter Herbs/Maror

Charoset

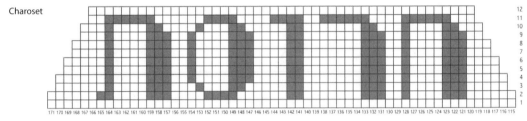

3. Word order shown: *Beitzah / Maror / Charoset / Chazaret / Z'roa / Karpas.* The words are worked in the sport-weight cotton CC yarn. *(Note: The order of the words may be changed to suit your personal preference.)*

4. After completing rounds 1–12 of the colorwork charts, continue in cotton MC yarn and continue with decreases as shown in Figure 22.3. If needed, switch to double-pointed needles as the number of stitches decreases.

## Star of David Background in Self-Striping Yarn

On round 41 of Figure 22.3, *make an additional stitch in the self-striping yarn before working the first left facing decrease in MC; work in MC to the

*Figure 22.2*

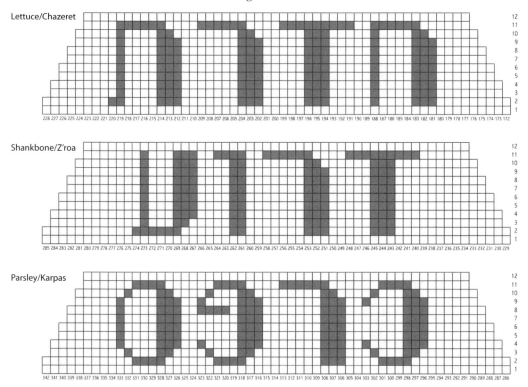

right facing decrease, k2tog as on other rounds, and then repeat from * to the end of the round.

Next round: Knit the MC stitches in MC and the self-striping stitches in the self-striping yarn.

Round 43: *M1, knit 1, M1 in the self-striping yarn before working the first left facing decrease in MC; work in MC to the right facing decrease, k2tog as on other rounds, and then repeat from * to end of round.

Round 44: Knit the MC stitches in MC and the self-striping stitches in the self-striping yarn.

Round 45: *M1, knit 3, M1 in the self-striping yarn before working the first left facing decrease in MC; work in MC to the right facing decrease, k2tog as on other rounds, and then repeat from * to the end of the round.

*Figure 22.3*

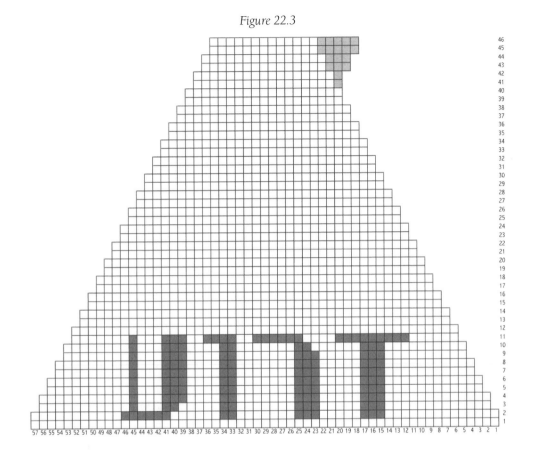

Round 46: Knit the MC stitches in MC and the self-striping stitches in the self-striping yarn—108 stitches remain.

## Making Box Pleats

Change to work entirely with the self-striping yarn.

Box Pleat round: *Knit 5, slip the next 3 stitches onto a cable needle or other short needle and hold the slipped stitches in front of the left-hand needle; insert the right-hand needle in the 1st stitch on the cable needle and also in the 1st stitch on the left-hand needle, knit them off as a single stitch. Continue this way until all 3 stitches on the short needle are worked off. Knit 1.

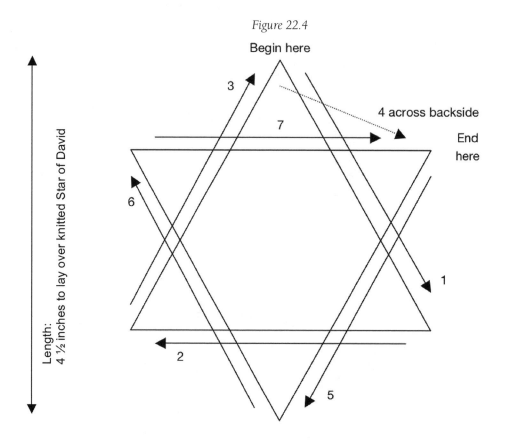

*Figure 22.4*

Begin here

3

7

4 across backside

End here

6

1

2

5

Length: 4 ½ inches to lay over knitted Star of David

Slip the next 3 stitches onto the cable needle, hold this in back of the left-hand needle, knit off these 3 stitches with the corresponding stitches on the left-hand needle as above. Repeat from * to end.

End with 72 stitches.

## Continuing Star of David Background in the Center of the Seder Plate with Self-Striping Yarn

Round 1: Knit.
Round 2: *Knit 1, k2tog; repeat from * to end—48 stitches.
Round 3: Knit.
Round 4: *Knit 1, k2tog; repeat from * to end—16 stitches.

Round 5: Knit.

Round 6: *K2tog, repeat from * to end—8 stitches.

Round 7: *K2tog, repeat from * to end—4 stitches.

Round 8: *K2tog, repeat from * to end—2 stitches.

Pull yarn through remaining stitches and fasten off.

## Finishing

Block the seder plate.

With a tapestry needle, weave in loose yarn ends, fasten off, and clip yarn ends close to the surface.

With a single strand of the self-striping yarn, embroider a Star of David on top of the center Star of David background created in the middle of the seder plate, following the Star of David pattern on page 164 (Figure 22.4). Secure the Star of David by sewing the long strands of the 2 triangles together at the points where they cross one another—6 small connections.

Weave in yarn ends, fasten off, and clip.

You may sew a lining on the back side of the seder plate with cotton or linen fabric if you do not want the stitching on the wrong side to show.

Grace your seder table with this stunning knit seder plate!

# PART FOUR

# Through the Jewish Life Cycle

For many Jewish people, a love for Judaism is interwoven in the fabric of our lives. Jewish traditions start at birth and carry through the rest of life. Even as young children, we observe, absorb, and experience the Jewish influences around us.

Judaism lays out a plan to help us navigate through daily life. Rituals in place for generations are rooted in rich customs surrounding birth, entering adulthood, marriage, daily prayer, keeping the Sabbath, observing dietary laws, celebrating holidays, comforting the sick, and mourning those who pass on. Judaism's tried-and-true guidelines for a fulfilling life range from caring for others to *tzedekah* (giving charity), mitzvot (doing good deeds and following the commandments), and developing a strong and joyful household. These guidelines draw on the wisdom of biblical and talmudic teachings.

Fabric crafts figure in many of the familiar traditions that punctuate the Jewish life cycle and play an important role in Jewish consciousness (see Hannah's Baby Quilt by Claire Sherman, chapter 23, and Julia's Bat Mitzvah Challah Cover by Lois Gaylord, chapter 25). In the opening to part two, we saw the role that *wimpels* play, not only traditionally in the birth of a son but in his Bar Mitzvah and wedding as well. Contemporary traditions have evolved for making *wimpels* to celebrate the birth of girls as well. (See Vicki Pieser's Cross-Stitch

*Wimpel,* chapter 24.) Even more significant are religious ritual items made of fabric, like the tallit, which are mentioned in the Bible.

## Tallitot

The tallit, or *tallis* as it is called in Ashkenazi and Yiddish references, is worn to fulfill the commandment in the Bible (Numbers 15:37–40) that Jewish people wear *tzitzit* (fringes) at the four corners of an outer garment. Wearing *tzitzit* is also noted in Deuteronomy 22:12. There are two types of tallitot (the plural of *tallit*)—a *tallit gadol* (a large tallit) and a *tallit katan* (a small tallit). The *tallit gadol,* the large outer rectangular garment with *tzitzit* attached to its four corners, is worn only during prayer services. The *tallit katan,* sometimes just called *tzitzit,* is an undergarment, like an open T-shirt with *tzitzit* attached to the four corners. It is a mitzvah to wear *tzitzit* all the time, and the *tallit katan* is an easy way to perform this mitzvah. Wearing *tzitzit* reminds Jewish people to follow the commandments in the Torah, therefore weaving a life of good deeds, just as a tallit is woven of fine threads.

Tallitot have long been a favorite stitchwork project of craft artists who see the completed prayer shawl as having both functional and sentimental value. (See Julian M. Brook's Traditional Tallit, chapter 26, and Susan M. Rappaport's Tallit & Tallit Bag for her daughter, Debra, chapter 28.) One of the most popular presents, family heirlooms, and keepsakes in the Jewish religion, tallitot have been lovingly created and presented to family members and close friends for centuries—a very personal, meaningful, and thoughtful gift.

A ritual garment, the tallit must be worn the same way each time it is used. So every tallit has an *atarah,* or crown. The *atarah* appears on the top of the tallit, on the side that shows; this makes it simple to don the prayer shawl properly. Fancy needlework often enhances the *atarah,* with the blessing or part of the blessing recited when putting on the tallit. Other *atarah* designs have become popular among contemporary fabric artists as well. Because it stands out, the *atarah* is often the focal point of the prayer shawl, a design element that makes that particular tallit special and in some cases one-of-a-kind.

Tallitot play important roles in the lives of many Jewish people. Some are given to a boy or girl celebrating a Bar or Bat Mitzvah by parents or grandparents. Wives often give husbands a tallit as a wedding or anniversary gift. According to Jewish tradition, a talented bride-to-be would make her betrothed a tallit, along with a *kippah,* and present the gifts to her new husband right after the marriage ceremony. Tallitot accompany Jewish people on long trips, go with soldiers deployed abroad, are carried onto battlefields, and are carefully packed as families move from home to home. The tallit may serve as a chuppah during wedding ceremonies, too. In that case, the garment is held over the heads of the bride and groom by four people during the marriage service. Even as young children, we may sense the importance of tallitot and patiently wait for the day when we receive a tallit of our own.

Because our tallitot can follow us through all stages of life—both good and troubled times—and they can be such an important part of our spiritual lives, many Jews choose to be buried in their tallit, either one they have worn for many years or one specially chosen for this solemn occasion. Oftentimes, Jewish people have several tallitot and decide ahead of time which one(s) to leave to family members as keepsakes or to be worn through the generations, and which one to be buried in. It is a comfort to a Jewish person to know that this tradition will be followed, and soothing to those mourning the loss of a loved one. Though at one time only men were buried in a tallit, today women may also choose to be buried wearing a tallit.

Family histories are often wrapped up in a tallit. The oldest tallit believed to exist in America belonged to Abraham Isaacks, who immigrated to the United States from Europe in 1698. When Isaacks arrived in the colonies, there were only about three hundred Jews living in America. A merchant, he settled in New York and served as president of Shearith Israel, the oldest congregation in the New World. He wore the same tallit throughout his life; it is not known if Isaacks brought the garment with him from Europe. When he died, circa 1743, Abraham Isaacks left his tallit to his wife, Hannah. Hannah died about two years later, and the tallit went to the couple's son, Jacob. The tallit was handed down through the generations—about ten generations in all. The historic garment traveled with family members throughout the country, going as far away from New York City as Eugene, Oregon. In 2006, descendants of the family donated the heirloom tallit to the American Jewish Historical Society in Manhattan, and the tallit returned to New York City, coming full circle.

Tallitot have changed through the centuries. Historians believe the first ones were actual robes, matching the outer clothing worn in ancient times. They began to become smaller as clothing styles changed. Though tallitot were worn only by men at one time, some women in Reform, Reconstructionist, and Conservative congregations have now taken to wearing tallitot during prayer services. As a result, tallitot are designed with both men and women in mind.

## Tallit & Tefillin Bags

Since so many tallitot are handmade, used for years, and become family heirlooms, it's not surprising that creative needlecrafters started designing tallit bags to protect these prized prayer shawls. Early tallit bags were made out of leather or velvet. The first ones were string tied, but now zippers are generally used as closures. With the growing number of different designs decorating tallitot, many tallit bags are made to coordinate with the tallit itself. Today tallitot and tallit bags are made as sets, and many Jews cherish their tallit bags nearly as much as the tallit itself. (See Judith S. Paskind's Garden of Eden Tallit Bag, chapter 27, and Debra's Tallit & Tallit Bag, chapter 28.)

Variations of tallit bags have also been made to carry tefillin. Tefillin are two small black leather cube boxes that contain scrolls with verses from the Torah on parchment. Each of the two tefillin contain two black leather straps. Tefillin are worn by men (and by some women as well) during morning prayers on weekdays. This is considered an important part of daily Jewish life and a mitzvah. One tefillin, *shel rosh,* is worn just above the forehead. The other, *shel yad,* is worn on the upper arm with the straps wrapped around the arm, hand, and fingers. Boys in traditional Jewish homes receive their first pair of tefillin about a month before their Bar Mitzvah and are taught how to use them at that time. They are then supposed to don the tefillin at morning prayers for the rest of their lives, following their Bar Mitzvah. Women are not required to use tefillin, but some participate in the practice. The practice of tefillin is mentioned four times in the Torah, twice in Exodus (13:9 and 13:16) and twice in Deuteronomy (6:8 and 11:18). These are the verses that are handwritten on the tiny scrolls in the tefillin.

Bags for tefillin are often coordinated with tallit bags. The Torah calls on us to wear tefillin to remember that God delivered the people of Israel from Egypt. Jewish scholars point out that it is not the tallit or the tefillin that are holy in and of themselves, but the actions of the one wearing them. Following the ways of the Torah, the teachings of the Talmud, performing mitzvot, and living a life of goodness and kindness show a respect and understanding for the tallit and tefillin and the reason they are worn.

## Chuppot

Chuppot (plural of *chuppah*) are another fabric craft that can play an integral part in the Jewish life cycle. The chuppah, or wedding canopy, symbolizes the home the couple will build together. There are no possessions under the chuppah, to show that, in the Jewish tradition, it is the people who form the basis of a home, not the items in it. The four poles supporting the chuppah represent the trust and faith that will keep the marriage strong. Some chuppot display simple stitchwork; others feature a mélange of complicated fabric artwork. Beginning in the sixteenth and seventeenth centuries, in the small Jewish villages in Europe known as shtetls, women would get together and make a chuppah for their community. That canopy would be used through the years by couples in the village who were getting married.

In contemporary times, many couples commission a chuppah for their wedding. The chuppah might even be made by family members who are handy with a needle and thread, though making the wedding canopy can be rather tricky, time-consuming, and difficult. (See stories about two chuppot in the "Inspirations" section.) Most couples who have a chuppah made just for them hope to start a family tradition whereby other members of the family marry under the same specially made chuppah. This chuppah may be used by children and grandchildren, cousins, nieces, and nephews, and it would then be handed down through the generations as a family heirloom. The chuppah can even be made with specific family references on it, such as the names, embroidered in English and Hebrew, of everyone married under the canopy. As children are born, their names can be embroidered on this chuppah as well. The creative possibilities that make the chuppah distinct to one family are unlimited.

## Healing Quilts

Just as chuppot are made with a particular theme in mind, so are healing quilts. The tradition of healing quilts is not deep-rooted in any one religion, but healing and caring for the sick are both important aspects of Judaism and Jewish practice. Long before healing quilts became popular, a prayer for the sick was always included during Shabbat services every week, showing that Judaism considered prayer crucial to the healing process. The tradition continues today, as congregants request that their rabbi say a *Mi Sheberach* (prayer for the sick) for a particular person. The prayer is usually said during the Shabbat Torah reading. In some synagogues, the rabbi pauses before saying the prayer for the sick and asks members of the congregation to call out the names of anyone they know who is in need of healing, so those people may be included in the prayer.

The Torah makes it the obligation of every Jewish person to tend to the sick as well as anyone in need of help. Healing quilts are a creative way to carry out this mitzvah. (See Stuart's Healing Quilt by Holly Levison, chapter 29.) These lovingly handmade quilts go a long way toward raising the spirits of people with protracted illnesses and show the support of family, friends, and the community at large. They provide comfort and warmth, along with a combination of good wishes, inspirational sayings, positive thoughts for strength and recovery, Jewish prayers, and symbols of hope written, painted, or sewn on them. Memorial quilts, like the Shalva Quilts created by the Quilting Group with No Name (chapter 30), extend the sentiment of healing to those left behind when a loved one passes on.

—*Robert Grayson*

# 23 Hannah's Baby Quilt

## *Project designer:* Claire Sherman

In the past year, Claire Sherman has become very close to a new friend whose family includes an adorable young daughter, Hannah Rose. Although they are not related to her, they are starting to feel like part of her family.

Reflecting on the relationship she's forged with Hannah Rose and her family, Claire observes, "While I worked on Hannah's quilt, I spent a lot of time thinking about everything I wish for her as she grows up. I thought about her learning to read her name and excitedly reading it on the front of the quilt, in Hebrew and English. I also imagined her picking out the Hebrew letters in the *aleph-bet* fabric on the back."

Although the world is safer now than it was for Claire's ancestors in a Russian shtetl, whenever she makes a baby quilt, she thinks about all the ways in which this covering protects the baby from the negative forces in the world. "A quilt is a labor of love. As I work on it, I am pouring my love for this baby into each stitch. When I gave Hannah her quilt, it was a way of claiming her as part of my extended family. Maybe I'll become her extra aunt," Claire says hopefully.

Inspired by a neighbor's Victorian crazy quilt, Claire started her first quilt at age thirteen. Because she hand-sewed and hand-embroidered it, this debut quilt took five years for her to complete. Thirty years passed between the time Claire finished her first quilt and started her second.

In the meantime, she pursued a passion for ceramic sculpture, majoring in ceramics at Rhode Island School of Design and making ceramic Judaica pieces while living in Israel after she graduated from college. After moving to the West Coast of the United States, Claire read Jennifer Chiaverini's quilt novels and fell in love with quilting once more. She has been an avid quilter ever since.

Today Claire conducts art workshops in paper cutting and Jewish ritual objects for adults and children throughout California. She is also a member of the Quilting Group with No Name, whose Shalva Quilts are featured in chapter 30. A founding member of Congregation Netivot Shalom, where she enjoys chanting Torah and leading services, Claire lives in Berkeley with her architect husband and two daughters.

Baby quilts like Hannah's are among her favorite pieces to design and make because they embody wishes for a happy and healthy future for the next generation.

# Getting Started

*Finished size:* 24 inches by 29 inches

Refer to "General How-To's for Quilt Making," pages 245–251, and "General How-To's for Lettering," pages 252–254.

## WHAT YOU'LL NEED

Fabric (approximately 3 yards of fabric, total):

Center panel, 13 inches by 18 inches

$\frac{1}{4}$ yard each of 4 or 5 fabrics for the quilt top

33-by-28-inch piece of fabric for the backing, or sew together rectangular scraps to this size

$\frac{1}{4}$ yard of paper-backed fusible web

Thread for sewing and quilting (Claire uses transparent nylon monofilament thread to zigzag around the multicolored appliqué butterflies, and cotton for all other stitching)

1 yard of quilt batting

Light- and dark-colored fabric pencils

## HOW-TO'S

### *Quilt Top*

1. Hannah Rose's quilt started with some fabric that had a large-scale rose design. Claire cut a big rectangle for the center—$12^3/_4$ inches by $17^3/_4$ inches—though this size was determined in order to feature a large flower motif in the center, with smaller ones on the sides. Let your fabric choice determine the square or rectangular size for this center piece.

2. Next, try out various fabrics for a border with squares in the corners. The borders in Hannah's quilt are $4^1/_2$-inch-wide strips, cut from selvage to selvage. Sew one to each long side, and trim off the extra. Use the cut-off pieces for the shorter top and bottom borders, cutting them to $4^1/_2$ inches by $12^3/_4$ inches. (These were $12^3/_4$ inches long because that was the width of the center rectangle.) Before sewing these onto the center rectangle, sew a corner square to each end of the top and bottom fabric strips. These corner squares measure $4^1/_2$ inches by $4^1/_2$ inches. Claire chose fabric with zaftig fairies for this, because she wanted to put a little magic into the quilt.

   At this point, the quilt seemed too small to Claire—even for a baby quilt—so she added another fabric for an outer border. She cut $2^1/_2$-inch-wide strips. To get the right length for these strips, measure the quilt down the center, in both directions. Measuring this way helps keep your quilt flat and squared up.

3. To make the letters to spell the baby's name, pick a fabric that contrasts well with the border fabric. See "General How-To's for Lettering," pages 252–254. Iron fusible web onto the back of the fabric. Use a fabric pencil in a color that will show up to mark the letters on the right side of the fabrics. It may be helpful to first use a ruler to mark a rectangle for each letter, $2^1/_2$ inches tall by about $1^3/_4$ inches wide. Start with the English letters, then mark the Hebrew

ones. Cut out each letter along the marked lines with small, sharp scissors. Peel the paper backing off after cutting out the letters. The paper backing stiffens the fabric, which makes the letters easier to cut.

4. Since *Hannah* in English is so much longer than the Hebrew version, this quilt needed something to balance out the border designs. So Claire added butterflies in colors that complemented those of the quilt. Ironing fusible web onto this fabric, she then cut out the butterflies and fused them to the quilt. She playfully placed the butterflies crossing from the borders to other parts of the quilt. As a final touch on the quilt top, she added a tiny ladybug to one of the flowers.

5. Secure fusible appliqués in place: Using fine, close zigzag stitches, sew around the raw edges of the letters in a matching cotton thread. Zigzag-stitch around the edges of the fused butterflies using clear nylon or polyester monofilament in the top of the machine, and sewing thread in the bobbin.

## *Assembly*

1. For the back of the quilt, sew 3 rectangles of fabric together (see photo on this page) to produce a rectangle at least 2 inches larger than the quilt top all around. Claire was pleased to include a piece of her favorite *aleph-bet* fabric. ("I imagine Hannah pointing out which Hebrew letter is which, on her quilt, when she's older," the designer interjects.

2. Make a quilt sandwich, laying the backing facedown on a table. Place the batting, trimmed to the same size, over the backing. Center the quilt

top on top of the batting, right side up. Baste the quilt sandwich with safety pins or large basting stitches. Then quilt as desired by hand or sewing machine.

3. After quilting, cut the batting to the same size as the quilt top, and the backing 1 inch larger all around. Bind the quilt by folding the edges of the backing ¹/₂ inch to the wrong side, then ¹/₂ inch over the front, and stitch close to the fold. *Alternatively,* trim all quilt layers to the same size, make a binding (see "General How-To's for Quilt Making," pages 250–251), and apply it.

Now, schedule a get-together with the baby's parents so you can present them with their one-of-a-kind quilt.

# 24 Vicki's Cross-Stitch *Wimpel*

*Project designer:* Vicki Pieser

As a self-described "small-town Jew" all her life, Vicki Pieser, a Minnesotan, felt compelled to fashion her own religious milieu for her three children. For her, this has meant creating out of fabric all sorts of handmade ritual pieces.

Over the years, Vicki has held a variety of jobs, reflecting an eclectic array of interests—from probation officer to sociology and women's studies instructor, and program coordinator and later administrator for a small museum. Focusing her women's studies courses on women in history and religion, she co-created a Women and Spirituality course at Minnesota State University. This course spotlighted women's penchant (or gifts) for creating ritual and religious objects. "Women seem to have a strong affinity for this form of creativity," Vicki contends.

Prompted by the birth of her first grandchild (she now has three), Vicki designed this *wimpel,* a unique, egalitarian piece of material culture to celebrate the arrival of the firstborn of a new generation. *Wimpels,* which are decorated pieces of cloth, date back to the fourteenth century, when they were first used to tie Torah scrolls together. According to Vicki, "*Wimpels* were originally made from the cloth that traditionally swaddled an infant boy at his *brit milah.* It was then decorated by the mother and taken to the synagogue to be used as a

181

Torah binder at his Bar Mitzvah." The word *wimpel* itself derives from an old German word for "veil" or "cloth." (See the introduction to part two, pages 40–41, for more information on *wimpels*.)

Vicki's research has revealed that this custom is believed to have begun in the north of Italy and spread to other Western European countries. "The cloth used to hold the infant was cut into strips, which were sewn together to make one longer strip. The inscriptions embroidered or painted on them expressed the hope that the boy would grow up to study Torah, marry, and do good works," she explains. "As an expression of folk art, the *wimpel* also reflected the spiritual impulses and personal passions of the women who decorated them, revealing their outlook on life and religion, their ethnicity, Jewish dress and customs of the times, even political and national trends."

Like many of the fabric artists whose work is represented in *Jewish Threads,* Vicki has adapted this centuries-old custom to address contemporary needs and impulses, making *wimpels* for female namings as well as *brit milahs*: "Unlike the original *wimpels*, I decorate mine before the birth, partially to enhance the *brit* or naming and also to educate those in attendance about this custom and the amazing women who made them centuries ago. I also separate the designs so that the *wimpel* can eventually be joined into three or four strips to encircle the Torah. With a nod to superstition, I add the child's name after the ceremony."

Vicki's *wimpel* designs tend to incorporate traditional religious symbols—a Torah scroll, because the *wimpel* ties the child to Torah; *hamsas* and tablets of the Ten Commandments, which also adapt well to the limitations of the counted cross-stitch cloth. Trees or greenery add interest, as do family trees, which connect family history to the blessed event. She sometimes inserts scenes from the Land of Israel as well. The white background on the *wimpel* shown here comes from a treasured family heirloom. To make the background, the fabric artist drew from a duvet in her mother's trousseau, with her mother's initials, A.E., embroidered on it. This duvet was sent to the United States from Prague in 1939, ahead of her parents' daring escape from the Nazis.

Vicki does most of the lettering on her *wimpels* in English, but with some Hebrew phrases added as well. Says the artist, "One of my favorite biblical quotes expresses the spirit of Hannah, who took her newborn son, Samuel, to the Temple to allow him to be raised by the priests, as an expression of gratitude to God for his birth. Loosely translated, this line, which comes from the Book of Samuel, reads: 'For this child I prayed and the Lord has granted my petition' [1 Samuel 1:27]." The *wimpel* shown here, stitched in two panels, could be used as a Torah binder by attaching a ribbon or tie to each end of it. Vicki chose to have it sewn onto a fabric background, so she could present it to the new parents to use as a blanket at the *brit*.

In her *wimpels,* the fabric artist tends to use traditional colors—gold, blue, maroon, green, and white or cream—as in the sample. Sometimes she cross-stitches with more than one color thread, using lighter and darker strands for shading.

While Vicki has no formal visual arts training or background in textiles, she has loved and collected folk art for decades. In making *wimpels* like this one for members of her family, she looks forward to creating more of them as the family grows. "My pieces have been completed thanks to the cajoling and support of a group of non-Jewish women who are talented textile artists," she notes. "They have helped me continue when I became frustrated, often tearing out mistakes for me and helping me join the pieces together." Vicki's mentors, Nancy Sponholz, Cindy Hillesheim, and Mary Anne Baumgart, are a big help when it comes to sewing her *wimpels* together.

Much like the *wimpels* of old, Vicki's reflect her own passion for Jewish life and her desire to express her love of Judaism through fabric crafts that are destined to become family heirlooms.

# Getting Started

*Finished size:* Left-hand panel: 27 inches by 9¹/₂ inches; right-hand panel: 23 inches by 9¹/₂ inches; 2-panel *wimpel:* 50 inches by 9¹/₂ inches; 2-panel *wimpel* with borders: 50 inches by 22 inches

Refer to "General How-To's for Lettering," pages 252–254.

## WHAT YOU'LL NEED

1½ yards of 14-count even-weave white cross-stitch cloth, 60 inches wide, in washable polyester (Vicki used Zweigart; see "Resources," page 257)

6-strand embroidery floss in blue, maroon, white, gray, green, and gold

Fabric marking pen (Vicki used Dritz)

Gold metallic thread (Vicki used DMC)

Embroidery needle and hoop

Approximately 80 glass 2-millimeter seed beads

Fabric of your choice for backing, 25 inches by 56 inches (A fabric with special meaning works well here—a piece of a wedding dress or an heirloom tablecloth from a beloved relative, for example)

2 pieces of thin woven fabric in a contrasting color, each measuring 9 inches by 54 inches, for borders

*Figure 24.1*    *Figure 24.2*

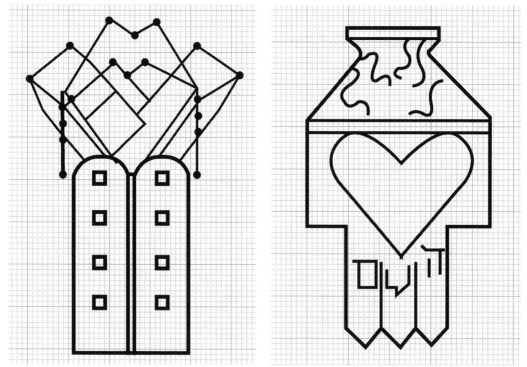

## HOW-TO'S

1.  Enlarge Figures 24.1, 24.2, and 24.3, and trace them onto the cross-stitch cloth. Leaving a 3-inch border around the images to allow for finishing and a border, sketch out the wording you want to insert as well. Count each square on the graph paper as a stitch.

2.  Separate the floss, and use 3 strands in the needle. Cut an 18-inch length, and thread it onto needle. To begin, leave a tail on the back, and do stitches over the end; do not make knots. To end, thread the tail under stitches on the back. Make a row of diagonal stitches in one direction, then complete the cross-stitches with stitches on the other diagonal. Use backstitches for fine lines.

3.  To insert beads, bring the threaded needle up through the fabric, thread a bead onto it, then bring the needle back through the fabric, pulling taut.

4.  For the left panel, using gray embroidery floss, stitch Hannah's request for a child—*For this child I prayed, and the Lord granted my petition. I will give thanks to the Lord with my whole heart.* Then, using the same-color thread, stitch the tablets of the Ten Commandments, topped by a gold crown. Stitch seed beads into the crown above the Ten Commandments. For the *hamsa*, use gray thread for the

*Figure 24.3*

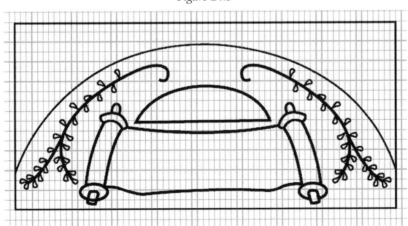

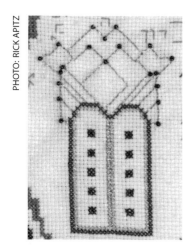

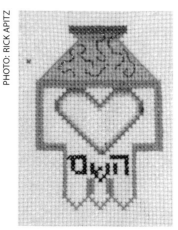

hand and gold thread for the word *Hashem* in the center. Stitch the border in maroon.

5. For the right panel of the *wimpel,* stitch in gray the English prayer—*Blessed is he who enters*—and the Hebrew translation beneath it in gold (see photo below).

6. For the rectangle featuring the open Torah scrolls (see photo on page 187), stitch the background in gray, the Torah handles in maroon, the Torah parchment in gray, and the leaves surrounding the Torah in green. Stitch seed beads into the vines running under the Hebrew lettering, the leaves on either side of the Torah scrolls, and the wide rectangle surrounding the Torah scrolls and the vines. Trim the unused even-weave cloth, leaving a ⅝-inch margin beyond the stitching. Stitch the border in maroon.

7. With right sides facing, sew the 2 panels together on the short side, making sure they're both right side up. Press the seam open.

8. To make the borders: With right sides facing, pin the top of the *wimpel* to one border piece and the bottom of the *wimpel* to the other. Sew the borders to the *wimpel,* with a ¼-inch seam allowance. Press open.

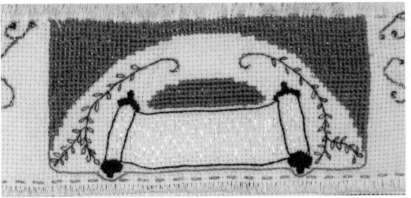

9. To sew the completed cross-stitch canvas, with borders, to the backing, place the backing material and the cross-stitch canvas together, right sides facing. Trim the backing material so it's the same size as the bordered *wimpel*. With a $1/2$-inch seam allowance, sew around the outside edge, leaving a 6-inch opening. Trim the excess. Turn the *wimpel* right side out. Fold in the seam allowance at the opening, and hand-stitch it closed using a slip stitch. Press, avoiding areas where there are beads.

Present your beautifully cross-stitched *wimpel* to the new parents as a gift from your heart.

# 25 Julia's Bat Mitzvah Challah Cover

*Project designer:* **Lois Gaylord**

Celebrating Shabbat is one of the central observances of Jewish practice. And challah figures prominently in that celebration. So for Lois Gaylord, a fiber artist, making a one-of-a-kind challah cover for her niece, Julia Bond, on the occasion of her Bat Mitzvah, seemed like an inspired gift. Julia enthusiastically agreed, saying, "The challah cover was one of the more personal and thoughtful gifts I received for my Bat Mitzvah. Many of them were money, jewelry, and the obligatory fountain pen, but none of the others actually promoted an involvement in the Jewish faith."

Since challah covers come in a myriad of designs, Lois looked for design elements to include that would set the intention for its use. Lois recalls, "I chose to use the Hebrew word *Shabbat* as the central motif. This would indicate when the piece was to be used. You could also make a round cloth with *Rosh Hashanah* for the High Holy Days."

The artist's design went further, painting wheat motifs to suggest the challah itself and the *motzi* prayer—bringing forth bread from the earth. "I chose to make this challah cover in natural linen to evoke the earth, with the blue as a reference to the sky. Blue is also a traditional color used in Jewish art. The gold represents the spirit and richness of Shabbat," she contends.

A native of San Francisco who grew up in San Jose, California, in a culturally Jewish home, Lois developed a passion for textiles and

189

fiber crafts early in life, when she learned how to sew, embroider, cro-chet, and weave. This led her to earn a BA degree in textile design from the University of Washington, with classes focusing on surface design as well as additional fiber construction. "I also completed the University of Washington Extension Fiber Arts Certificate program, which is designed to help fiber artists find their artistic voice and encourage them to take their work to the next level," she says. Lois now lives in Seattle, with her husband and son, and their cat, named Mouse.

Over the years Lois has experimented with many different fiber art techniques. "In college I started working with painted warps and wove fabric for wall pieces and clothing. Later, I had a crafts business making origami cloth boxes, and most recently I've been fashioning fiber jew-elry. I use the techniques of bobbin lace, cord-making, and braiding to make pins, necklaces, and earrings," says the imaginative fabric artist.

These days, Lois focuses her artistic energies on creating fiber art-work and other objects with a spiritual dimension. "I draw on my personal connection with Shechinah—the feminine sense of God's presence—for inspiration," she notes. "Flowing from this inspiration, I create work that expresses my worldview and the philosophy that all things are connected in some way. Through this work, I hope to make some contribution to *tikkun olam,* the healing of the world. As a holis-tic thinker and abstract artist, I choose from a variety of materials and techniques to find the ones that best illustrate my ideas."

Lois's Shabbat challah cover—her first piece made for spiritual or ritual use—reflects the spiritual inclination that now infuses so much of her work. Her most recent piece is a bimah cloth for the Women's Torah Project, sponsored by the Kadima Reconstructionist Community in Seattle (see the story about this bimah cloth in the "Inspirations" section). She weaves tallitot, *atarot* (tallit neckpieces), and other "cer-emonial cloths," which are showcased at www.LoisGaylord.etsy.com. In pieces like this lovely Shabbat challah cover, she shares her love of Jewish tradition as she draws inspiration from it to help mend the world.

# Getting Started

*Finished size:* 16 inches by 20 inches
Refer to the "Stitch Guide," pages 255–256.

## WHAT YOU'LL NEED

Prewashed, preshunk fabrics, pressed smooth:

    White linen, 9 inches by 5 inches

    Natural linen fabric, 17 inches by 21 inches

    $1/2$ yard of blue cotton fabric, 42 inches wide

    1 piece, 17 inches by 21 inches, for the backing

    2 strips, 3 inches by 21 inches, for the border

    2 strips, 3 inches by 17 inches, for the border

Metallic textile fabric paints in royal blue, antique gold, and umber

White thread

Blue 6-strand embroidery floss

Heavy (3-ply) gold metallic thread (Lois used Madeira number 15, Gold 22)

Small, tapered paintbrushes

Embroidery needle

Parchment paper

*Note: See "Resources," page 258, for linens and gold metallic yarn indicated above.*

## HOW-TO'S

### Assemble the Top

1.    Press the edges of the white fabric $1/2$ inch to the wrong side, to form an 8-by-4-inch rectangle.

2.    Center it on the natural linen; pin in place. Using white thread, top-stitch close to the pressed edges.

*Figure 25.1*

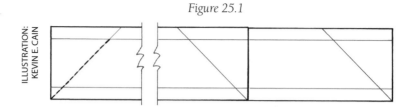

ILLUSTRATION: KEVIN E. CAIN

3. To miter the corners of the outside blue border, press under ¹/₂ inch to the wrong side of the fabric, along the long edges of the border strips (see Figure 25.1). Open the folds back out. There will now be a crease on the long edges. Fold the corner diagonally, wrong sides together, aligning each end to one of the long edges. Press, then open back out. This will give you a 45-degree angle to stitch along. Make sure that the ends are folded to the same long edge. Sew the long strips to the shorter strips to form a rectangle. Line up the ends of one short and one long strip, and sew from the point along the 45-degree crease to the crease at the inside edge of the border. Sew all 4 corners. Trim seam allowance and press open.

4. Re-press the ¹/₂-inch crease along the inside of the rectangle, and flatten the crease on the outside edge. Place the sewn-together border on the linen, lining up the outer edges. Pin and baste in place. Sew the border onto the background thread using gold metallic thread and blanket stitch.

## *Embellishing*

1. Following the pattern on page 193 (Figure 25.2), enlarge the Hebrew letters to 8 inches by 4 inches and, centering carefully, trace them onto the center white linen rectangle. Fill in the letters with royal blue paint, and heat-set the paint according to the manufacturer's directions. When the paint is dry, outline the letters in gold thread using stem stitch.

2. Embroider over the topstitching in featherstitch using 2 strands of blue embroidery floss (see photo on page 193).

3. Enlarge the wheat motif at right (Figure 25.3), trace it onto parchment paper, and cut out the oval and stem only. Iron at a 45-degree angle, and with a pencil trace around the shape onto the natural linen. Repeat in each corner of the linen rectangle. Paint over the pencil lines in antique gold. Let the paint dry, heat-set it, then use umber or a darker color to add detail lines as shown.

4. Embroider over the inner edge of the border with gold metallic thread in blanket stitch (see photo below).

*Figure 25.2*

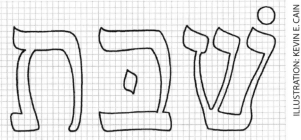

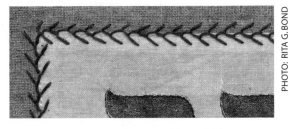

ILLUSTRATION: KEVIN E. CAIN

PHOTO: RITA G. BOND

## *Assembly*

1. Place the embroidered top on the fabric for the backing, with right sides facing. Sew around, 1/2 inch from the edges, leaving about 6 inches unstitched along one of the short sides.

2. Trim the corners, turn right side out, and press, folding the edges of the opening 1/2 inch to the inside. Slip-stitch the opening closed.

Sign and date the back before giving this lovely piece to the intended recipient.

*Figure 25.3*

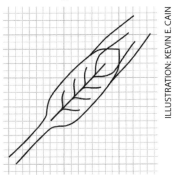

ILLUSTRATION: KEVIN E. CAIN

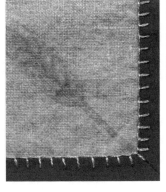

PHOTO: RITA G. BOND

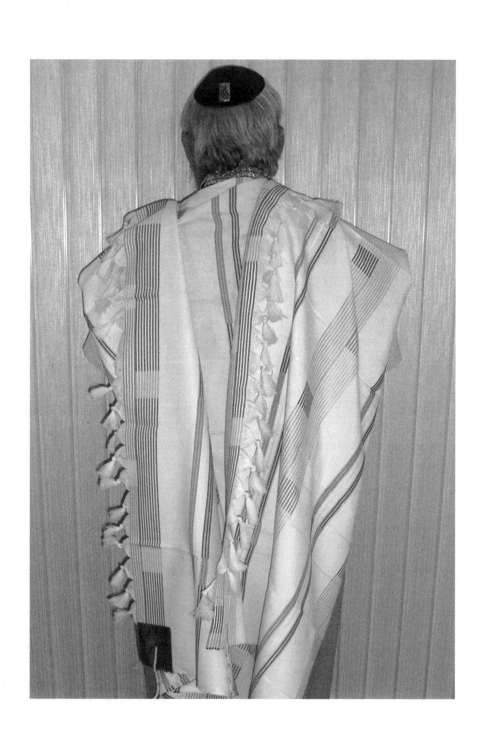

# 26 Julian's Traditional Tallit

*Project designer:* **Julian M. Brook**

For more than thirty years, Julian Brook, the international financial secretary of the United Synagogue of Conservative Judaism, has made several dozen tallitot of his own as well as a number for friends. He's conducted classes at his synagogue on tallit making, too. Julian's goal is to fashion a tallit for each *parashah* (the Torah portion of the week), but he still has a ways to go.

"I think the reason I am so fond of this one is that it has a very traditional flair with the black on white, but also the stripes have a modern look and feel as well," Julian notes. "It is the blending of old and new that makes this one interesting to me."

As a young man, Julian figured out a simple way to make tallitot. Since then, he's become a tallit-making maven. And he's happy to share his approach to making a prayer shawl that has personal meaning to the wearer: "When people ask me what kind of fabric to select, I usually tell them that I walk through a fabric store looking for something that jumps up and says, 'Make a tallit from me.' Some fabrics whisper, some shout." The Birmingham, Alabama, resident goes on to explain, "My most unusual one is from a Mexican blanket like those you sometimes see at sidewalk sales and flea markets. It had great fringe already on the ends and very colorful stripes. I simply put *tzitzit* on each corner and an *atarah* [the neckpiece] and I was done—perfect for a cold day."

Serendipity figured in the fashioning of this traditional tallit. Julian was in a fabric store helping a friend find something that said "tallit" to him when Julian spotted this material. "I pointed it out to him, and he immediately loved it. He made a very handsome tallit with it," the tallit maker remembers. "I, on the other hand, immediately regretted not having bought that fabric myself, since I loved it as well, and there was only the one piece and it was just enough for a single tallit."

A few days later, Julian was again walking the aisles of the fabric store, this time looking through remnants for something that would seize his imagination. "Lo and behold, I saw another piece of this fabric, and it was just large enough for one tallit!" the fabric artist recalls. "I pounced on it, and this tallit is the result. I have never again seen another piece or bolt of this material."

As an unusual side note, the surface of this fabric was very smooth and slick, so the finished tallit tended to slide off Julian's shoulders. After fighting with his new tallit to stay in place, Julian finally decided to try something completely off the wall: "I laid it out on a table, took a very fine piece of sandpaper, and went very lightly over the whole surface. That roughened the surface just enough. It now lies nicely and does not slide off."

In general, for his own tallitot Julian looks for materials with a striped pattern, which tends to be customary. Stripes running across the fabric are found often in Jewish prayer shawls, but tallitot with stripes running the long way and even sans stripes are not the least bit unusual anymore. For Julian, it is easier if the pattern, if any, graces both sides of the fabric. Many prints appear on one side only, but both sides of a tallit are visible—at least partially. *Alternatively,* if the "back" side is different, but interesting or attractive, that may work, too. Generally, coarse, knobby, or tweedy fabrics, which have some texture, are more interesting as candidates for tallitot and are easier to fray (for making the fringes).

A "full" tallit takes a generous arm span (fingertip to fingertip) of material, about 6 feet (2 yards) in length. The height (top to bottom, when it's placed horizontally) is normally the width of the fabric as it comes off the bolt, but it can be trimmed if the tallit maker likes. However, trimming requires gluing, rolling, or hemming that edge to keep it from fraying. The height generally falls from chin to calf.

In making tallitot, Julian cautions against *shatnes,* the blending of linen and wool, which is forbidden in the Torah. So even if a particular fabric "speaks" to your soul, if it blends linen and wool, it is off-limits as a fabric for a tallit.

Julian poses this question to his students: "What is the most important part of the tallit?" That's actually a trick question. "The only important part is the *tzitzit* on each corner," he points out. "All the rest is decoration. The corner patches reinforce where the *tzitzit* go through the corners.

"The *atarah* lets you know which side is up. You can get premade *atarot* from some Judaica shops and on the Internet. But creating your own *atarah* can be fun as well."

According to Julian, there are many ways to proceed once you've chosen your fabric. "I try to use approaches that take a minimum of special skills, knowledge, or equipment," he explains. "For example, corners and the *atarah* are usually attached by sewing, but they can be affixed with fabric adhesive if you do not sew or don't have access to a sewing machine. Iron-on adhesive patches can also be used. Tie-dyeing, painting, and other decorating can certainly be done, too—it all depends on the interest and abilities of the maker. I generally look for fabrics that do not need further embellishment. Of course, the corners and the *atarah* can add considerable decoration and interest." Making a tallit is a mitzvah, Julian observes, and to beautify or enhance a mitzvah is also a mitzvah (known in Hebrew as *hiddur mitzvah*).

Besides making tallitot, Julian does leatherwork and silk-screens the logos of the various organizations he is involved with onto ties, suspenders, and other items. He has served as regional president of United Synagogue of Conservative Judaism, as president of Ramah Darom (a Jewish summer camp and retreat center), as president of his synagogue, and as president of his Jewish Community Center. In addition, the talented tallit maker does woodworking and radio restoration—a renaissance man of many stripes.

# Getting Started

*Finished size:* Approximately 6 feet by 42 inches (but size yours as you wish)
*(Note: If you'd like to make a shawl tallit, the same instructions apply, but the size is approximately 6 feet by 30 inches.)*

## WHAT YOU'LL NEED

Approximately $2^1/_2$ yards of woven fabric of your choice

Sequin and/or trim for the *atarah*, approximately 4 inches by 27 inches

4 reinforcement patches or 4 pieces of fabric (complementing or contrasting with the *atarah*), approximately $3^1/_2$ inches square

Sewing needle and thread to match your fabric (or transparent thread)

Large needle with a large eye or a crochet hook (to pull *tzitzit* through the corner holes)

Small embroidery scissors to make the corner holes

A set of kosher *tzitzit* (available online and from many Judaica shops)

### *Optional*

Purchased fringe, to trim desired edges

Small amount of upholstery fabric for the *atarah*

Decorative trims for the *atarah*

Needlepoint canvas for the *atarah*

Crochet hook

Fabric glue or fusible web (to secure the *atarah*, if you prefer a no-sew project)

## HOW-TO'S

### *Getting Started*

1.  Once you have chosen your material, cut it to the desired dimensions. For clean-finished edges, hem by folding twice and sewing with small stitches or by securing with fabric glue.

2. If you are going to fringe the fabric, proceed as follows: About 3¹/₂ inches from each short side, make a slit. The slit should be perpendicular to the end and also about 3¹/₂ inches long. For now, ignore the flap created on each corner by the slits you just made. Begin unraveling the woven fabric, gently pulling out threads between the 3¹/₂-inch cuts. Use a needle or pin to separate the strands. It may be helpful to pull a few threads from the edge of the slit toward the middle in order to expose the ends of the threads to be pulled out and removed. Depending on the looseness of the weave, you may be able to pull several threads all the way across at one time. If the weave is tight, it may help to cut additional slits to divide the area into more manageable sections to be frayed. Fray each edge to the full depth of the slits. Keep the fringes you are creating smooth and untangled. Once you have frayed each end, you are ready to tie knots in the fringes. How wide a section to gather into each knot depends very much on the thickness of the strands and the amount you unraveled to create the fringe. Some trial and error may be necessary. Starting from one end of the unraveled threads, gather together about 1 inch if the threads are heavy, 2 inches if the threads are fine. Smooth and flatten the threads. Twist them into a cord and tie a single loose knot in the center. Assess the effect: If you don't like the way it looks, untie it and try a smaller or a larger gathering of the threads. In addition, you may wish to increase or decrease the increments of strands to ensure equally full bundles all the way across the unraveled edge. However, Julian generally starts tying knots from both sides and adjusts or "cheats" on the width as he gets toward the middle so the knots seem to be evenly spaced and evenly full. When you're satisfied with the look, adjust this first knot so it is roughly in the middle of the length of the gathered fringe, and pull it tight. *(Note: Some people find a large crochet hook useful for knotting fringe.)*

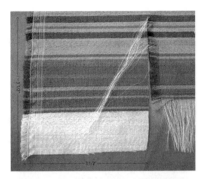

## Making the Atarah

*Note: There are so many choices for an* atarah *that you can let your own creativity be your guide, according to Julian. Commercial atarot (like those found on tallitot on the racks in most synagogues) are available with and without the blessings on them. Some people prefer to use those. Other folks make their own* atarot *from photographs printed on fabric, needlepoint designs, painting on fabric, or just by attaching an interesting piece of fabric that complements the fabric of the tallit itself. Among the simpler variants are woven belt or trim fabric; gold trim sewn or glued on top of a shiny blue fabric; and needlepoint designs.*

1.  For Julian's traditional tallit, he used 5 rows of sequin trim sewn on a black fabric background. Keep in mind that the average size of an *atarah* is 3 inches by 24–30 inches.

2.  To attach your *atarah,* first decide which side of your tallit is "up." That is the edge the *atarah* will go on. Now fold the tallit in half lengthwise to find the middle. Put a pin at the fold to mark the spot. Next, fold your *atarah* in half as well, and mark the fold with a pin. Pin the *atarah* to the tallit, $1/8$ inch to $1/4$ inch from the tallit edge and matching the center pin marks. If desired, fold the short ends of the *atarah* under to form a V. Hand-stitch the *atarah* to the tallit, using thread that matches the *atarah. Alternatively,* the *atarah* can simply be glued on with fabric glue or ironed on with a fusing layer between it and the tallit.

## Corner Squares & Tzitzit

*Note: Corner squares are designed to reinforce the tallit fabric, to hold the* tzitzit *securely. Most often the corner squares are on the same side of the tallit as the* atarah, *though they sometimes appear on the opposite side, and even on both sides! Choose a fabric to match the* atarah, *contrast with it, complement it, or be rather plain and inconspicuous. They can be made from a different part of the* atarah *fabric or a shiny fabric that complements the* atarah.

1.  Cut fabric $3 1/2$ inches square (larger if desired); the squares should cover the tallit corners beyond the knotted fringe. Fold the edges

under, hem, and press. *Alternatively,* glue or fuse the fabric squares in place at each corner.

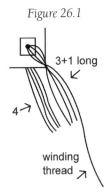

Figure 26.1

2. Once the corners are in place, make a small, round hole in the center of each corner patch. If desired, blanket-stitch around the hole to finish it. Take the *tzitzit,* and pull 3 short strings and 1 long string (called the *shammas*) through the eyelet hole until all the ends but the 1 long strand are even with each other (see Figure 26.1). You may use a large needle or a crochet hook to do this, ending with 7 short strings and 1 long string. *(Note: In Jewish mysticism, seven is the number representing perfection in the physical realm. Eight, therefore, transcends the physical realm and symbolizes a direct link to the spiritual realm.)* The short strings should all be the same length; the *shammas* is longer.

3. Tie the 4 strings on one side together in a slip knot to hold them together while you work. Wind the 7 strings together (all but the *shammas*), and then wrap the *shammas* around the other 7 strings 7 times. Make a double knot at that point (the first of 5 sets of double knots, all tied right over left, then left over right [a "Boy Scout" or "square" knot, not a "granny" knot]).

4. Wind the 7 strings together again, and wrap the *shammas* around the 7 strings 8 times. Make another knot at that point.

5. Wind the 7 strings together again, and then wrap the *shammas* around the 7 strings 11 times. Make another double knot.

Figure 26.2

6. Wind the 7 strings together again, and wrap the *shammas* around the 7 strings 13 times. Make another double knot.

7. Release the slip knot that has been keeping the strings in order (see Figure 26.2).

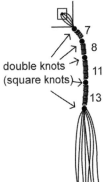

double knots
(square knots)

8. Working in the same way, knot each group of 8 strings 5 times to form a *tzitzit.*

Head for synagogue and enjoy your new tallit. Remember to say a *Shehecheyanu* the first time you wear it.

# 27 Judy's Garden of Eden Tallit Bag

*Project designer:* Judith S. Paskind

------------------------------------------------

J udith S. Paskind began expressing her love of Judaism, Jewish culture, and Jewish life through arts and crafts more than forty years ago. She was originally inspired by a stunning counted cross-stitch challah cover, handmade in Israel, which she received as a wedding gift. Since then, Judy has created her own patterns for *atarot* (tallit neckpieces), tallit bags, challah covers, and other items of Jewish interest for members of her family—her husband, Lee, and their three grown children—and for others who have requested them.

A talented fiber artist, Judy, who works professionally as an accountant, also designs and makes quilts. She notes, "When the inspiration strikes me, I design. And then I have fun making the items."

Judy created this exquisite Garden of Eden Tallit Bag for the Bat Mitzvah of her daughter, Miriam. "The pattern is based on the very beautiful and inspiring stained-glass panels in the sanctuary of our former synagogue, Congregation Ahavat Shalom. These were designed by Eric Roseff, the son of members," Judy points out. "The stained-glass panels recount the stories in the Torah of the Garden of Eden through the burning bush, and use lush colors like these, which engage the eye and soothe the spirit. From the first time I viewed these stained-glass panels, I knew that I wanted to use their colors in a craft project."

The opportunity presented itself serendipitously: "When my daughter requested a tallit and a matching tallit bag for her upcoming Bat Mitzvah, I decided to base the design on the stained glass that we enjoyed each Shabbat morning as the sun shone through them."

Recalling how she felt while creating the tallit and its matching tallit bag, Judy says, "I loved making them for my daughter. Our synagogue had recently voted to allow women and girls to read from the Torah on Shabbat mornings, to lead all parts of the service, and to wear tallitot. Miriam got to learn so much and incorporate it into her Bat Mitzvah. She enjoyed her Bat Mitzvah tremendously and was happy to be wrapped in her tallit that morning."

From a spiritual perspective, the Garden of Eden sets the stage for a number of themes that recur throughout the Bible: the loss of innocence, the mixed blessing of the knowledge of good and evil, the dangers that lurk in the larger world. Yet looking back to the Garden of Eden, we can still recall the imagined natural beauty our first ancestors savored under date palms and other fruit trees like those pictured in Judy's Garden of Eden Tallit Bag.

# Getting Started

*Finished size:* 12 inches by 10³/₈ inches

## WHAT YOU'LL NEED

2 pieces 16-count Aida cloth, cut to 15 inches by 13³/₈ inches (see "Resources," page 258)

6-strand DMC embroidery floss: 2 skeins each of dark, medium, and light Delft; and 1 skein of all other colors listed on legend (page 212)

2 pieces 15-by-13³/₈-inch cotton fabric in a color to match or contrast with the Aida cloth, for lining

12-inch zipper

## HOW-TO'S

1. To personalize the design for your tallit bag, use the lettering chart
   below to plot out the Hebrew name toward the bottom. (Judy's says
   "Miriam," her daughter's name, in Hebrew.) Photocopy and align the
   6 sections of the chart (Figures 27.2 through 27.7, also available on

*Figure 27.1*

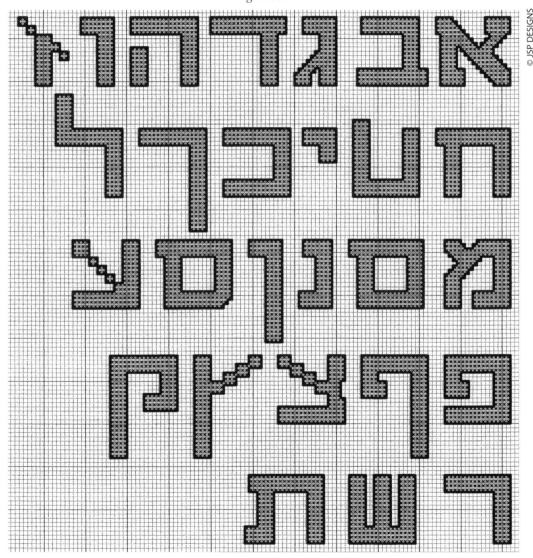

*Figure 27.2 (top left)*

Figure 27.3 (top center)

*Figure 27.4 (top right)*

*Figure 27.5 (bottom left)*

*Figure 27.6 (bottom center)*

*Figure 27.7 (bottom right)*

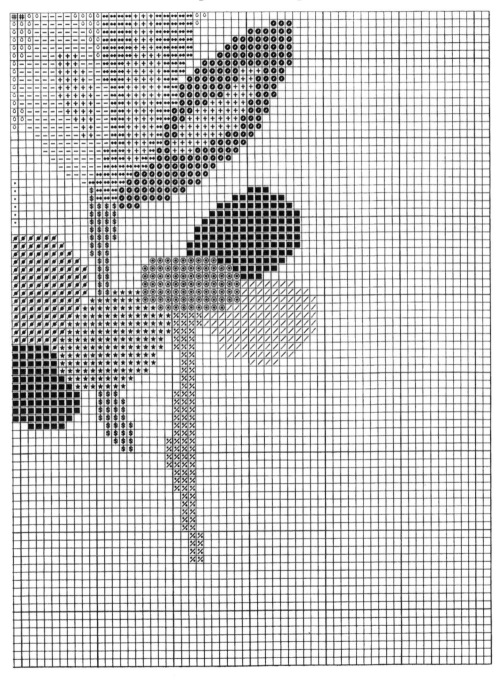

## Legend

(Numbers are DMC; see "Resources," page 258)

| Symbol | No. | Color | Symbol | No. | Color | Symbol | No. | Color |
|---|---|---|---|---|---|---|---|---|
| + | 99 | Metallic Gold | ■ | 553 | Violet | # | 742 | Tangerine—light |
| ø | 209 | Lavender—dark | ★ | 554 | Violet—light | ( | 798 | Delft—dark |
| / | 211 | Lavender—light | ✦✦ | 606 | Bright Orange-Red | ✎ | 799 | Delft—medium |
| ✳ | 310 | Black | — | 608 | Bright Orange | 0 | 800 | Delft—light |
| ❖ | 349 | Coral—dark | 2 | 666 | Christmas Red—light | ↑ | 839 | Beige Brown—dark |
| ◉ | 350 | Violet—very dark | % | 699 | Christmas Green | $ | 910 | Emerald Green—dark |
| ■ | 552 | Violet—medium | ◙ | 740 | Tangerine | ✳ | 911 | Emerald Green—medium |

Jewish Lights' website at www.jewishlights.com/JewishThreads/ Chapter27Charts.pdf), drawing a red line between charts. Decide on the best location for the name, and draw it in another color of pencil on the chart, replacing the letters for the floral pattern. Choose a color for stitching the name that contrasts well with the design around the letters. (Judy used black for the letters.)

2. To prevent the edges of the Aida cloth from unraveling, stitch around the raw edges, either zigzag-stitching by machine or overcast-stitching by hand.

3. Fold the Aida cloth crosswise in half, and baste along the crease. Fold it lengthwise in half, and baste along the crease. Follow the chart to work stitchery on each section. When work is complete, carefully remove the basting stitches.

4. Separate the floss, and use 2 strands of embroidery floss in the needle to make each cross-stitch, working over one square of Aida cloth to correspond to each symbol on the charts. To begin, cut an 18-inch length of floss and thread it onto the needle. Leave a tail on the back, and make stitches over the end; do not make knots. To end, thread each tail under stitches on the back. Use backstitches for fine lines.

5. First, cross-stitch the letters with which you personalized the design. Then, work the rest of the design, referring to the chart and the legend. Work from the center outward, but cross-stitch all the same color before switching to a different color.

## Finishing

1. Press the piece, blocking it to shape. Trim unused Aida cloth, leaving a $5/8$-inch margin beyond the stitching.

2. For the back of the bag, cut a 2nd piece of Aida cloth to the same size as the cross-stitched piece. For the lining, cut 2 more rectangles the same size as the cross-stitched Aida cloth.

3. Following the manufacturer's instructions on the zipper package, stitch the zipper between the bag front and back. With right sides facing and edges even, sew around the remaining three sides. Open the zipper, turn to the right side, and press the bag.

4. Place the 2 lining fabric rectangles together with right sides facing. Stitch around the two short sides and one long side, $1/4$ inch from the edges, making the lining the same size as the cross-stitched bag. Sew together, leaving one long side open at the top. Leaving the wrong sides out, press, turning in the seam allowance remaining on one long edge. Insert the lining in the bag. Hand-stitch the folded edges of the lining to the tallit bag on the inside, close to the zipper opening, and press.

Present your beautiful, handcrafted tallit bag to the person whose name is stitched with love on the front.

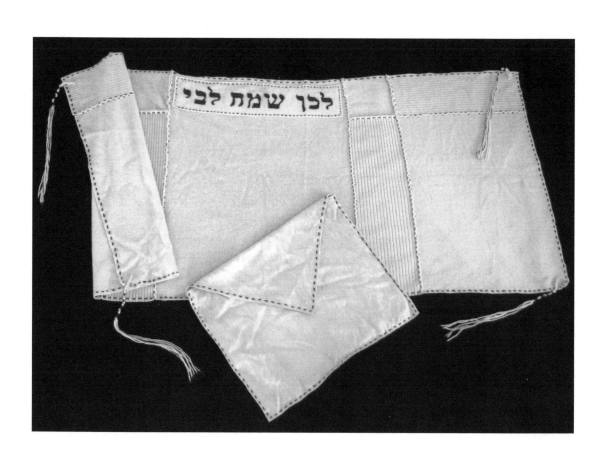

# 28 Debra's Tallit & Tallit Bag

---

*Project Designer:* **Susan H. Rappaport**

F or Susan H. Rappaport, making this tallit was a family affair. First of all, she fashioned the tallit for her daughter, Rabbi Debra Rappaport, who is the spiritual leader at B'nai Vail Congregation in Vail, Colorado. Then, in choosing the materials for the tallit, Susan used white cashmere from sweaters worn by her husband, Gary; by Debra; by her other daughter, Lissie Schifman; and by Susan herself to ground the tallit in a sense of family heritage. Susan sewed everything by hand, making the *tzitzit* from directions she found on the Web. "The directions were very specific about keeping focused on your intention and not being distracted by the things around you," she points out. "It was a very profound process for me."

A multimedia artist who lives in Deephaven, Minnesota, Susan draws inspiration from a wide variety of found objects, noting that "these objects have power, energy, and meaning for me. I work to transform and combine them in nontraditional ways." She especially loves working with cashmere because of its gorgeous texture and says, "I like to reuse and repurpose beautiful objects, rather than throwing them away." In addition to this tallit, she has made decorative pillows, scarves, and clothing for children and adults from cashmere. "I always sew by hand, and I often decorate using needle felting."

While the pattern for Debra's tallit was dictated by the size of the good pieces of cashmere Susan had on hand, she chose to make it symmetrical and to incorporate contrasts in textures as well. She sewed the entire tallit by hand, using blue thread in a wool/silk blend. Wanting to give this tallit family history and power, Susan embroidered Debra's initials (DLR), her own (SHR), and those of Debra's grandparents (NHH, ILH, MER, BBR) on the back of the prayer shawl.

The Hebrew phrase on the *atarah*, "*Lachen samach libi*—So my heart rejoices ..." (Psalm 16:9), was chosen by Debra as a reminder that God's presence is with us always—from the prior verse of the psalm—and that is a cause for rejoicing. Susan first cut out Hebrew letters from a piece of blue cashmere, and then needle-felted the letters onto the *atarah*.

"Making this tallit was a very meditative and spiritual experience for me," Susan recalls. "My daughter was entering a whole new and challenging part of her life, and this was a way for me to give her my blessings and the blessings of her family and her ancestors. I wanted to wrap her in love—both literally and figuratively."

And this magnificent tallit holds extraordinary meaning for Debra, who notes, "Though my mom invited quite a bit of collaboration on this project, I was moved to tears when I received this tallit. The thoughtfulness and love that went into it were profound. I feel deeply blessed, held, and joyful every time I put it on."

Because such a beautiful tallit calls for its own special carrying case, Susan handmade the accompanying tallit bag out of raw silk.

## Getting Started—Debra's Tallit

*Finished size:* 60½ inches by 25 inches
Refer to "General How-To's for Lettering," pages 252–254, and the "Stitch Guide," pages 255–256.

### WHAT YOU'LL NEED

A large quantity of 100% pure fabric: cashmere, wool, silk, or linen (be sure to have more fabric on hand than you think you'll need; traditionally, tallitot are made from pure, natural fabrics, rather than synthetics)

A complementary contrasting color of cashmere for the words on the *atarah* (Susan used a 12-by-14-inch piece of blue cashmere, but the amount of cashmere you need depends on the number of letters or images in your *atarah* and how large you make them; this is the piece to be cut into Hebrew letters and needle-felted)

Blue, medium-weight embroidery thread (100% wool, silk, cotton, or a combination of any of these; Susan used a wool/silk blend that matched the color of the letters on the *atarah* and contrasted with the white of the tallit fabric)

Fusible web (optional)

Kosher *tzitzit* (available in Judaica stores and online)

## HOW-TO'S

*Note on this project: In creating this lovely tallit, Susan drew on her artistic, intuitive nature, rather than proceeding in a regimented way. She calls the process "adventurous" and encourages readers to tap into their own imagination and intuition to make a tallit that reflects their own passions and love of Judaism.*

*Notes on needle felting: Needle felting is done with a barbed needle (available at yarn stores). Before you begin, place a dense foam pad (also available at yarn stores) on a tabletop to protect the surface. Place the 2 pieces to be needle-felted on top of the foam pad. Then punch the barbed needle many, many times into the 2 fabrics until their fibers are meshed, or woven, together. In order for the needle felting to "hold," punch it until you see that the fabrics look and feel completely integrated. Needle felting works on both cashmere and wool. If you don't want to needle-felt, you could cut the letters from fusible-backed fabrics and embroider the letters on the atarah by hand.*

1. Decide on the overall size of the tallit you want to make. Tallitot usually span the length from outstretched fingertip to outstretched fingertip, and fall from the chin to the calf, but sizes vary, depending on your preference. Susan gathered several old, white cashmere sweaters—her own, her husband's, and her daughters'. She cut them

apart along the seams, and then cut them to get as many large pieces as possible. Then she arranged them in an artistic pattern. (She notes, "Each sweater I used was different, and if I were to make another tallit from cashmere sweaters, it would have a different pattern.")

2. Lay out the flat, rectangular pieces in a pattern that works both from a design standpoint and from the perspective of the fabric size you have available. Susan notes that the design you choose is totally arbitrary, depending on the sizes of the fabrics and your artistic vision. The design may be done in completely random fashion—say, as patchwork—or it may be done symmetrically, as Susan made Debra's. That contributes to the artistry and unique character of the piece. ("There is some magic that goes into this process," Susan points out. "That's what made it fun and wonderful—both for me and for my daughter.")

3. Once you have the pattern designed, cut out the pieces and sew them together using a running stitch so that it will look good on the reverse side as well, remembering that the back of the tallit will sometimes show. Susan butted the edges together, with no seam allowances.

4. Make the *atarah*: Cut out a 27-by-4-inch piece of fabric for the *atarah*. Susan used the same color (white) as for the rest of the tallit. Cut out the Hebrew letters from a piece of blue cashmere. Needle-felt the letters onto the *atarah* (see "Notes on needle felting," page 217). *Alternatively,* cut the letters out of scrap material, backed by fusible web, and simply sew them onto the *atarah*. Sew the completed *atarah* onto the tallit with the same running stitch used to sew the tallit pieces together.

5. Make the *tzitzit*. See "Corner Squares & *Tzitzit*" in Julian's Traditional Tallit, pages 200–201, for directions on how to do this. (Susan chose not to reinforce the corners on Debra's tallit, but this, again, is up to you.)

Now bless your tallit and either wear it yourself or present it to the person for whom you've made it with love.

# Getting Started—Debra's Tallit Bag

*Finished size:* 14 inches by 10 inches

Refer to the "Stitch Guide," pages 255–256.

## WHAT YOU'LL NEED

Raw silk or any firm fabric, 30 inches by 16 inches

Blue, medium-weight, wool/silk embroidery thread (the same thread used for the tallit)

A large snap

## HOW-TO'S

1. Fold the fabric crosswise into thirds, with right sides in. The top third will become a triangle flap that snaps closed.

2. Open out the flap. Using very small stitches, stitch $1/4$ inch from the side edges of the other layers. Trim seam allowances to $1/8$ inch. Clip the corners, and turn the bag to the right side. Press. Use blue embroidery thread (matching the thread used on the tallit) and a running stitch to topstitch along the sides and the bottom of the bag, $1/4$ inch from pressed seams.

3. Cut the flap so it covers only half the bag. Use a pencil and ruler to draw lines from the center of the flap out to the top corners, then cut the flap into a triangular shape. Press the edges $1/8$ inch to the wrong side twice, then topstitch with running stitches as before.

4. Sew a male snap onto the inside point of the flap, and a corresponding female snap on the bag.

Carry your lovely cashmere tallit to synagogue in its gorgeous matching bag, or present both to the intended recipient with your blessings.

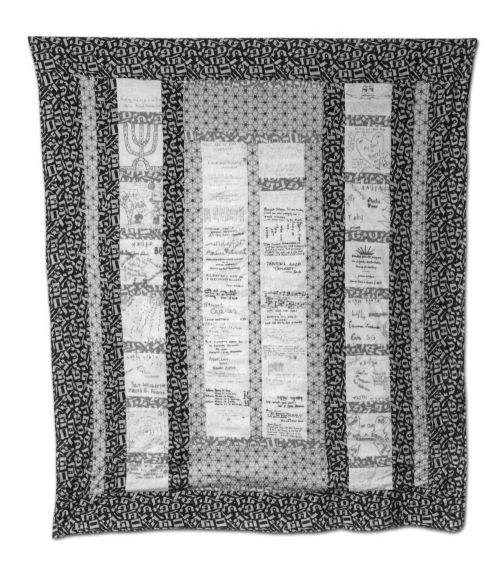

# 29

# Stuart's
# Healing Quilt

*Project designer:* Holly Levison

When someone in a close-knit community becomes gravely ill, members of that community join together to comfort the one who is suffering. Oftentimes, the illness itself makes it impossible for people to visit, whether for fear of spreading germs to the patient whose immune system may be compromised or because the person does not have the physical or emotional stamina for visitors. Still, well-wishers want to share their strength, their prayers, and their spiritual sustenance with their ailing friend. One solution is the healing quilt, a collaborative creation imbued with heartfelt good wishes, which surrounds the person undergoing treatment with support and love like a "virtual hug."

Members of the Woodstock (Vermont) Area Jewish Community / Congregation Shir Shalom were devastated to hear that their lay spiritual leader and the founder of the congregation, Stuart M. Matlins, had been diagnosed with colon cancer several years ago. (He had a complete healing and recovery.) Stuart is also the founder of Jewish Lights Publishing, the publisher of *Jewish Threads*, and a visionary who first thought of establishing a Jewish community in this quiet corner of the Green Mountain State over two decades ago, together with his wife, Antoinette. In response to his then-impending surgery, local members of the congregation, as well as seasonal members from across the United States, created a beautiful healing quilt in just three weeks.

Although healing quilts are not new, the design of this quilt reflects the desire to visually support the patient's climb back to health. Squares were created by adult congregation members and by each of the Shir Shalom Hebrew School classes. "It was our gift to the man who paved the way for our spiritual home," says Holly Levison, who coordinated the healing quilt project. "We were able to give back to someone who had given us so much."

According to Holly, pulling together all the threads involved in fashioning a healing quilt requires organization and the support of friends and colleagues close to the ailing person. With healing quilts, you're often working under a deadline (Holly chose to finish the quilt before Stuart went in for surgery—a matter of mere weeks). You need to orchestrate sending the quilt squares out to everyone you think might be interested in participating, make the return process easy and user-friendly, and schedule time for assembling and finishing the quilt. The turnaround time can be quite unforgiving, often mirroring the ailment that you are hoping your quilt will help heal.

In the case of Stuart's quilt, some well-wishers lived close by and could be called or approached in person. Others were farther afield, so their squares had to be sent by round-trip mail. A packet was created with a cover letter, outlining the idea of the quilt, the basic process, and the return date; a piece of fabric on which the well-wisher could write or embroider a thought or prayer; and a stamped, self-addressed return envelope. "Families are frequently not up to the burden of generating support or soliciting squares; they are focused on the impending event or illness. They may also resist the concept because it adds a reality to the situation that they are not ready to accept," Holly notes. "It is important to ask the family if they would like to contribute a square. Some may want to participate; some may not. Either way, the finished quilt will offer a healing moment for the family or loved ones, as well as the patient."

Because healing is a climb from illness back to health, Holly chose a ladder design for Stuart's quilt. "Between each rung is a set of thoughts, prayers, or wishes to ease the burden of the climb," she explains. "The layout incorporated two ladders and two additional columns of wishes, laid out like the tablets of the Ten Commandments. The number of ladders included in the quilt design can be adjusted to reflect the number of participants in the quilt."

A longtime quilter, Holly made her first quilt in high school, back in the 1970s. Since then, she has given quilts as baby gifts, wedding gifts, auction donations, and to bring comfort to those in need. "Although each quilt has its own unique story and motivation, they all have one thing in common: the recipient has a deeply emotional response to receiving a quilt," she says.

Stuart was no exception. When he was presented with his healing quilt the night before his surgery, he wrote an e-mail that said, in part, "To say that I am deeply moved by this does not begin to describe my feelings.... It will be like being wrapped in the wings of angels. To be wrapped in so much love and caring has to be helpful in the healing ... [and] brings great comfort."

While she is not a full-time artist, Holly has pursued fabric art, especially quilting and costume design, as an artistic outlet through-out her life. After a career in the banking industry, she retired and had two daughters, now teenagers, and then went back to work at the local arts council. Among her recent Jewish fiber works are several projects through the Congregation Shir Shalom Hebrew School, including a community tallit that measures 21 feet by 4 feet and a hand-painted community chuppah, and she has been assisting the students of the Hebrew School in creating individual quilts based on life-cycle events and significant Hebrew words.

"Creating fiber art, by drawing on the power of the human spirit, can change the soul," Holly points out, noting that this kind of project falls within the Jewish imperative of *tikkun olam* (mending the world). "The amazing outcome of a healing quilt is the power infused in each fabric piece, each handwritten note, each stitch sewn. Together, we can lift an ailing soul up each rung of the ladder. There are times when that ailing soul is the patient, and times when that ailing soul is the family or loved ones of the patient. Either way, the collective spirit of love, friendship, and hope embodied in the healing quilt intensifies its potential to heal. The simple act of putting your heart into cloth, stitching it in place, and sharing that love with someone in need makes the world a better place."

# Getting Started

*Finished size:* 66 inches by 72 inches
Refer to "General How-To's for Quilt Making," pages 245–251.

## WHAT YOU'LL NEED

*Notes:*

- For this healing quilt, Holly worked in organic white cotton sateen, with fleece for the backing.

- She favors cottons or cotton/flannels because they're soft, warm, and rejuvenating, and organic, sustainable materials because they feel more restorative.

- For the batting, Holly likes to use Warm and Natural Needled Cotton Batting or Nature-Fil Bamboo batting—50% rayon fiber from bamboo, 50% certified organic cotton.

- For the white cotton, on which participants will write with fabric markers, Sharpies, Bic Mark-Its, or other permanent markers, choose a tightly woven fabric so bleeding of the ink is minimal.

White, tightly woven cotton, 1¹/₂ yards, for personalized submissions to position between the ladder rungs:

Fourteen 7-inch squares

Twenty 4-by-7-inch rectangles

2 yards of fabric, for background bars (this fabric was a neutral color with Stars of David):

Two 23-by-7-inch rectangles

Two 23-by-3-inch rectangles

Two 5-by-41-inch strips

One 3-by-41-inch strip

Two 3-by-61-inch strips

2 yards of light blue print, for horizontal spacers and ladder rungs (Holly used light Hebrew-letter fabric for this):

Four 3-by-61-inch strips

Fourteen 3-by-7-inch strips

2 yards of dark blue print for ladder uprights and surrounding quilt edges (Holly used dark Hebrew-letter fabric for this):

Four 5-by-61-inch strips

Two 9-by-61-inch strips, for wide binding

Two 9-by-67-inch strips, for wide binding

Thin fleece or flannel for backing, 66 inches by 72 inches (if you cannot find 66-inch-wide fabric, you can piece the backing)

Thin batting, 66 inches by 72 inches

Parchment paper (optional)

*Figure 29.1*

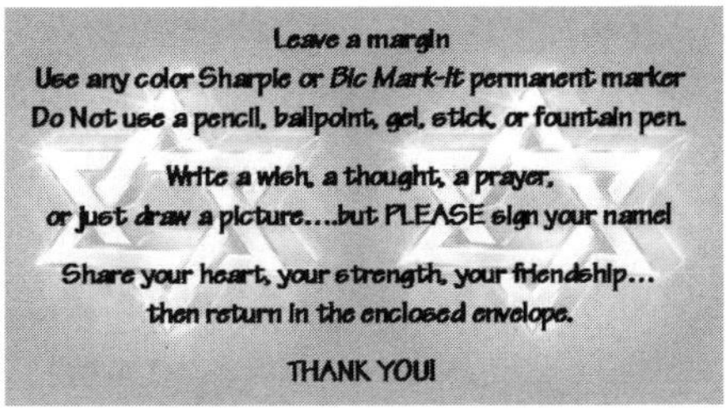


*Figure 29.2*

**Shhhhhh!!!!!!!!!!**

It's a Surprise!

As you know, our dear friend and guide Stuart Matlins is going in for some surgery. We are asking you to be a part of his 'get well' quilt. Your piece of the quilt is enclosed.

Please write your thoughts on the fabric using a SHARPIE permanent marker or Bic Mark-It permanent pen. Do not use any type of water-soluble ink, ballpoint, gel, or fountain pen, pencil, or markers that do not specifically state they are permanent ink.

It is important to leave about half an inch around the edges. These pieces will be sewn together and anything close to the edge will be in the seams.

When your quilt piece is complete, please return it to:
Xxxxxxxxxxxxxxxx
xxxxxxxxxxxxxxxxx

We need the quilt pieces back no later than ____________. Our goal is to deliver the quilt by his surgery date which is__________. The sooner you send your quilt piece back, the sooner our gift of support will reach Stuart.

Remember – this is a secret!

**We thank you for joining us in wrapping Stuart in the warmth of our love and prayers.**

*If you have any questions, please call* ____________________

## HOW-TO'S

### *Signed Patches*

Send white cotton fabric squares and rectangles out to all prospective well-wishers with a note specifying what you're looking for and sample instructions (see Figures 29.1 and 29.2). The larger squares are intended for collective signing by groups; the smaller rectangular patches are meant for individuals, couples, and families. You might want to suggest the following ideas:

- Sketch out your design and decide what you want to write on scrap paper before you write or draw it in permanent marker.
- Iron the fabric to parchment paper for a firm, stabilized surface to write on.
- If you're artistic, the sky's the limit.

Once all the patches are returned, press them with a hot, dry iron to heat-set the writing.

## Making the Quilt Top

1. Arrange the patches: Divide the individual wish pieces between the ladders and columns. Lay them out side by side to determine the most appealing arrangement. Then figure out how many rungs you need by mapping out your quilt on graph paper (Figure 29.3).

2. Join the signed patches and rungs, stitching with right sides together and pressing the seam allowances.

3. Stitch the ladder uprights to either side of the joined signed patches and rungs.

4. Sew the smaller wish patches into columns. These will form the 2 center columns. Stitch narrow vertical spacers between the 2 center columns. Add background strips to each side of the columns. Then sew a horizontal spacer, measuring 23 inches by 3 inches, to the top and bottom of the widened column. Add a large rectangle of background fabric, measuring 23 inches by 7 inches, to the top and bottom and finish with 2 more horizontal spacers, measuring 23 inches by 3 inches, framing the center columns of wishes.

*Figure 29.3*

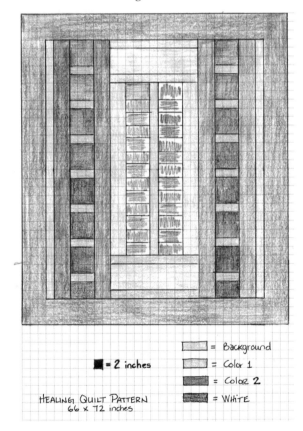

■ = 2 inches

▭ = Background
▭ = Color 1
▭ = Color 2
▦ = White

HEALING QUILT PATTERN
66 × 72 inches

## *Finishing*

Make a quilt sandwich with the quilt top faceup on top, the batting in the middle, and the fleece or flannel backing on the bottom (right side out). Quilt "in the ditch," so the ladders show on the back of the quilt as well. ("I believe that gives the wishes a way to seep through the quilt, which is the goal with a healing quilt," Holly says.) Bind the quilt all around.

*(Alternative without batting: With right sides facing, pin the quilt top to the backing. Sew around 3 sides, like a pillowcase, then turn the quilt right side out and hand-sew the open side closed with a slip stitch. Press.)*

Arrange to deliver your healing quilt so all the love stitched into it can speed the patient's healing and offer immeasurable comfort.

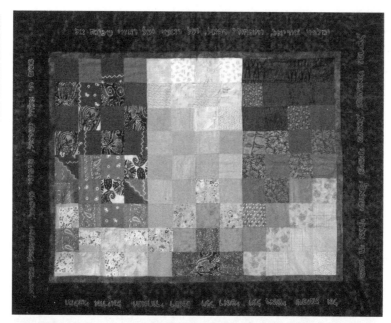

# 30

# Shalva Quilts

*Project designers:* **The Quilting Group with No Name: Diane Bernbaum, Carol Dorf, Lee Feinstein, Karen Benioff Friedman, Rivka Greenberg, Shari Rifas, and Claire Sherman**

The Quilting Group with No Name began with Rivka Greenberg, who wanted to bring together women to pursue fiber arts and text study in a group setting. A professional fiber artist offered her studio as a meeting place, and the group evolved over several years, eventually focusing more on quilting than study of sacred texts.

Members learned to listen closely to each other, to compromise in design, to know who is best on a machine, who has a trusted eye for color, who can do anything with embroidery and beads, who knows how to dye fabric, who knows how to draw a free-form *hamsa,* and who will be the most dependable one to buy notions at the fabric store.

Among the projects they have created have been a chuppah for one member's daughter's wedding and a tallit when another member's daughter became a bat mitzvah. They have made quilts to give to local Jewish organizations to be raffled in their fund-raisers. They fashioned a quilt in loving memory of one of the group members; this hangs in the synagogue where most of them are members. They helped the community as a whole say good-bye to a beloved artist who moved away, by taking squares crafted at a good-bye party and making them into a quilt.

But the project of which they are most proud are their Shalva quilts. After they had been making fabric art together for several years, someone approached them and asked for help. Shalva, *z"l*, a woman in their community, had died a year earlier. She had left two very young daughters. A group of her friends had gathered some of her clothing at the time of her death, not knowing what they would do with it, but determined to make something for these girls. However, none of them could sew. The woman who brought the group the bundle of clothes showed obvious relief that something would finally happen with the contents of the large plastic bag.

Some of the group members had known Shalva. Some knew her mother; some, her daughters. None had known her well. They poured the clothing onto the table in the studio where they met. Both the sadness and the profound act of what they were trying to create overwhelmed them. Eventually, they threw themselves into the easy part, ripping seams out of jeans and skirts and blouses so that they would have flat pieces of fabric. At first they thought of making a quilt where parts of the clothing kept its identity as a sleeve or a pant leg. But when they laid out the fabric for that idea, they could see that they needed to step away from such a direct and visceral reference to Shalva. Once they were holding a piece of pink patterned cotton— and not a blouse—the grief involved in what they were doing became manageable.

They wanted to make two separate quilts that would be similar to each other, yet distinctive, so that each girl could have her own piece of her mother's life. They began to cut the material into 6½-by-6½-inch squares, which they affixed to their batting wall, and then they began arranging and rearranging them. This process took a number of months. They were concerned not only with creating a design that would please all of them, but one that would be replicable and balanced between the two. If the quilt on the right had a square with a preserved jeans pocket, what did the quilt on the left have with a similarly unique piece of fabric? The delicate Indian fabrics were beautiful, but would they hold up in the quilt? How to arrange the colors and patterns to their liking, while keeping in mind the memory a particular piece might evoke for the girls? When it was time to select the border fabric, they deliberated for a very long time over the color until one member fortuitously walked into a meeting wearing a strong purple sweater and stood near the quilts. That was it—two slightly different purples, one for each quilt, resolved that dilemma.

They talked with Shalva's mother. Had there been anything special that Shalva would say to the girls that they would remember? Her mother recounted that each night, when Shalva put her daughters to bed, she sang Shlomo Carlebach's "Angel Song." They wrote the words on the computer in Hebrew, printed them out, and then traced them on the border fabric using tailor's chalk. Painstakingly, they embroidered the Hebrew words so they encircled the quilt, just as Shalva had encircled her daughters with her love.

Finally, after many months of work, they finished and let the family know they were ready to give the girls their gifts. Their grandmother created a beautiful ceremony. Shalva's family, members of the Quilting Group, and Shalva's friends who had participated in her healing circle when she was ill—the friends who had saved her clothing without really knowing why—all came together one May afternoon. Several people spoke, a musician led the gathering in singing some songs, they ate beautifully decorated homemade heart-shaped cookies, and they presented the quilts to the girls.

When they started as a group, they weren't sure where they were going. But over time theirs has developed into a group of Jewish women who meet a few times a month to create works from their hands, doing *hiddur mitzvah* (beautifying and enhancing a mitzvah). They come together to help people get married, to become b'nei mitzvah, to help Jewish organizations raise enough money to balance their budgets, to make beautiful things for Jewish public spaces, and to help people mourn their losses and celebrate the lives of those lost. They started out thinking they could do this by studying sacred texts, but instead found that in creating beautiful things through fabric they were stitching a tangible link to their Jewish spirituality.

# Getting Started

*Finished size:* 85 inches by 77 inches

Refer to "General How-To's for Quilt Making," pages 245–251, and "General How-To's for Lettering," pages 252–254.

## WHAT YOU'LL NEED

Clothing and linens (tablecloths, scarves, etc.) of the person being memorialized or honored

Fabric for backing, 81 inches by 89 inches (piece as necessary to obtain dimensions at least 2 inches larger all around than the quilt top)

Batting, 89 inches by 81 inches

Sewing and quilting thread to match most fabrics

Embroidery needle and 6-strand embroidery floss in colors to contrast with the border fabric

Fabric pencils in light and dark colors

## HOW-TO'S

*Notes:*

- The process used in making these quilts would work for anyone making a memorial quilt out of fabrics from someone who has died. *Alternatively,* as in the book *The Keeping Quilt* by Patricia Polacco, you could use worn-out or outgrown children's clothing, fashioned into a quilt as a keepsake of childhood.

- Unless otherwise indicated, pin pieces together with right sides facing. Stitch ¼ inch from the raw edges. Press the seam allowances to one side, if not as you go, then at least before joining stitched rows together.

1. Decide whether or not to keep any pockets, buttons, sleeves, or the like in the quilt. (Children love having a pocket to store secret things in.)

2. Choose the size of the blocks: These quilts feature 6-by-6-inch squares. With ¼-inch seam allowances, you will need to cut 6½-inch

squares. Cut a 6½-inch-square template from cardboard. Look through the garments to find that expanse of fabric. If helpful, cut or rip the seams apart first. Lay the template on the garment piece so that the threads run parallel to the edges of the square. Use a pencil to trace around the template, and then cut out the square along the marked lines.

3. A design wall is extremely useful for the next step. You can make your own by draping some flannel or batting over a door. For optimal results, stretch white flannel over a piece of 4-by-8-foot foam core board from the lumberyard; staple edges to the other side to secure. The squares of fabric stick to your design wall and allow you to stand back and look at your design to better judge the composition. (In the studio the Quilting Group uses, the design wall is a plain white wall on which large pieces of quilt batting hang. As a square was cut, they would stick it up on the batting, which gripped it in place without the need for pins. Then, they would look for another fabric that would go well beside it, and cut out a square of this 2nd fabric.)

4. Arrange and rearrange the squares until you find groupings in which the colors of the 16 adjacent squares work well together. Before you sew them together, make sure they work well with the grouping of 16 next to them. You might wish to design the layout of the entire quilt before sewing a single square. For the Shalva quilts, the Quilting Group arranged 12 squares across and 9 squares top to bottom.

5. When you are sure you like the final design, machine-stitch the squares in each row together, leaving ¼-inch seam allowances. Press the seam allowances to the right on odd rows, and to the left on even rows. Then pin the rows together: to obtain crisply matched angles at the corners, nestle the seam allowances that go in opposing directions together, and secure each of these junctures with a pin. As you stitch across, ¼ inch from the edges, remove each pin before the sewing machine needle reaches it. Press these seam allowances downward.

6. For inner borders, measure the quilt center. Here, the 9 by 12 squares measure 54 inches by 72 inches, including seam allowances all around. Cut two strips 2 inches by 56$\frac{1}{2}$ inches—or the width of your quilt center plus 2$\frac{1}{2}$ inches—from high-contrast fabric. Pin, then stitch them to the narrower ends of the quilt center. Press seam allowances outward, then trim the ends of the inner borders so they are flush with the quilt center edges. Next, cut 2 strips 2 inches by 74$\frac{1}{2}$ inches or the length of your quilt center plus 2$\frac{1}{2}$ inches; pin, sew, press, and trim as before.

7. For the wide, outer border, measure the width of the piece, and add 2 inches. Cut 10$\frac{1}{2}$-inch-wide strips to this measurement. Measure the length, add 24 inches, and cut 10$\frac{1}{2}$-inch strips to this measurement.

8. If you want to embroider a design on the outer borders, as the Quilting Group did on the Shalva quilts, mark and embroider the design before sewing the outer borders to the quilt top. It is easier to embroider a strip of border fabric than the whole quilt top. An embroidery hoop can be used, if desired. Look for appropriate phrases in English or Hebrew on the Internet. Paste your phrase into a document, and increase the font size as desired. Print it out, and position it under the border, pinning to secure. Hold the border, with the pattern underneath, over a sunny window, and trace the text using fabric pencils that show up well. To embroider the outer borders, separate the 6-strand embroidery floss, and use 3 strands in the needle. Work a chain stitch along the marked pattern lines.

9. Attach the outer borders, following step 6. Beginning with each of the narrower strips, pin, sew, press, and trim as before. Then join the longer borders in the same way.

10. Make a quilt sandwich: First, lay the backing right side down on a large, flat surface. Center the batting over the backing. Then, center the quilt top right side up, on top of the batting. Baste the layers together to keep them from shifting. Quilt as desired by hand or sewing machine. The Quilting Group cut out *hamsas* (see patterns on page 16) from parchment paper. They pressed the patterns, shiny

side down, on the quilt over the intersections of 6-inch squares. They used quilting thread and quilted around the shapes by hand. Then they peeled off the patterns.

11. Again lay the quilt on a large, flat surface. Cut the batting even with the quilt top. Cut the backing so it extends only 1 inch beyond the quilt top. Fold the extending edge $\frac{1}{2}$ inch to the wrong side, then $\frac{1}{2}$ inch over the batting and quilt top. Pin, then slip-stitch in place.

This chapter is dedicated to Shalva's memory.

# About the Quilters

**Diane Bernbaum** has been the director of Midrasha, a community Hebrew high school in Berkeley, California, for thirty years. She makes a lot of baby quilts, many for past faculty and students. She learned to knit when she was four, to sew in home economics class, and to quilt about twenty-five years ago when her children were home with the chicken pox.

**Carol Dorf** is a poet and math teacher. She has almost no background in fabric arts, but her grandparents owned a sewing notions shop. She loves sewing by hand, and is OK with ironing.

**Lee Inman Feinstein**, who holds a BS in textile design, has worked as a travel agent and has been a spinner/weaver in her spare time. She has sewn many of her own clothes since the 1960s. She started quilting five years ago, when she retired.

**Karen Benioff Friedman** is a visual artist working in the San Francisco Bay Area. After attending Amherst College, she moved west and worked as production manager for an East Bay magazine, married, and became a mother. In 2003 Karen decided to devote her time to printmaking (primarily monotype) and creating art quilts. Her skills in quilting are self-taught, and she adores the group process for its collaborative qualities and the educational potential for each member.

**Rivka Greenberg** has embroidered from childhood and made most of her clothes in high school. Raising three daughters, working as a consultant and evaluator with children and families at risk, and teaching in universities meant putting her sewing aside until she got involved in the Quilting Group with No Name. Quilting with these creative and multifaceted Jewish women adds a wonderful texture to her life.

**Shari Rifas** was taught to sew by her sister when she was ten years old, and she made her first quilt as a high school senior project. She gave up quilting when her children were born, until she discovered the Quilting Group with No Name. Shari loves the collaborative process with these talented women. Every decision is an adventure and no path is linear.

Inspired by a neighbor's Victorian crazy quilt, **Claire Sherman** started her first quilt at age thirteen. She finished it five years later and took it with her to the Rhode Island School of Design, where she majored in ceramics and received her BFA. She spent the next twenty-five years making ceramic Judaica and teaching art workshops, but she made no quilts. In 2006, after reading Jennifer Chiaverini's quilt novels, she fell in love with quilting once again and has been quilting avidly ever since. Claire contributed three individual projects to *Jewish Threads* as well: her *Ushpizin* Quilt (chapter 15), *Afikomen* Envelopes (chapter 21), and Hannah's Baby Quilt (chapter 23).

# Inspirations

As I was gathering projects and stories for *Jewish Threads*, I came across a number of pieces that seemed too complicated for relative newcomers to needlecrafts or even experienced fabric artists to make on their own. Even working on them in a group might be challenging, and most of these drew on the expertise of fiber art professionals. For me—and I hope for you, too—these advanced projects fall under the heading of "Inspirations."

## NCJW, West Morris Chuppah

This magnificent appliquéd and quilted chuppah, or bridal canopy, was made by members of the National Council of Jewish Women (NCJW), West Morris (New Jersey) Section. As co-president of NCJW, West Morris Section, and as one of those who appliquéd a square and made many grape clusters for the chuppah, I take immense pride in this exquisite piece of fabric art and share with my fellow NCJW, West Morris members a wonderful sense of accomplishment.

A small core group of women—Donna Gross and Lesley Frost (two contributors to *Jewish Threads*), plus Dorothy Cohen, Susan Neigher, and Lois Dornfeld—met weekly over a two-year period to sew and schmooze together. Many others, including my mother-in-law, Stella Hart Grayson, and I, stitched panels or made clusters of fabric grapes at home. (I sewed the Doves panel, which was placed at the center of the chuppah; my mom-in-law stitched the Apples & Honey panel, which was the basis for Donna's Apples & Honey Challah Cover, chapter 13.)

בורא פרי הגפן

Panels of Stars of David also grace the 8-by-8-foot chuppah. June Shatken, an NCJW, West Morris member and a professional artist, created a signature quilt with the names of everyone who contributed to the chuppah in one way or another: this forms the top, outside part of the chuppah. Under the guidance and general design of master quilter Mark Lipinski and with additional designs created by Donna Gross, the chuppah slowly came together.

Mark had been the special guest speaker at one of our NCJW events. Afterward, inspired by his talk, several members came up with the idea of making a quilted chuppah. Little did we realize how much time and effort would be involved in this mammoth project. Beyond the small sewing circle, dedicated sewers appliquéd thousands of fabric grape clusters, which were later sewn onto the valances and pole covers. Also sewn as appliqués were lilies of the valley and pomegranates, both species cited in the Torah.

A breathtaking piece, this chuppah was the product of many hands working together under the guidance of a talented professional. It holds a special place in my heart: not only was it the inspiration for this book, but my brother-in-law, Lee March Grayson, and his wife, Judy, were married under it in the summer of 2009.

## Arna's Tallit Bag

Arna Shefrin's stunning needlepoint tallit bag pictures a scene of Jerusalem in glorious colors. Arna, who also contributed a needlepoint piece to *Jewish Threads* called Arna's *Ahavah* Needlepoint (chapter 3), used an array of different needlepoint stitches and threads to create this exquisite tallit bag for her husband. Working on this stunning bag with threads of silk, metallic polyester, wool, and satin, the fabric artist thinks of needlepoint as "painting with threads."

As a passionate knitter, needlepointer, and fabric artist, who makes many of her own clothes, Arna wanted to create a special piece for her husband, Hersh, who has always supported and encouraged her efforts. She had knit a *kippah* for him, which he wears to synagogue frequently. But she was determined to make him something more elaborate and personal, something that expressed her deep feelings for him and his

love of Judaism. So she decided to make him a bag to hold his tallit, a treasured Jewish ritual garment. Arna's husband cherishes this one-of-a-kind tallit bag. "He truly appreciates all the love, creativity, and time that went into making it," Arna points out.

And time it did take! Recalls Arna: "Over a six-month period, I spent between 250 and 300 pleasurable hours working on this tallit bag." She started with the City of Jerusalem, a Judaic needlepoint canvas from Needlepoint Unlimited. The design is hand-painted on a 10-by-11-inch 13-mesh rectangle. "I wanted the various stitches and threads to convey texture and perspective." Arna, who lives in Menlo Park, California, used about twenty-five different stitches and fifteen different threads on the canvas. After she had completed the needlepoint, the canvas was professionally finished to create a deep gold velvet tallit bag, which has a finished size of 9 inches by 12 inches; it is lined in white satin, has a braid around the perimeter, and features a zippered, tasseled closure.

## Another Chuppah

Sandy Eichengreen Bailen's mother, Ursel Behr Eichengreen-Fuchs, also enjoyed doing needlepoint. Over the course of four years, she designed and hand-stitched a stunning needlepoint chuppah with upward of one million stitches, a feat hard to imagine in today's world of instant gratification. For Sandy, who lives in Louisville, Kentucky, this chuppah has become part of her family's heritage, a loving legacy her mother left to future generations.

The designs embroidered on the chuppah are intended to impart specific meaning to those who join their lives together beneath it, presumably future generations of her family. "The trunk of the tree shows the strength of our family now and in the future, while the roots symbolize the importance of our past generations, who will never be forgotten," Sandy points out, in describing the meaning of the designs gracing her mother's needle-pointed chuppah. "On this tree is an abundance of fruit. This signifies the hope that those who stand under this cover will have many children to carry on the name and traditions of our family.

"The red roses stand for health and beauty. It is the artist's wish that all who come together under this chuppah have lives that reflect the characteristics of this noble flower. Among the beauty and strength of the roses are concealed thorns. This shows us that life will have painful moments. However, with trust and understanding, these difficulties can be faced and overcome.

"The final symbol is the white dove. Beneath its wings all who are joined together are blessed with peace for themselves and all humanity."

## Hannah's Woven *Shalom* Wall Hanging

Hannah Sue Margolis, who settled in San Antonio after twenty-seven years as a physical therapist in the U.S. Air Force, changed course entirely when she was drawn to spinning and weaving, taking professional classes at the Southwest School of Art (SSA), also in San Antonio. For the past twenty-five years, she's been weaving all sorts of pieces—for herself and others—and working with novice weavers to enhance their skills.

A perennial student of weaving, Hannah decided to make this 16-by-30-inch wall hanging to infuse one of her pieces with her sense of Jewishness. Recalling how this came about, she says, "A friend had asked me to weave a tapestry for her sister's congregation, in her sister's memory. I wanted to make something light and airy. Determining to use the word *shalom* was easy. The feeling of peace I exuded as I wove made this especially meaningful for me. Using many colors added to the brightness of my thoughts."

The yarn, a natural-color cotton-linen blend, allows the weaver to maintain an openness in the background weave. This adds yet another design element to the tapestry—an airiness that suffuses the weaver's sense of peace as she weaves this beautiful piece. Hannah feels this wall hanging shows up best with light behind it, such as a sunny window, but displaying it on a white wall works just as well.

Hannah's love of Yiddishkeit comes through in this woven wall hanging, whose doves—plus the English and Hebrew lettering—give it the kind of subtle beauty and majesty that imbue the word *shalom.* Beyond a sense of "peace," *shalom* resonates with meanings, from "wholeness" to "integrity"—all foundations of Judaism, Jewish observance, and Jewish life through the ages.

## Women's Torah Project Bimah Cloth

In 2003 Kadima, now the Kadima Reconstructionist Community of Seattle, commissioned modern history's first woman-scribed Torah (www.womenstorah.com). The community was astonished to realize that this had never been done before. Kadima started with a single scribe in the usual tradition. In the end this beautiful Torah was scribed by six different women from three continents and is adorned and accompanied by the work of eight women artists, also from three continents. The Torah was completed in October 2010 at a *siyyum,* or completion celebration, where the scribes, artists, and the larger community gathered and sewed the panels together.

Lois Gaylord, who contributed two projects to *Jewish Threads* (Lois's *Sefer* Placekeepers, chapter 8, and Julia's Bat Mitzvah Challah Cover, chapter 25) and whose family joined Kadima in 2005, volunteered soon after to weave a bimah cloth for the woman-scribed Torah. Says Lois, "I saw this women-scribed Torah as a manifestation of *tikkun olam,* part of the process to help restore the balance of female and male energies in the world, and I wanted to express that in my design."

The design begins with a blue border to symbolize the energy defining sacred space—the space where the Torah would be unrolled to be read. Two concepts are represented in the design. Torah is called a Tree of Life, and the wings of Shechinah (the feminine divine presence) have been over this project since its inception. To honor both these concepts, the painted warp design evokes either a leaf or a feather. The tablet-woven band acts as the spine of the leaf/feather, with the Hebrew inscription: "She is a Tree of Life to all who hold her tight."

Lois wove the cloth, measuring 38 inches by 75 inches, with a linen warp and two different silk yarns for the weft; she wove the tablet-woven band with the inscription out of silk. The artist painted the leaf/feather design, with fiber-reactive dyes, onto the warp threads before putting them on the loom. The color in the band is also a painted warp.

The merging colors of red for male and blue for female, in a lovely chromatic smear, represent the rebalancing of those energies. Lois fashioned this bimah cloth (also known as a *shulchan,* or table, cover) in the spirit of *hiddur mitzvah,* the beautification of a mitzvah.

While these pieces may be beyond the skills of most of us, I wanted to share with you some magnificent Jewish fabric crafts that talented craft artists have produced either on their own or in a group with the help of professionals. It's amazing what you can do with a needle and thread, fabric, yarn, and the spiritual intention to make something Jewishly meaningful, beautiful, and destined to be handed down from generation to generation.

# Final Threads

## General How-To's for Quilt Making

For enthusiastic novices—relative newcomers to needlecrafts who want to share their love of Judaism with others by making their own Jewish fabric crafts—this section offers a clear overview of quilt-making basics. Beginners: Please read this over before you begin any of the quilting projects in this book. You might also want to consult some of the resources in "Suggested Reading for Beginners" on pages 265–266. Experienced quilters: Refer to this information on an as-needed basis.

### Materials

Yardage amounts for quilter's cottons are based on 42-inch widths unless otherwise indicated. When possible, the "How-To's" suggest that you can use fat quarters (18 inches by 21 inches) or fat eighths (9 inches by 21 inches). Prewash all cotton fabrics in hot water, and dry in the dryer to preshrink them—loosely woven fabrics, such as flannel, will shrink a lot—and to remove excess dyes and prevent bleeding. Always remove the selvages—the tightly woven, lengthwise edges of the yardage. Iron the fabric after drying, so you will be working with crisp, unwrinkled fabric.

Use 50- or 60-weight cotton thread in the sewing machine needle and bobbin for sewing (the same for hand-appliqué), and heavier thread for hand- or machine-quilting (top of machine only).

## Tools

Here's what you'll want to have handy:

Paper, tracing paper, and parchment paper, for patterns

Rotary cutting supplies: rotary cutter, cutting mat, acrylic quilting rulers

Sewing machine in good working order

Thread snips or small embroidery scissors

Pins and a pincushion

Sewing and quilting needles

Fabric markers for light and dark fabrics (always test on your fabrics before you use them to be sure the marks will come out, unless you want a permanent mark, as on Menorah Rotenberg's Challah Cover, chapter 12)

Steam iron, ironing surface, and nonstick presser sheet

## Cutting

Most of the quilting projects in this book are made more quickly and with greater precision if you rotary-cut your pieces. Generally, use a cutter with a 45-millimeter blade that's sharp. Always work on a cutting mat. Use quilter's rulers—thick acrylic rulers to measure and ensure straight cuts. A large 15-inch square and a large rectangle, 6 inches by 24 inches, are the most versatile for cutting backgrounds, borders, and backings, as well as doing the squaring up accurately. Keep your fingers away from the edge, and keep the blade flat against the ruler. Close the blade when you're done cutting.

For scissors cutting, use a sharp pair designed for cutting fabrics. Be sure to measure and mark lines before you cut them.

## Borders

The "What You'll Need" lists often include fabric yardages for extra-long borders. Your quilt may very well end up a little shorter or longer than the dimensions indicate, depending on your seam allowances, cutting, and pressing techniques. It's best to wait and measure your quilt top before cutting borders to the exact lengths you need. Pin the border strips in place along the sides of your quilt top, with right sides together and raw edges even. Stitch ¼ inch from the raw edge. Press seam allowances toward the borders. Trim the borders evenly along the ends before adding borders along the perpendicular edges in the same way.

## Piecing

Unless otherwise indicated, place pieces together with right sides facing and edges even. If helpful, insert pins at the corners, at intervals in between, and wherever you'd like to match seams. Take care to remove pins as your machine needle reaches them, as stitching over them will often break the needle. Machine-stitch, leaving ¼-inch seam allowances.

## Pressing

For piecing, you can often finger-press seams until you finish a unit, make a lot of units, and then do all the pressing with an iron. Use a hot, dry iron set for cotton, a lower setting if your project includes synthetics or delicate fabrics.

## Hand Appliqué

Choose threads to match the color of fabric appliqués. Knot the end of the thread, and insert the needle under the appliqué to begin, ³⁄₁₆ inch from the edge. Use the length of the needle to guide the fabric edge under about ³⁄₁₆ inch, and hold in place with the thumb of your non-stitching hand. Bring the needle into the background fabric, and back up to the folded edge of the appliqué, passing through the folded edge and emerging about ¼ inch farther along. Take a tiny stitch through just a couple of threads of the fabric, before stitching through the background again. Continue in this way. End with a backstitch on the back to secure, guide the thread under the background behind the appliqué, bring the needle out a little ways away, and clip the tail end close to the surface.

## Fusible Appliqué

Fusible web is available by the yard at any fabric store; use the paper-backed type. Before applying it to fabrics, wash the fabrics to remove any sizing or finishes. Follow the manufacturer's instructions for the fusible web you are using. All product information will direct you to place fusible web with the rough side down on the wrong side of your fabric. Protect your iron and ironing surface with a presser cloth or with a Teflon or other nonstick pressing sheet. You can also use parchment paper, sold in grocery stores for lining baking sheets, for this purpose. If the fabric is synthetic, use a press cloth over the fabric as well, so the heat of the iron does not melt the fibers. Place a hot iron on the fabric for several seconds. Repeat across the surface so that every part of the fusible web gets properly and completely adhered.

Many quilters prefer to trace or pin patterns to the right side of the fabric, to avoid the need to reverse designs and to allow for the removal of the paper backing before cutting out the shape. Peeling off the release paper after the shape is cut can be more difficult and often results in appliqué edges that become stretched or distorted. If you have difficulty removing the release paper on a cutout shape, use a pin to score the paper backing, and remove the paper in pieces, working from the center outward.

Cut out fused fabrics with sharp scissors. Position the appliqué on the background. Either pin pieces in place, or fuse-tack them by pressing with an iron for just 2–3 seconds. When you are ready to secure everything permanently, press for about 10 seconds, using a steam iron or, if you prefer, a damp pressing cloth. Steam-press from the back as well.

Fused appliqués may, in time, lift away from the background. Therefore, you really should secure all fused appliqués with stitching. If you do this after sandwiching the quilt, your stitches will simultaneously quilt your piece. Zigzag-stitch along the raw edges, using a clear, monofilament thread in the top of the machine and standard sewing thread in the bobbin. Or, use a very fine, wide zigzag stitch to satin-stitch along the raw edge in a matching or contrasting color and a heavier thread in the needle, such as a 40-weight rayon or cotton. Be sure to test your machine's tension, as the fused fabric and background are a firmer surface than usual.

## Sandwiching Your Quilt

Cut batting and backing fabric 2 inches larger all around than the quilt top. For securing the layers together quickly, use fusible batting, or apply basting spray in a ventilated area. Place the backing right side down on a large, flat surface, and spray. Smooth the batting on top. Spray again. Center the quilt top right side up over the batting and backing. *Alternatively,* use giant basting stitches, safety pins, or even straight pins to keep the layers from shifting.

## Quilting

Quilt the major elements of your quilt, such as the center design and the borders, in the ditch—the seam between two pieces, as in Stuart's Healing Quilt (chapter 29). Do the longest straight lines or consistent, gentle curves with a walking foot, which keeps the backing from shifting, so the quilting is neat on the back. For all other quilting, start at the center of your quilt sandwich, and work outward in all directions.

For **echo quilting**, which follows the contours of a shape in concentric rounds, use the width of the presser foot to keep the lines equally spaced, as in Ruth Lenk's ChanuCats Quilt (chapter 17, at right).

PHOTO: JONATHAN SCHROTT

For **free-motion quilting**, use a darning foot, which allows you to move the quilt sandwich in any direction. Practice until you are able to move the piece and run the machine smoothly and produce stitches that are fairly consistent in length. Free-motion quilting can follow a shape, like the vines of Ruth's *Hamsa* Wall Hanging (chapter 2), or they can be truly freehand, meandering over the surface to fill the space nicely, like the curlicue pattern used in Susan's Tree of Life Wall Hanging (chapter 1, at left).

## Finishing

After quilting, trim the edges, so the edges of the quilt sandwich are even and square. If your quilt is to hang on a wall, you'll want to make a sleeve or channel casing for a rod or piece of lattice to pass through. Cut a rectangle of fabric 3 inches shorter than the edge that will be at the top, and 8½ inches wide. Hem the short ends of the rectangle, fold it lengthwise in half, and lightly press. Center it along the top edge of the backing, with raw edges even. As you bind your quilt, these raw edges will be enclosed. After the binding is attached, slip-stitch along the bottom fold of the casing to secure it to the backing.

**To bind the quilt,** cut strips: Unless otherwise indicated, cut them 2½ inches wide along the grain of the fabric. For a double-fold binding, press the strip or strips lengthwise in half, with the right side facing out. Beginners may wish to simply prepare binding for each edge, equal in length to the sides, and ½ inch extra for binding the top and bottom edges. Bind the sides first, then the top and bottom, tucking in the ends to neatly finish the corners. More experienced quilters may wish to piece the strips together so you have 8 inches more than will fit all around the quilt, press the seam allowances open, miter the corners, and overlap the ends of the binding strips neatly. In either case, pin the binding to the right side of the quilt, with raw edges even, and stitch through all layers, leaving ¼-inch seam allowances and removing pins as you come to them. Bring the long folded edge of the binding over the edges of the quilt sandwich, and pin it to the backing so it covers the machine stitching. Using thread in a color that matches the binding, slip-stitch the folded edge to the back of the quilt.

**Add a label** to the back of the quilt to properly document your tribute. Quilt labels generally include your name, possibly your relationship to the recipient (such as *Aunt, Grandma,* or the like), the recipient's name, the date, and the city and state where you live. Future generations will thank you for it! Either fuse the label to the back, or turn the edges under and slip-stitch them in place, penetrating the backing only. If desired, keep the label open on one side, like a pocket. Slip in a letter, photos, or anything that helps you chronicle the occasion for which you made this quilt.

# General How-To's for Lettering

As you're designing your Jewish fabric craft, consider personalizing your work by inserting words or phrases that have special meaning for you or the intended recipient. Here are some suggestions for ways to incorporate lettering—in English and/or Hebrew—in your project.

## For Even-Weave Fabric or Needlepoint Canvas

Use the chart for Hebrew letters in chapter 27 ("Judy's Garden of Eden Tallit Bag"), or seek out a different style or an English alphabet in books or online. On graph paper, copy the appropriate letters, spacing them out consistently. Trim the paper and fold it to locate the center, and then stitch the letters from the center of the space on the fabric or canvas where you wish to place them.

## For Writing Directly on Fabric

Iron a piece of parchment paper to the back of the fabric to stabilize it, so it's easier to write on. Practice writing on scrap paper cut to the same size as the space you wish to fill. Place this "test" sample beside the fabric as a guide. Use a permanent marker or a fabric marker to do the writing. Iron to heat-set the ink.

## For Writing or Painting

Use your computer to plan the font style and size of the letters you want. Your computer's document software undoubtedly includes many choices for English; do a search for free downloads of Hebrew letters. At press time, www.shalom-peace.com/pdf/alephbetcards.pdf offered a number of easy-to-use Hebrew fonts. Print out the words you'd like to grace your project. Trace them onto the shiny, waxy side of parchment paper. Iron to the wrong side of your fabric. Trace the letters with a permanent marker. Or trace just the outlines with fabric pencil. Leave parchment paper in place, to act as a stabilizer, and fill in using a small, flat paintbrush and fabric or acrylic paint. Use a small, pointy or tapered brush to neaten. Let dry, then add a second coat.

## For Stenciling

There are countless choices for alphabet stencils. For *aleph-bet* stencils, consider www.stencilease.com (800-334-1776), which features Hebrew letters 1 inch high and 3 inches high; or Benny's Educational Toys Aleph-Bet hard plastic stencil—GAN455 for letters ⅝ inch high, at www.tjssc.com (800-984-3616).

Achieve neat, consistent looks by drawing guidelines on fabric lightly with pencil or with a dressmaker's chalk pencil (also known as tailor's chalk). Do a test, stenciling on paper or scrap fabric to determine spacing, and use that measurement between letters. Spray the back of the stencil with repositionable spray adhesive, and press tightly to the surface of the fabric. Dip a stencil brush into textile paint, acrylic craft paint, or stenciling paint; be sure to test it on scrap fabric. If needed, tamp the brush on a paper towel first, to remove excess paint. Keep brushes dry so paint does not run. To change colors, use another brush, or wash and thoroughly dry the brush between colors.

## For Rubber Stamping

Seek out rubber stamps for alphabets and *aleph-bets* on the Internet. Use guidelines, test on a separate piece of scrap fabric, and measure to space consistently, the same as you would do for stenciling.

## For Embroidery

Print out, trace, or draw lettering onto paper. Position on the wrong side of the fabric, pinning to secure. If you are working on a quilted project, mark the top before it is sandwiched with batting and backing. Hold up the fabric, with the pattern underneath, over a light box or against a sunny window; tape to secure. Trace the text using fabric pencils in a color that contrasts with the fabric and therefore shows up well. Do not work embroidery over one layer of fabric; stitches will generally pull and distort the surface. For quilted projects, add batting and backing, and then embroider. For single-layer items, iron or baste a tearaway stabilizer to the back, and remove it carefully after embroidery. Separate six-strand embroidery floss and use only two, three, or four strands in the needle to backstitch, stem-stitch, or chain-stitch the letters. See the "Stitch Guide" on pages 255–256.

## For Appliqué

Enlarge and use patterns in this book (see, for example, those in chapters 9, 10, and 20). *Alternatively,* use your computer to plan the font style and size for the letters you want (see "For Writing or Painting," page 252).

**For needle-turn appliqué:** Using permanent marker, trace outlines of each letter onto the matte side of parchment paper. Cut out along the marked edges. Iron to the right side of fabric so letters are at least ½ inch apart. Cut out ¼ inch beyond the marked edges, for seam allowances, and press edges to wrong side. Use slip stitches to secure the edges of the appliqué as you work, traveling a few thread lengths under the background.

**For raw edge or fusible appliqué:** First back desired fabrics with fusible web, following manufacturer's instructions. Remove the paper backing. Trace the desired letters to the right side of the fabrics, using a fine-tip permanent marker. Cut out just to the inside of the marked lines. Iron fusible-backed appliqué to the background, following manufacturer's instructions. To prevent appliqués from lifting over time, stitch over the edges, using straight stitch, zigzag stitch, or blanket stitch, by machine or by hand, and working over stabilizer or over sandwiched layers.

# Stitch Guide

These graphics illustrate how to do the specified stitches. See also "Suggested Reading for Beginners," pages 265–266.

## Embroidery

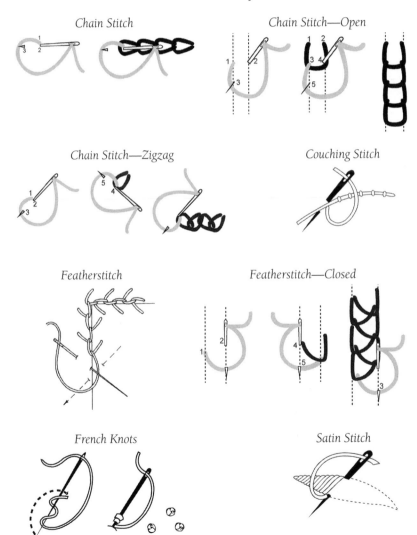

Chain Stitch

Chain Stitch—Open

Chain Stitch—Zigzag

Couching Stitch

Featherstitch

Featherstitch—Closed

French Knots

Satin Stitch

# Needlepoint

### Basketweave Stitch

### Slanted Gobelin Stitch

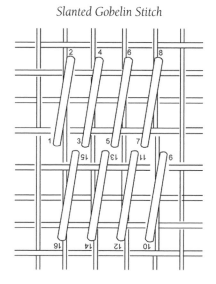

### Straight Gobelin Stitch

# Sewing

### Blanket Stitch

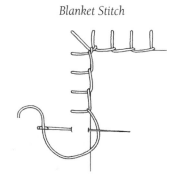

### Running Stitch

### Slip Stitch

### Stem Stitch

# Resources

Most of the supplies needed for the projects in *Jewish Threads* can be found at your local yarn, craft, or fabric store. For a few of the more unusual materials, here are some online sources—plus one Minnesota store that ships for free—to check out if your local store does not carry them.

## Chapter 5: Barbara's Felted Grapes Purse

*Grayson Purse Handles*

  www.jimmybeanswool.com

## Chapter 8: Lois's *Sefer* Placekeepers

*Metallic Fabric Paint*

  Lumiere by Jacquard:

    www.jacquardproducts.com/products/paints/lumiere
    www.dharmatrading.com
    www.dickblick.com

## Chapters 9 and 10: Sukkot & Shavuot Torah Mantles

*Needlepoint Yarn*

  Frosty Rays needlepoint yarn:

    www.mscanvashouse.com/shop/thread_frostyrays.html

## Chapter 24: Vicki's Cross-Stitch *Wimpel*

*Even-Weave Cross-Stitch Cloth, 60 inches (Zweigart or Salem)*

  Nadelkunst
  212 North Minnesota St.
  New Ulm, MN 56073
  (507) 354-8708
  (The owner, Cindy Hillesheim, ships for free.)

## Chapter 25: Julia's Bat Mitzvah Challah Cover

*Linens*

www.fabrics-store.com

Check the "Doggie Bag" for smaller pieces.

*Gold Metallic Yarn*

Madeira number 15, Gold 22:

www.madeiramart.com

## Chapter 27: Judy's Garden of Eden Tallit Bag

*Aida Cross-Stitch Cloth*

www.needleworkersdelight.com/aidacloth.html

*DMC Floss*

www.dmc-usa.com

# The Blessing of Working Together

Jewish tradition encourages us to worship together, celebrate holidays and other *simchahs* (joyous occasions) together, and sit shiva together when a loved one passes on—all as a way to enrich our lives and sustain our community. So if you're inspired to make a piece based on one or more of the projects in this book, consider working together with others to bring your idea to fruition. No need to be discouraged from stitching an heirloom piece with spiritual intention when others can help you shape your idea for a Jewish fabric craft and make it a reality.

## Projects for Sewing Circles

As you work in a group with people of varied levels of expertise in sewing, knitting, crocheting, cross-stitching, and other needlecrafts, you exchange design ideas, learn new techniques, and explore unexpected ways to combine colors, fabrics, threads, and yarns. Among the *Jewish Threads* projects that lend themselves to group work are the following:

Ruth's *Hamsa* Wall Hanging, chapter 2

Esther's Crazy Quilt *Shulchan* Cover, chapter 7

Sukkot Torah Mantle, chapter 9

Shavuot Torah Mantle, chapter 10

Stuart's Healing Quilt, chapter 29

Shalva Quilts, chapter 30

## Projects for Parents & Children

While you need some background in needlecrafts to make most of the Jewish fabric crafts in *Jewish Threads,* parts of certain projects can be done together with a child or a number of children, including the following:

Claire's *Ushpizin* Quilt, chapter 15

Dancing Hamantaschen, chapter 18

Lesley's Purim Puppets, chapter 19

# Projects for Holidays

A number of projects in *Jewish Threads* focus on holiday themes, so consider making one of more of these for an upcoming holiday.

## Shabbat

Esther's Crazy Quilt Challah Cover, chapter 11
Menorah's Challah Cover, chapter 12
Donna's Apples & Honey Challah Cover, chapter 13
Julia's Bat Mitzvah Challah Cover, chapter 25

## Rosh Hashanah

Donna's Apples & Honey Challah Cover, chapter 13
Heather's High Holy Day Inspiration, chapter 14

## Sukkot

Sukkot Torah Mantle, chapter 9
Claire's *Ushpizin* Quilt, chapter 15

## Chanukah

Eleanor's *Chanukiah* Vest, chapter 16
Ruth's ChanuCats Quilt, chapter 17

## Purim

Dancing Hamantaschen, chapter 18
Lesley's Purim Puppets, chapter 19

## Passover

Shellie's Ten-Plagues Matzah Cover, chapter 20
Claire's *Afikomen* Envelopes, chapter 21
Zoë's Knit Seder Plate, chapter 22

## Shavuot

Shavuot Torah Mantle, chapter 10

# An Array of Techniques

The projects in *Jewish Threads* incorporate a wide range of needlecraft techniques.

## Quilting

Susan's Tree of Life Wall Hanging, chapter 1
Ruth's *Hamsa* Wall Hanging, chapter 2
Donna's Quilted *Shalom* Wall Hanging, chapter 4
Eleanor's Tree of Life Runner, chapter 6
Sukkot Torah Mantle, chapter 9
Esther's Crazy Quilt Challah Cover, chapter 11
Heather's High Holy Day Inspiration, chapter 14
Ruth's ChanuCats Quilt, chapter 17
Hannah's Baby Quilt, chapter 23
Stuart's Healing Quilt, chapter 29
Shalva Quilts, chapter 30

## Embroidery

Esther's Crazy Quilt *Shulchan* Cover, chapter 7
Lois's *Sefer* Placekeepers, chapter 8
Sukkot Torah Mantle, chapter 9
Shavuot Torah Mantle, chapter 10
Esther's Crazy Quilt Challah Cover, chapter 11
Menorah's Challah Cover, chapter 12
Shellie's Ten-Plagues Matzah Cover, chapter 20
Julia's Bat Mitzvah Challah Cover, chapter 25
Shalva Quilts, chapter 30

## Needlepoint

Arna's *Ahavah* Needlepoint, chapter 3
Sukkot Torah Mantle, chapter 9
Shavuot Torah Mantle, chapter 10

## Cross-Stitch

Vicki's Cross-Stitch *Wimpel*, chapter 24
Judy's Garden of Eden Tallit Bag, chapter 27

## Crochet

Sukkot Torah Mantle, chapter 9
Shavuot Torah Mantle, chapter 10

## Knitting

Barbara's Felted Grapes Purse, chapter 5
Zoë's Knit Seder Plate, chapter 22

## Felting

Barbara's Felted Grapes Purse, chapter 5

## Needle Felting

Debra's Tallit & Tallit Bag, chapter 28

# Jewish Imagery

In many *Jewish Threads* projects, symbols grounded in Jewish tradition abound. Here are some Jewish images to consider incorporating in your own fabric crafts:

Apples and honey

*Chai*

Challah

Doves

Dreidel

Hamantaschen

*Hamsa*

*Kiddush* cup

*Lulav* and *etrog*

Menorah/*chanukiah*

Olive branch

Rainbows

Shabbat candles

*Shalom*

Shofar

Star of David

Tablets of the Ten Commandments

The Hebrew letter *hey*

The Hebrew letter *shin*

The seven biblical fruits

Torah scrolls

Tree of Life

# From Sea to Shining Sea ... and Beyond

Contributors to *Jewish Threads* come from eleven U.S. states, plus the State of Israel.

*Alabama*
Julian M. Brook

*California*
Barbara D. Levinson
Quilting Group with No Name: Diane Bernbaum, Carol Dorf, Lee Feinstein, Rivka Greenberg, Karen Benioff Friedman, Shari Rifas, and Claire Sherman
Arna Shefrin
Claire Sherman

*Kentucky*
Sandy Eichengreen Bailen

*Massachusetts*
Zoë Scheffy

*Minnesota*
Vicki Pieser
Susan M. Rappaport
Judy Snitzer

*New Jersey*
Lesley Frost

Donna Gross
Ellen Muraskin and Marcy Thailer
Menorah Lafayette-Lebovics Rotenberg

*New York*
Judith S. Paskind
Susan Schrott
Heather G. Stoltz

*Pennsylvania*
Eleanor Levie

*Texas*
Hannah Sue Margolis

*Vermont*
Holly Levison

*Washington*
Shellie Black
Lois Gaylord

*Israel*
Ruth Lenk
Esther Tivé-Elterman

# Suggested Reading
# for Beginners

If you're new to fabric crafts, these books can ease your way into whichever craft you'd like to learn.

## Cross-Stitch

Greenoff, Jane. *The New Cross Stitchers' Bible: The Definitive Manual of Essential Cross Stitch and Counted Thread Techniques.* Rev. ed. Cincinnati: Dave & Charles Ltd., 2010.

Knox, Gerald M., contributing editor. *Better Homes and Gardens America's Best Cross-Stitch.* Des Moines, IA: Meredith Corporation, 1988.

## Embroidery

Eaton, Jan. *The Complete Stitch Encyclopedia.* Hauppauge, NY: Barron's Educational Series, A Quarto Book, 1986.

Hart, Jenny. *Embroidered Effects: Projects and Patterns to Inspire Your Stitching.* San Francisco: Chronicle Books, 2009.

## Knitting & Felting

Allen, Pam, Tracy L. Barr, and Shannon Okey. *Knitting for Dummies.* 2nd ed. Hoboken, NJ: Wiley Publishing, 2008.

Skolnik, Linda, and Janice MacDaniels. *The Knitting Way: A Guide to Spiritual Self-Discovery.* Woodstock, VT: SkyLight Paths Publishing, 2005.

Taylor, Kathleen. *Knit One, Felt Too: Discover the Magic of Knitted Felt with 25 Easy Patterns.* North Adams, MA: Storey Publishing, 2003.

## Needlepoint

Christensen, Jo Ippolito. *The Needlepoint Book: A Complete Update of the Classic Guide.* Rev. ed. New York: Fireside, 1999.

# Quilting

Fall, Cheryl. *Quilting for Dummies.* 2nd ed. Hoboken, NJ: Wiley Publishing, 2006.

McClun, Diane, and Laura Nownes. *Quilts! Quilts!! Quilts!!!: The Complete Guide to Quiltmaking.* 2nd ed. New York: McGraw-Hill, 1998.

Polacco, Patricia. *The Keeping Quilt.* New York: Aladdin Paperbacks, 2001.

Simon, Jeri. *Quilting: The Basics & Beyond.* Urbandale, IA: Landauer Books, 2010.

Witzenburg, Lynn. *Machine Quilting: The Basics & Beyond.* Urbandale, IA: Landauer Books, 2008.

Zimmerman, Darlene. *Quilting: The Complete Guide.* Iola, WI: Krause Publications, 2006.

# Sewing

Moebes, Deborah. *Stitch by Stitch: Learning to Sew One Project at a Time.* Cincinnati: Krause Publications, 2010.

Rupp, Diana. *Sew Everything Workshop: The Complete Step-by-Step Beginner's Guide.* New York: Workman Publishing, 2007.

Stewart, Martha. *Martha Stewart's Encyclopedia of Sewing and Fabric Crafts.* New York: Potter Craft, 2010.

# And Also Keep in Mind ...

Leaf, Reuben. *Hebrew Alphabets: 400 B.C.E. to Our Days.* New York: Bloch Publishing, 1976.

Ungerleider-Mayerson, Joy. *Jewish Folk Art: From Biblical Days to Modern Times.* New York: Simon & Schuster, 1987.

# Acknowledgments

Heartfelt thanks to all the contributors to *Jewish Threads*. Your understanding, infinite patience, and endless cooperation made writing this book an amazing journey for me. Your good spirits buoyed mine throughout the process. The creativity and spiritual intention that underlie all your projects are a marvelous testament to the collective Jewish spirit, which has sustained us through countless generations. I deeply appreciate how graciously you shared with me your work, your stories, and your time.

A big bouquet of thanks to Eleanor Levie, who kindly offered a critical eye to all the project write-ups on the first go-round. Her thoughtful and insightful comments made the project instructions much clearer and easier to follow. I am very much in Elly's debt for the time she took to review these "How-To's" and share her boundless knowledge of fabric crafts with readers of *Jewish Threads*. (She also contributed two lovely projects to this book—Eleanor's Tree of Life Runner, chapter 6, and Eleanor's *Chanukiah* Vest, chapter 16.)

Thanks, too, to Kevin Greene, whose clear and well-executed illustrations appear throughout these pages. Kevin's work gives many of the project instructions a visual complement that makes the patterns much easier to follow than they would have been otherwise.

I am grateful to the National Council of Jewish Women—especially the West Morris Section, of which I share the position of president with my friend, Susan Neigher—for giving me a wonderful circle of friends, many of whom tirelessly worked on the quilted chuppah that was the inspiration for this book. Among them: Lesley Frost and Donna Gross (both contributors to *Jewish Threads*—Lesley's Purim Puppets, chapter 19; Donna's Quilted *Shalom* Wall Hanging, chapter 4; and Donna's Apples & Honey Challah Cover, chapter 13), Susan Neigher, Lois Dornfeld, and Dorothy Cohen. June Shatken, another NCJW friend, put me in touch with Susan Schrott, whose beautiful Tree of Life Wall Hanging appears in chapter 1. Michelle Bobrow, of

NCJW, Essex County Section, and a knitting teacher, read through a number of project write-ups and made terrific suggestions and comments on them. Eleanor Levie, mentioned above, also came to me by way of NCJW.

A simple thank-you hardly conveys my deep appreciation to Stella Hart Grayson, who encouraged me to write this book when it was nothing more than a germ of an idea, and kept me going when it seemed as if I would never get it done.

In this age of dwindling newspaper circulations, I extend thanks to all the Jewish newspapers throughout the country that ran stories about the book when I was seeking contributors. Without their help in spreading the word, I would never have gathered so many extraordinary projects from around the United States—and Israel. (The two Israeli contributors—Ruth Lenk and Esther Tivé-Elterman—found out about the book through friends and relatives in the States, who read about the project in their local Jewish newspapers.)

Sincere thanks as well to Jewish Lights' Emily Wichland, vice president of editorial and production, a source of great support and encouragement throughout the writing process; Daniela Cockwill, assistant editor, who shepherded this project through the editorial process with dedication, savvy, and good spirits; and Stuart M. Matlins, publisher of Jewish Lights, for publishing and championing *Jewish Threads*.

My husband, Robert Grayson—a professional writer in his own right—deserves thanks beyond measure for helping me pull together all the disparate threads of this manuscript, for researching and writing the beautiful part openings, and for his insightful and compassionate perspective on Judaism, Jewish life, and Jewish heritage, which infuses all the pages of *Jewish Threads*.

—*Diana Drew*

I extend a big *todah rabbah* (thank-you) to my grandparents, Frances and Sol Engelhard, *z"l*. Life is a series of special moments, and I spent many of those moments at the home of my grandparents in Brooklyn. By seeing firsthand their daily mitzvot—from Shabbat dinners and synagogue attendance to joyous observance of the holidays—I discovered what being Jewish was all about. Judaism became integral to my identity, and being Jewish was something I wanted to be, not something I had to be. In writing the part openings of this book, I shared some of what I learned growing up around my grandparents and my parents, Stella and Leonard Grayson, as they kept alive the wonderful traditions of Judaism handed down through the generations. What they taught me inspired what I write here and how I live.

My thanks to Stella Hart Grayson for reading every word I ever wrote.

My brother, Lee, inspires me every day with his courage, reminding me that Judaism calls on us to give life meaning by exemplifying the highest ideals despite setbacks and challenges. His example radiates throughout my work on this book.

I also thank Cheryl Wrigley, though *thank you* hardly expresses my feelings, for translating the words of the Talmud into action by saving a life—Lee's—as a marrow donor. Cheryl's selflessness added special meaning to the passages I wrote in this book.

In addition, I thank my beloved cats, both those who have passed on and those with me now, who have always sat by my side as I put words on paper or onscreen. As God's creatures, they have inspired me with their loving and giving nature, making tough days bearable and great days even better.

My appreciation, too, for the tireless efforts of Diana Drew, who doubles as my wife, in putting this project together and bringing it to fruition. I think it's finally done now.

—*Robert Grayson*

## *Congregation Resources*

**Spiritual Boredom:** Rediscovering the Wonder of Judaism  *By Dr. Erica Brown*
Breaks through the surface of spiritual boredom to find the reservoir of meaning within.  6 x 9, 208 pp, HC, 978-1-58023-405-4  **$21.99**

**Building a Successful Volunteer Culture**
Finding Meaning in Service in the Jewish Community
*By Rabbi Charles Simon; Foreword by Shelley Lindauer; Preface by Dr. Ron Wolfson*
Shows you how to develop and maintain the volunteers who are essential to the vitality of your organization and community.  6 x 9, 192 pp, Quality PB, 978-1-58023-408-5  **$16.99**

**Inspired Jewish Leadership:** Practical Approaches to Building Strong Communities
*By Dr. Erica Brown*  6 x 9, 256 pp, HC, 978-1-58023-361-3  **$27.99**

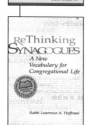

**Rethinking Synagogues:** A New Vocabulary for Congregational Life
*By Rabbi Lawrence A. Hoffman, PhD*  6 x 9, 240 pp, Quality PB, 978-1-58023-248-7  **$19.99**

**The Spirituality of Welcoming:** How to Transform Your Congregation into a
Sacred Community  *By Dr. Ron Wolfson*  6 x 9, 224 pp, Quality PB, 978-1-58023-244-9  **$19.99**

# *Children's Books*

**Around the World in One Shabbat**
Jewish People Celebrate the Sabbath Together
*By Durga Yael Bernhard*

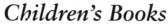

Takes your child on a colorful adventure to share the many ways Jewish people celebrate Shabbat around the world.
11 x 8½, 32 pp, Full-color illus., HC, 978-1-58023-433-7  **$18.99**  *For ages 3–6*

## What You Will See Inside a Synagogue
*By Rabbi Lawrence A. Hoffman, PhD, and Dr. Ron Wolfson; Full-color photos by Bill Aron*
A colorful, fun-to-read introduction that explains the ways and whys of Jewish worship and religious life.
8½ x 10½, 32 pp, Full-color photos, Quality PB, 978-1-59473-256-0  **$8.99**  *For ages 6 & up*
*(A book from SkyLight Paths, Jewish Lights' sister imprint)*

## Because Nothing Looks Like God
*By Lawrence Kushner and Karen Kushner*  Introduces children to the possibilities of spiritual life.  11 x 8¼, 32 pp, Full-color illus., HC, 978-1-58023-092-6  **$17.99**  *For ages 4 & up*

**The Book of Miracles:** A Young Person's Guide to Jewish Spiritual Awareness
*Written and illus. by Lawrence Kushner*
6 x 9, 96 pp, 2-color illus., HC, 978-1-879045-78-1  **$16.95**  *For ages 9–13*

**In God's Hands**  *By Lawrence Kushner and Gary Schmidt*  9 x 12, 32 pp, Full-color illus., HC, 978-1-58023-224-1  **$16.99**  *For ages 5 & up*

**In Our Image:** God's First Creatures  *By Nancy Sohn Swartz*
9 x 12, 32 pp, Full-color illus., HC, 978-1-879045-99-6  **$16.95**  *For ages 4 & up*

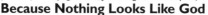

**The Kids' Fun Book of Jewish Time**
*By Emily Sper*  9 x 7½, 24 pp, Full-color illus., HC, 978-1-58023-311-8  **$16.99**  *For ages 3–6*

## What Makes Someone a Jew?  *By Lauren Seidman*
Reflects the changing face of American Judaism.
10 x 8½, 32 pp, Full-color photos, Quality PB, 978-1-58023-321-7  **$8.99**  *For ages 3–6*

*Or phone, fax, mail or e-mail to:* **JEWISH LIGHTS Publishing**
Sunset Farm Offices, Route 4 • P.O. Box 237 • Woodstock, Vermont 05091
Tel: (802) 457-4000 • Fax: (802) 457-4004 • www.jewishlights.com
**Credit card orders: (800) 962-4544** (8:30AM–5:30PM ET Monday–Friday)
*Generous discounts on quantity orders. SATISFACTION GUARANTEED. Prices subject to change.*

# Life Cycle

## Marriage/Parenting/Family/Aging

**The New Jewish Baby Album:** Creating and Celebrating the Beginning of a Spiritual Life—A Jewish Lights Companion
*By the Editors at Jewish Lights; Foreword by Anita Diamant; Preface by Rabbi Sandy Eisenberg Sasso*
A spiritual keepsake that will be treasured for generations. More than just a memory book, *shows you how—and why it's important*—to create a Jewish home and a Jewish life. 8 x 10, 64 pp, Deluxe Padded HC, Full-color illus., 978-1-58023-138-1 **$19.95**

**The Jewish Pregnancy Book:** A Resource for the Soul, Body & Mind during Pregnancy, Birth & the First Three Months *By Sandy Falk, MD, and Rabbi Daniel Judson, with Steven A. Rapp* Medical information, prayers and rituals for each stage of pregnancy. 7 x 10, 208 pp, b/w photos, Quality PB, 978-1-58023-178-7 **$16.95**

**Celebrating Your New Jewish Daughter:** Creating Jewish Ways to Welcome Baby Girls into the Covenant—New and Traditional Ceremonies *By Debra Nussbaum Cohen; Foreword by Rabbi Sandy Eisenberg Sasso* 6 x 9, 272 pp, Quality PB, 978-1-58023-090-2 **$18.95**

**The New Jewish Baby Book, 2nd Edition:** Names, Ceremonies & Customs—A Guide for Today's Families *By Anita Diamant* 6 x 9, 320 pp, Quality PB, 978-1-58023-251-7 **$19.99**

**Parenting as a Spiritual Journey:** Deepening Ordinary and Extraordinary Events into Sacred Occasions *By Rabbi Nancy Fuchs-Kreimer, PhD*
6 x 9, 224 pp, Quality PB, 978-1-58023-016-2 **$17.99**

**Parenting Jewish Teens:** A Guide for the Perplexed
*By Joanne Doades* Explores the questions and issues that shape the world in which today's Jewish teenagers live and offers constructive advice to parents.
6 x 9, 176 pp, Quality PB, 978-1-58023-305-7 **$16.99**

---

**Judaism for Two:** A Spiritual Guide for Strengthening and Celebrating Your Loving Relationship *By Rabbi Nancy Fuchs-Kreimer, PhD, and Rabbi Nancy H. Wiener, DMin; Foreword by Rabbi Elliot N. Dorff, PhD*
Addresses the ways Jewish teachings can enhance and strengthen committed relationships. 6 x 9, 224 pp, Quality PB, 978-1-58023-254-8 **$16.99**

**The Creative Jewish Wedding Book, 2nd Edition:** A Hands-On Guide to New & Old Traditions, Ceremonies & Celebrations *By Gabrielle Kaplan-Mayer*
9 x 9, 288 pp, b/w photos, Quality PB, 978-1-58023-398-9 **$19.99**

**Divorce Is a Mitzvah:** A Practical Guide to Finding Wholeness and Holiness When Your Marriage Dies *By Rabbi Perry Netter; Afterword by Rabbi Laura Geller*
6 x 9, 224 pp, Quality PB, 978-1-58023-172-5 **$16.95**

**Embracing the Covenant:** Converts to Judaism Talk About Why & How
*By Rabbi Allan Berkowitz and Patti Moskovitz* 6 x 9, 192 pp, Quality PB, 978-1-879045-50-7 **$16.95**

**The Guide to Jewish Interfaith Family Life:** An InterfaithFamily.com Handbook
*Edited by Ronnie Friedland and Edmund Case*
6 x 9, 384 pp, Quality PB, 978-1-58023-153-4 **$18.95**

**A Heart of Wisdom:** Making the Jewish Journey from Midlife through the Elder Years
*Edited by Susan Berrin; Foreword by Rabbi Harold Kushner*
6 x 9, 384 pp, Quality PB, 978-1-58023-051-3 **$18.95**

**Introducing My Faith and My Community:** The Jewish Outreach Institute Guide for the Christian in a Jewish Interfaith Relationship
*By Rabbi Kerry M. Olitzky* 6 x 9, 176 pp, Quality PB, 978-1-58023-192-3 **$16.99**

**Making a Successful Jewish Interfaith Marriage:** The Jewish Outreach Institute Guide to Opportunities, Challenges and Resources *By Rabbi Kerry M. Olitzky with Joan Peterson Littman*
6 x 9, 176 pp, Quality PB, 978-1-58023-170-1 **$16.95**

**A Man's Responsibility:** A Jewish Guide to Being a Son, a Partner in Marriage, a Father and a Community Leader *By Rabbi Joseph B. Meszler*
6 x 9, 192 pp, Quality PB, 978-1-58023-435-1 **$16.99**; HC, 978-1-58023-362-0 **$21.99**

**So That Your Values Live On:** Ethical Wills and How to Prepare Them
*Edited by Rabbi Jack Riemer and Rabbi Nathaniel Stampfer*
6 x 9, 272 pp, Quality PB, 978-1-879045-34-7 **$18.99**

# Spirituality/Women's Interest

## New Jewish Feminism
### Probing the Past, Forging the Future
*Edited by Rabbi Elyse Goldstein; Foreword by Anita Diamant*

Looks at the growth and accomplishments of Jewish feminism and what they mean for Jewish women today and tomorrow.

6 x 9, 480 pp, Quality PB, 978-1-58023-448-1 **$19.99**; HC, 978-1-58023-359-0 **$24.99**

## The Divine Feminine in Biblical Wisdom Literature
### Selections Annotated & Explained
*Translation & Annotation by Rabbi Rami Shapiro*

5½ x 8½, 240 pp, Quality PB, 978-1-59473-109-9 **$16.99**
*(A book from SkyLight Paths, Jewish Lights' sister imprint)*

## The Quotable Jewish Woman
### Wisdom, Inspiration & Humor from the Mind & Heart
*Edited by Elaine Bernstein Partnow*

6 x 9, 496 pp, Quality PB, 978-1-58023-236-4 **$19.99**

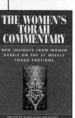

## The Women's Haftarah Commentary
### New Insights from Women Rabbis on the 54 Weekly Haftarah Portions, the 5 Megillot & Special Shabbatot
*Edited by Rabbi Elyse Goldstein*

Illuminates the historical significance of female portrayals in the Haftarah and the Five Megillot. 6 x 9, 560 pp, Quality PB, 978-1-58023-371-2 **$19.99**

## The Women's Torah Commentary
### New Insights from Women Rabbis on the 54 Weekly Torah Portions
*Edited by Rabbi Elyse Goldstein*

Over fifty women rabbis offer inspiring insights on the Torah, in a week-by-week format.
6 x 9, 496 pp, Quality PB, 978-1-58023-370-5 **$19.99**; HC, 978-1-58023-076-6 **$34.95**

# Social Justice

## Confronting Scandal
### How Jews Can Respond When Jews Do Bad Things
*By Dr. Erica Brown*

A framework to transform our sense of shame over reports of Jews committing crime into actions that inspire and sustain a moral culture.
6 x 9, 192 pp, HC, 978-1-58023-440-5 **$24.99**

## There Shall Be No Needy
### Pursuing Social Justice through Jewish Law and Tradition
*By Rabbi Jill Jacobs; Foreword by Rabbi Elliot N. Dorff, PhD; Preface by Simon Greer*

Confronts the most pressing issues of twenty-first-century America from a deeply Jewish perspective. 6 x 9, 288 pp, Quality PB, 978-1-58023-425-2 **$16.99**

**There Shall Be No Needy Teacher's Guide** 8½ x 11, 56 pp, PB, 978-1-58023-429-0 **$8.99**

## Conscience
### The Duty to Obey and the Duty to Disobey
*By Rabbi Harold M. Schulweis*

Examines the idea of conscience and the role conscience plays in our relationships to government, law, ethics, religion, human nature, God—and to each other.
6 x 9, 160 pp, Quality PB, 978-1-58023-419-1 **$16.99**; HC, 978-1-58023-375-0 **$19.99**

## Judaism and Justice
### The Jewish Passion to Repair the World
*By Rabbi Sidney Schwarz; Foreword by Ruth Messinger*

Explores the relationship between Judaism, social justice and the Jewish identity of American Jews. 6 x 9, 352 pp, Quality PB, 978-1-58023-353-8 **$19.99**